Britain's
Best**Pubs**

AA

© Automobile Association Developments Limited 2007.

Automobile Association Developments Limited retains the copyright in the current edition © 2007 and in all subsequent editions, reprints and amendments to editions.

 This product includes mapping data licensed from Ordnance Survey® with the permission of the Controller of Her Majesty's Stationery Office. © Crown copyright 2007. All rights reserved. Licence number 100021153.

Maps prepared by the Cartography Department of The Automobile Association.

Maps © Automobile Association Developments Limited 2007.

Advertising Sales:
advertisementsales@theAA.com

Editorial:
lifestyleguides@theAA.com

The contents of this publication are believed correct at the time of printing. Nevertheless, the Publisher cannot be held responsible for any errors or omissions or for changes in the details given in this guide or for the consequences of any reliance on the information provided by the same.

Assessments of AA inspected establishments are based on the experience of the hotel and restaurant inspectors on the occasion of their visit(s) and therefore descriptions given in this guide necessarily dictate an element of subjective opinion which may not reflect or dictate a reader's own opinion on another occasion. We have tried to ensure accuracy in this guide but things do change and we would be grateful if readers would advise us of any inaccuracies they may encounter.

Typeset by AA Lifestyle Guides

Printed and bound by Graficas Estella, Spain

Editorial contributors: Julia Hynard and Penny Phenix

Cover credits
Front cover: The New Inn, Shalfleet, Isle of Wight
Back cover: The Green Dragon Inn, Cowley

A CIP catalogue record for this book is available from the British Library

ISBN-10: 0-7495-5177-1
ISBN-13: 978-0-7495-5177-3

Published by AA Publishing, which is a trading name of Automobile Association Developments Limited, whose registered office is:
Fanum House, Basing View
Basingstoke
Hampshire RG21 4EA

www.theAA.com

Registered number 1878835

A03174

Britain's
Best**Pubs**

Contents

Welcome

Britain's Best Pubs is for anyone who enjoys eating and drinking well in formal or informal surroundings. Where diamonds or stars have been awarded, you can relax in the knowledge that the rooms have been inspected and rated by the AA.

Britain's Best

In this fully updated and revised guide you'll find a selection of "olde worlde" country pubs in hidden-away locations, smart gastropubs in towns and cities, and cosy inns on old coaching routes. Though very different in conception and setting, they all share a commitment to serving good food based on fresh (and local where possible) produce cooked to order. Hospitality is warm and welcoming, and well-kept real ales are offered alongside decent wines. The index and map sections at the back of this guide will help you to find a wide range of towns and villages to visit, in search of an authentic experience, whether it be traditional or modern. To help you make the most of your visit we've included recommended places to see in the area.

A Place to Stay

Room prices for single and double occupation are shown where the accommodation has been inspected and rated by the AA under the Hotel and Guest Accommodation Schemes. Many places will also offer variable rates and special offer breaks so it's worth asking when you book.

Accommodation varies from pubs with two or three rooms, to grander inns and hotels with all the extras, although most of the places included in this guide have fewer than 20 rooms. Whatever their size or style, all the places selected for inclusion in Britain's Best Pubs have the same things in common: good food, beer served in relaxed and inviting surroundings and great value for money.

Using the Guide

Britain's Best Pubs has been designed to enable you to find an establishment quickly and efficiently. Each entry provides clear information about the opening hours, food, facilities, AA-rated accommodation and nearby recommended places to visit.

Use the contents (page 3) to browse the main gazeteer section by county and the index to find either a location (page 329) or a specific Pub (page 334) by name.

Finding your way

The main section of the guide is divided into three main parts covering England, Scotland and Wales. The counties within each of these sections are ordered alphabetically as are the town or village locations (shown in capital letters as part of the address) within each county. Finally, the establishments are listed alphabetically under each location name. Towns names featured in the guide can also be located in the map section (page 315).

The Old Inn

★★★ ⊚ INN

Address:	Ash Lane, WHITCHURCH, Salisbury, SA38 2PP
Tel:	01963 300123
Email:	oldinn@pubgroup.co.uk
Website:	www.pubgroup.co.uk/oldrectory
Map ref:	3, TQ32
Directions:	Next to church at S end of Whitchurch

Open: 11.30–3 5.30–11 (Sun 12-3) ⊯ L 11–2 D 7–9 ⊙
L 12–2 D 6–9 Rooms: 8 rooms S £35–40
D £75–100 Facilities: Gardens Children welcome Outdoor seating Parking: 22 Notes: ⊨ ⊕ Free House ₹ 7

Tucked away down a leafy lane, The Old Inn is the perfect place for a relaxing drink and a good meal. This old inn has been beautifully restored and extended, with its character carefully preserved. The perfect place for walkers hiking the nearby Ridgeway, the garden offers a shady retreat for lunch and in colder weather log fires and leather sofa's provide a warm and welcome resting place. There are two bars, where meals can also be enjoyed, as well as a comfortable and spacious oak-beamed restaurant providing a more formal environment. The menu makes good use of local organic produce with well-cooked dishes that will satisfy the heartiest appetite. The en suite bedrooms are simply furnished and decorated with many of the thoughtful extras usually associated with superior hotels.

Recommended in the area
Salisbury Cathedral; New Forest National Park; Stonehenge and Salisbury Plain

❶ Stars/Diamonds and Symbols

A star or diamond rating denotes where an entry has been inspected under one of two separate schemes; either the AA Guest Accommodation Scheme or the AA Hotel Scheme.

Establishments in the AA guest accommodation scheme are rated for quality with a grading of either one to five diamonds ♦ or stars ★. The majority of the establishments in this guide have been rated using the new system of common quality standards in which they are rated for quality with a grading of one to five stars.

Pubs with a new star rating have been given a descriptive category designator: B&B, GUEST HOUSE, FARMHOUSE, INN, RESTAURANT WITH ROOMS or GUEST ACCOMMODATION.
Pubs in the hotel quality recognition scheme have their own descriptive designator: TOWN HOUSE HOTEL, COUNTRY HOUSE HOTEL, SMALL HOTEL, METRO HOTEL and BUDGET HOTEL.

See pages 8–10 for more information on the AA ratings and awards scheme.

Egg cups 🥚 and **Pies** 🥧: These symbols denote where the breakfast or dinner has exceeded the quality level for the rating achieved by the establishment.

Rosette awards ◉: This is the AA's food award (see page 9 for further details).

❷ Contact Details

The pub address includes a locator or place name in capitals (e.g. NORWICH). Within each county, entries are ordered alphabetically first by this place name and then by the name of the establishment.

Telephone and fax numbers, and e-mail and website addresses are given where available and are believed correct at the time of going to press but changes may occur. The latest establishment details can be found at www.theAA.com.

Website addresses have been supplied by the establishments and lead you to websites that are not under the control of Automobile Association Developments Ltd. AADL has no control over and accepts no responsibility or liability in respect of the material on any such websites. By including the addresses of third-party websites AADL does not intend to solicit business.

❸ Map Reference

The map reference is composed of two parts. The first number shows the atlas map number (from 1–13) at the back of the guide (see page 315 onwards). The second part is a National Grid reference. To find the town or village location on one of the maps, locate the lettered square and read the first figure across and the second figure vertically using the main gridlines to help guide you. For example, a map reference of '3, TQ28' refers to map 3 in the atlas section, grid square TQ on the map and a location of two across the grid square, running east-west, and eight in a north-south direction. The map section of this guide also provides road and county information.

Maps locating each establishment and a route planner are available at www.theAA.com.

❹ Directions

Where possible, directions have been given from the nearest motorway or A road. Distances are provided in miles (m) and yards (yds).

❺ Open

Indicates the opening hours of the establishment and, if appropriate, any dates when it may be closed for business.

🍽 Bar Meals

Indicates the times and days when the proprieters tell us bar food can be ordered, and the average price of a main course as supplied by the proprieter. Please be aware that last orders could vary by up to 30 minutes.

🍽 Restaurant

Indicates the times and days when proprietors tell us food can be ordered from the restaurant, and the average cost of a 3-course à la carte meal, as supplied by the proprietor.

❻ Room Information

Room information is only shown where accommodation has been inspected by the AA. The number of letting bedrooms with a bath or shower en suite are indicated. Bedrooms that have a private bathroom adjacent may be included as en suite. Further details on private bathroom and en suite provision may also be inlcuded in the description text (see ❿). Always phone in advance to ensure that the establishment has the room facilities that you require.

Prices: Charges shown are per night except where specified. S denotes bed and breakfast per person (single). D denotes bed and breakfast for two people sharing a room (double). In some cases prices are also given for twin (T), triple and family rooms, also on a per night basis. Prices are indications only, so check what is included before booking.

7 Facilities

This section lists a selection of facilities offered by the pub such as garden details or children's facilities. A minimum age may be specified, e.g. No children under 4 means no children under four years old. If you have very young children, check before booking. The facilities list is by no means exhaustive. If unsure, contact the establishment before your visit.

Additional facilities, such as access for disabled people, or notes about other services (e.g. if credit card details are not accepted) may be listed here.

8 Parking

The number of parking spaces available. Other types of parking (on road or Park and Ride) may also be possible; check the descriptions for further information. Phone the establishment in advance of your arrival if unsure.

9 Notes

This section provides details specific details relating to:

Smoking policy: The no smoking symbol by itself indicates a ban on smoking throughout the premises. If the establishment is only partly no smoking, the areas where smoking is not permitted are shown alongside the no smoking symbol.

The Smoking, Health and Social Care (Scotland) Act came into force in March 2006 (clearingtheairscotland.com). The law bans smoking in no-smoking premises in Scotland, which includes guest houses and inns with two or more guest bedrooms. The proprietor can designate one or more bedrooms with ventilation systems where the occupants can smoke, but communal areas must be smoke-free. Communal areas include the interior bars and restaurants in pubs and inns.

Similar laws covering England, Wales and Northern Ireland are due to come into effect during 2007. If the freedom to smoke or to be in a non-smoking atmosphere is important to you, we recommend that you check with the establishment when you book.

Dogs: Establishments that state no dogs may accept assist/guide dogs. Some places that do accept dogs may restrict the size and breed and the rooms into which they can be taken. Always check the conditions when booking.

🍺 Indicates the name of the brewery to which the pub is tied or the company which owns it, or where the pub is a free house and independently owned and run.

🍷 Indicates the number of wines available.

10 Description

The description of the pub includes the type of eating options available and, where relevant, information about the accommodation where it has been inspected and rated by the AA.

11 Recommended in the area

This indicates places of interest, local sights to visit and potential day trips and activities.

Key to symbols

★	Black stars (see page 8)
★	Red stars (see page 8)
♦	Black diamonds (see page 8)
♦	Red diamonds (see page 8)
◎	AA Rosette (see page 9)
3, TQ28	Map reference (see pages 471-485)
S	Single room
D	Double room
⊘	No smoking in area indicated
⊗	No dogs allowed in area indicated
🐕	Dogs allowed in area indicated
Wi-fi	Wireless network connection
🍽	Bar meals
🍴	Restaurant meals
🍺	Pub status (Chain or Free House)
🍷30	Wines available

AA Ratings and Awards

Diamond or stars shown in Britain's Best Pub guide indicate where the accommodation available has been rated by the AA under its guest accommodation or hotel schemes which use a new common standard rating.

Guest Accommodation and Hotel Schemes

The AA inspects and rates establishments under two different accommodation schemes. Guest houses, B&Bs, farmhouses and inns are rated under the Guest Accommodation Scheme and hotels are rated under the Hotel Scheme. Establishments recognised by the AA pay an annual fee according to the rating and the number of bedrooms. This rating is not transferable if an establishment changes hands.

Common Standards

The AA has introduced new quality standards for inspected accommodation. This follows extensive consultation by the inspection organisations (the AA, VisitBritain, VisitScotland and Visit Wales) with consumers and the hospitality industry in order to make the rating systems for hotels and guest accommodation easier to understand.

Since January 2006, each inspection organisation has used the same standard procedures to determine the new Star rating of any inspected guest accommodation. This replaces the previous Diamond rating, though the parallel one to five ratings indicate similar levels of quality. The new system of awards also uses six descriptive designators to classify the establishment (these are described on page 9).

Now, guests can be confident that, for example, a guest house anywhere in the UK and Ireland will offer consistent quality and facilities. The development of these new quality standards has also been supported by the government.

Stars & Diamonds

The AA Stars and Diamonds rate guest accommodation at five levels of quality, from one at the simplest, to five at the highest level of quality in the scheme.

Not all establishments have been inspected under the new quality standards in time for this edition of Britain's Best Pub guide, and so many are still rated with Diamonds. Check www.theAA.com for up-to-date information.

♦ Red diamonds highlight the best within the three, four and five diamond ratings for guest accommodation. A similar method of highlighting the best establishments within each rating under the common standards star system will be in place for 2008.

★ Red stars highlight the best within the three, four and five star ratings for hotels.

The Inspection Process

Establishments applying for AA recognition are visited by a qualified AA accommodation inspectors as a mystery guest. Inspectors stay overnight to make a thorough test of the accommodation, food, and hospitality. After paying the bill the following morning, they identify themselves and ask to be shown around the premises. The inspector completes a full report, resulting in a recommendation for the appropriate star rating. After this first visit, the establishment will receive an annual visit to check that standards are maintained. If it changes hands, the new owners must re-apply for rating, as standards can change.

Guests can expect to find the following minimum standards at all levels:

■ Pleasant and helpful welcome and service, and sound standards of housekeeping and maintenance

- Comfortable accommodation equipped to modern standards
- Bedding and towels changed for each new guest, and at least weekly if the room is taken for a long stay
- Adequate storage, heating, lighting and comfortable seating
- A sufficient hot water supply at reasonable times
- A full cooked breakfast. (If this is not provided, the fact must be advertised and a substantial continental breakfast must be offered.)

Designators (Guest Accommodation)

All guest accommodation inspected under the new common standards is given one of six descriptive designators to help the public understand the different types of accommodation available in Britain (see also ❶ on page 5).

B&B: Under the new Star rating, B&B accommodation is provided in a private house run by the owner and with no more than six guests. There may be restricted access to the establishment particularly in the late morning and the afternoon, so do check when booking.

GUEST HOUSE: A star-rated Guest House provides for more than six paying guests and usually offers more services than a B&B, for

example dinner, which may be served by staff as well as the owner. Some diamond-rated guest houses include the word 'hotel' in their name, though they cannot offer all the services required for the AA hotel star rating (for example evening meals). London prices tend to be higher than outside the capital, and normally only bed and breakfast is provided, although some establishments do provide a full meal service. Check on the service and facilities offered before booked as details may change during the currency of this guide.

FARMHOUSE: A farmhouse usually provides good value B&B or guest-house accommodation and excellent home cooking on a working farm or smallholding. Sometimes the land has been sold and only the house remains, but many are working farms and some farmers are happy to allow visitors to look around, or even to help

AA Rosette Awards

Out of the many thousands of restaurants in the UK, the AA identifies some 1,800 as the best. The following is an outline of what to expect from restaurants with AA Rosette Awards. For a more detailed explanation of Rosette criteria please see www.theAA.com

◉ Excellent local restaurants serving food prepared with care, understanding and skill, using good quality ingredients.

◉◉ The best local restaurants, which aim for and achieve higher standards, better consistency and where a greater precision is apparent in the cooking. There will be obvious attention to the selection of quality ingredients.

◉◉◉ Outstanding restaurants that demand recognition well beyond their local area.

◉◉◉◉ Amongst the very best restaurants in the British Isles, where the cooking demands national recognition.

◉◉◉◉◉ The finest restaurants in the British Isles, where the cooking stands comparison with the best in the world.

feed the animals. However, you should always exercise care and never leave children unsupervised. The farmhouses are listed under towns or villages, but do ask for directions when booking.

INN: Traditional inns often have a cosy bar, convivial atmosphere, good beer and pub food. Those listed in the guide will provide breakfast in a suitable room, and should also serve light meals during licensing hours. The character of the properties vary according to whether they are country inns or town establishments. Check your arrival times as these may be restricted to opening hours.

RESTAURANT WITH ROOMS: These restaurants offer overnight accommodation with the restaurant being the main business and open to non-residents. The restaurant usually offers a high standard of food and service.

GUEST ACCOMMODATION: This includes any establishment that meets the minimum entry requirements with a rating of three stars or more and has received outstanding results from an inspection visit.

Designators (Hotels)

All hotels inspected under the new common standards are given one of six descriptive designators to identify the different types of hotel available (see also ❶ on page 5).

HOTEL: The majority of establishments in this guide come under the category of Hotel.

TOWN HOUSE HOTEL: A small, individual city or town centre property, which provides a high degree or personal service and privacy

COUNTRY HOUSE HOTEL: These may vary in size and are located in a rural area.

SMALL HOTEL: Has less than 20 bedrooms and is managed by its owner.

METRO HOTEL: A hotel in an urban location that does not offer an evening meal.

BUDGET HOTEL: These are usually purpose built modern properties offering inexpensive accommodation. Often located near motorways and in town or city centres.

www.theAA.com

Go to www.theAA.com to find more AA listed guest houses, hotels, pubs and restaurants – some 12,000 establishments.

Routes & Traffic on the home page leads to a route planner. Simply enter your postcode and the establishment postcode given in this guide and click Confirm. Check your details and then click GET MY ROUTE and you will have a detailed route plan to take you door-to-door.

Use the Travel section to search for Hotels & B&Bs or Restaurants & Pubs by location or establishment name. Scroll down the list of finds for the interactive map and local routes.

Postcode searches can also be made on www.ordnancesurvey.co.uk and www.multimap.com, which will also provide useful aerial views of your destination.

Useful Information

If you're unsure about any of the facilities offered, always check with the establishment before you visit or book accommodation. Up-to-date information on contacting all pubs in this guide can be found at the travel section of the www.theAA.com

Fire Precautions and Safety

Many of the establishments listed in the guide are subject to the requirements of the Fire Precautions Act of 1971. All establishments should display details of how to summon assistance in the event of an emergency at night.

Dogs

Some establishments that accept dogs may restrict the size and breed of dogs permitted. Guide and Assist Dogs are accepted in all pubs.

Children

Restrictions for children are given at the end of entries. When booking a meal you would be advised to check that children are welcome.

Smoking Regulations

The Public Places Charter on smoking is a voluntary code which encourages establishments like pubs to indicate by signage whether or not they have facilities for non smokers. Establishments in this Guide which have told us they are fully non-smoking are shown by a logo indicating no smoking on the premises, at the end of the entry's notes. See also page 7. For more information see the AIR website at www.airinitiative.com.

Facilities for Disabled Guests

The final stage (Part III) of the Disability Discrimination Act (access to Goods and Services) came into force in October 2004. This means that service providers may have to consider making permanent physical adjustments to their premises. For further information, see the government website www.disability.gov.uk/dda. We indicate in entries if an establishment has ground floor bedrooms, and if a hotel or B&B tells us that they have disabled facilities this is included in the description. The establishments in this guide should all be aware of their responsibilities under the Act. We recommend that you always telephone in advance to ensure that the establishment you have chosen has appropriate facilities.

Complaints

Readers who have any cause to complain about accommodation, food and drink or service are urged to do so on the spot. This should provide an opportunity for the proprietor to correct matters. If a personal approach fails in connection with accommodation, readers should inform AA Hotel Services, Fanum House, Basingstoke, Hants RG21 4EA. For other complaints you may write in or e-mail us at lifestyleguides@theaa.com. The AA does not, however, undertake to obtain compensation for complaints.

Bank and Public Holidays 2007

New Year's Day	1st January
New Year's Holiday	2nd January (Scotland)
Good Friday	6th April
Easter Monday	9th April
May Day Bank Holiday	7th May
Spring Bank Holiday	28th May
August Holiday	1st August (Scotland)
Late Summer Holiday	27th August
Christmas Day	25th December
Boxing Day	26th December

ENGLAND

Yorkshire Dales National Park.

Luton Hoo country house.

The Falcon

Address:	Rushden Road, BLETSOE, MK44 1QN
Tel:	01234 781222
Fax:	01234 781222
Email:	info@thefalconbletsoe.co.uk
Website:	www.thefalconbletsoe.co.uk
Map ref:	3, TL05
Directions:	On A6 from Bedford just after Milton Ernest

Open: 12–3 6–11(Sat 12–11, Sun 12–10.30) ☕ L
12–2.15 D 6–9.15 ⬛ L 12–2.15 D 6.30–9.15
Facilities: Children welcome Garden **Parking:** 40
Notes: 🛢 Charles Wells 🍷 7

A beautiful centuries-old coaching inn, The Falcon is set in the rolling hills of north Bedfordshire with an extensive frontage onto the A6. Customers come from far and wide to this easily accessible and popular destination. A new dining terrace provides an attractive spot for summer meals, overlooking the large mature gardens, which sweep down to the Great River Ouse. Step inside and you'll be greeted by the relaxed ambience of a country inn, enhanced by the inglenook fireplace and an abundance of oak beams. Dark wooden panelling lines the walls of the dining room, and real log fires keep things warm and cosy in winter. At lunchtime there is a range of crusty sandwiches, farmhouse ploughman's and salad bowls in addition to a lengthy menu of steaks and traditional dishes, such as steak and kidney pie, and beer-battered cod and chips. For vegetarians there will be a tempting alternative, such as tagliatelle with roasted pepper, red wine and tomato. Home-made puddings are a particular treat here. As you might expect of such a venerable hostelry, there is reputed to be at least one resident ghost, and – more tangibly – there is a secret tunnel leading to nearby Bletsoe Castle. Private functions, weddings and corporate events are catered for. Children are made welcome, and coach parties can be accommodated.

Recommended in the area

Glen Miller Museum; Santa Pod Raceway; Body Flight – Europe's largest indoor skydiving tunnel

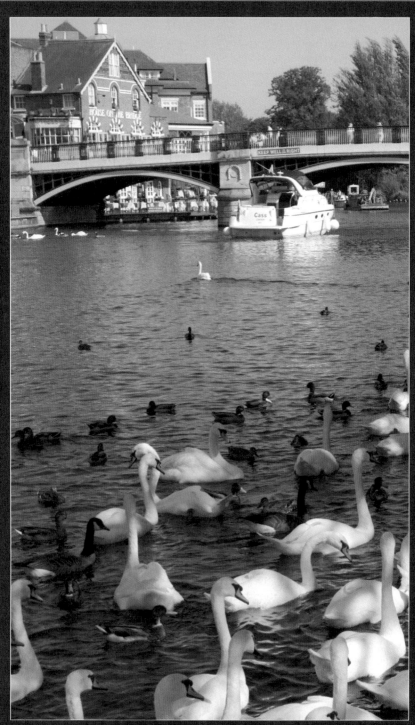

The River Thames at Windsor Bridge.

Chequers Brasserie

Address: Dean Lane,
COOKHAM DEAN, SL6 9BQ
Tel: 01628 481232
Fax: 01628 481237
Email: info@chequersbrasserie.co.uk
Map ref: 3, SU88
Directions: From A4094 in Cookham High St head towards Marlow, over railway line, 1 mile on the right
Open: 12–3 5.30–11 🍴 L 12–2.30 D 6.30–9.30
Facilities: Children welcome Garden Parking: 35
🛢 Free House 🍷 10

A well established gastro-pub in the pretty village of Cookham Dean, The Chequers Brasserie occupies a lovely old building with oak beams and open fires.

Kenneth Grahame, who wrote *The Wind in the Willows*, spent his childhood in this area – one of the most beautiful parts of the Thames Valley. Cookham Dean is also renowned for its associations with Stanley Spencer. The artist was born here and spent most of his working life in the village. Striking Victorian and Edwardian villas around the green set the tone, while the surrounding wooded hills and valleys are popular with walkers. The pub has a well-deserved reputation for its excellent food and wine. The blackboard menu changes regularly, with favourites that include seared king scallops with a crayfish tail risotto, piquant orange syrup and aged balsamic, or wild sea bass with asparagus spears, saffron fondant potato and bois boudran sauce. Traditional roasts are served on Sundays and bank holidays. Real ales, such as Morlands Original and Ruddles County Ale are offered alongside Scrumpy Jack cider. Seating is also available in the garden, where there is a small lawned area with benches and parasols.

Recommended in the area

Stanley Spencer Gallery; Cliveden House; Windsor Castle

The Crown & Garter

★★★★ GUEST HOUSE

Address: Inkpen Common, HUNGERFORD, RG17 9QR
Tel: 01488 668325
Email: gill.hern@btopenworld.com
Website: www.crownandgarter.com
Map ref: 3, SU36
Directions: From A4 turn off for Kintbury and Inkpen. At village store turn left onto Inkpen Rd, to Inkpen Common
Open: 12–3 5.30–11 (Sun 7–10.30) ⓑ L 12–2 D 6.30–9.30 ⓘⓞ L 12–2 D 6.30–9.30 Rooms: 8 en suite
S £59.50 D £90 Facilities: Children welcome Garden Parking: 30 Notes: ⊕ Free House ⓟ 8

Quiet lanes and honeysuckle-draped cottages mark the approach to this 17th-century family-run inn surrounded by beautiful Berkshire countryside. The oldest part is the bar, with a huge inglenook fireplace and beams, serving local and guest ales, malt whiskies and decent wines. Dishes, freshly prepared from local produce, can be eaten in the bar, restaurant or garden. The purpose-built rooms are set around a pretty garden with a pond. All have TV, DVD, tea and coffee tray and hairdryers.

Recommended in the area

Newbury Racecourse; Combe Gibbet; Highclere Castle

The Swan Inn

★★★★ INN

Address: Craven Road, Lower Green, Inkpen, HUNGERFORD, RG17 9DX
Tel: 01488 668326
Fax: 01488 668306
Email: enquiries@theswaninn-organics.co.uk
Website: www.theswaninn-organics.co.uk
Map ref: 3, SU36
Directions: From Hungerford High St (A338), take turning for Hungerford Common, then right to Inkpen 3m

Open: 12–2.30 7–11 (Open all day wknds summer) ⓑ L 12–2 D 7–9.30 ⓘⓞ L 12–2.30 D 7–9.30
Rooms: 10 en suite, S £60 D £80 Facilities: Children welcome Garden Parking: 50 ⊕ Free House

Just below Walbury Iron Age hill fort, the inn, though much extended, retains its character with exposed beams, stained glass door panels, open fires and old photographs. A good choice of real ales include the local organic Butts Traditional and Jester Bitter. The menu features fresh, organic produce. The owners are organic beef farmers, and their farm shop is adjacent. The garden has terraces, tables and chairs.

Recommended in the area

Kennet and Avon Canal; Combe Gibbet; Avebury Stone Circle

Bird In Hand Country Inn

Address: Bath Road, KNOWL HILL,
Twyford, RG10 9UP
Tel: 01628 826622
Fax: 01628 826748
Email: sthebirdinhand@aol.com
Website: www.birdinhand.co.uk
Map ref: 3, SU87
Directions: On A4, 5 miles W of Maidenhead, 7 miles
E of Reading
Open: 11–3 6–11 (Sun 12-10:30) 🍴 L 12–2.30
D 6.30–10 🍴 L 12–2.30 D 7–10 **Rooms:** 15 en suite, S £90 D £120 **Facilities:** Children welcome
Garden **Parking:** 86 **Notes:** 🐾 ⊕ Free House 🍷 12

Legend has it that George III granted a royal charter to this inn in the 1700s, for the hospitality shown
him following a hunting accident, and a royal welcome is still the order of the day. There's a light bar
menu or a more serious restaurant, where a mix of classic and modern dishes might include wild boar
in apricot and mushroom sauce; jambonette of guinea fowl; or grilled Dover sole.

Recommended in the area

Legoland; Odds Park Farm; Wellington Country Park

The Yew Tree Inn

Address: Hollington Cross, Andover Road, Highclere,
NEWBURY, RG20 9SE
Tel: 01635 253360
Fax: 01635 255035
Email: gareth.mcainsh@theyewtree.net
Map ref: 3, SU46
Directions: From Newbury, take the Andover road, A343,
drive through Highclere, pub is on right
Open: 10–12 🍴 L 12–3 D 6–10 🍴 L 12–3 D 6–10
Facilities: Garden **Parking:** 40 **Notes:** 🐾 ⊕ Free House 🍷 8

Just inside the Berkshire border at the foot of the Hampshire Downs, this fine 17th-century inn is full
of charm and character with oak beams and three inglenook fireplaces. With celebrated chef and
restaurateur Marco Pierre White at the helm as executive chef, the Yew Tree is really taking off. The
menu has been completely overhauled, and specials include grilled lobster with herbs and béarnaise
mousseline; braised pork belly with fricassée of butter beans and haricot blanc; grilled Dover sole with
tartare sauce; and confit of lamb a la Dijonaise with flageolet á la crème.

Recommended in the area

Highclere Castle; Hampshire Downs; Donnington Castle

BUCKINGHAMSHIRE

West Wycombe.

Crooked Billet

Address: 2 Westbrook End, Newton Longville,
BLETCHLEY, MK17 0DF
Tel: 01908 373936
Email: john@thebillet.co.uk
Website: www.thebillet.co.uk
Map ref: 3, SP83
Directions: Exit M1 at Junct 13, follow signs to
Buckingham. 6m signed at Buttledump rdbt to village of
Newton Longville.
Open: 12–2.30 5.3–11 (Sun 12-4, 7-10.30) ₤ L 12–2
D – ⏺ L 12.30–3 D 7–10 **Facilities:** Garden **Parking:** 25 ⊞ Greene King ☕ 300

This attractive thatched coaching inn started out as a farmhouse in the mid-17th century, serving
ale to its farm workers, and evolved into a typical country pub, but today it is nationally renowned
for its gastronomy and its top-class wine list. It is enclosed within a secluded garden, but the reason
for its popularity lies not so much in the setting as in those twin pleasures: wine and food. Emma
Gilchrist was once head chef at Nicole Farhi in London, while husband John was the award-winning
sommelier at nearby Brown's in Mayfair. They have brought considerable expertise and talent to the
Crooked Billet, offering an astounding 300-bin wine list, all available by the glass, as well as an
intriguing menu. Emma is passionate about using local produce, and acknowledges all her suppliers –
even the apiarist. Dishes – all cooked to order – range from lunchtime bar snacks like lobster club
sandwiches to the much more elaborate dinner menu and the ultimate, the six-course gourmet menu.
Starters might include beef fillet carpaccio with celeriac remoulade, followed by pan-fried sea bass
fillet, crushed Jersey Royal potatoes and roast salsify; or caramelized red onion tart with broad bean
and rocket risotto. For dessert, perhaps mango and passionfruit Pavlova with lemon and mint cream.
Booking, unsurprisingly, is essential.

Recommended in the area

Bletchley Park; Woburn Safari Park; Whipsnade Zoo

The Thames at Henley.

The Royal Oak

Address:	Frieth Road, BOVINGDON GREEN, Marlow, SL7 2JF
Tel:	01628 488611
Fax:	01628 478680
Email:	info@royaloakmarlow.co.uk
Website:	www.royaloakmarlow.co.uk
Map ref:	3, SU88

Directions: From Marlow, take A4155. In 300 yds turn right signed Bovingdon Green. After 0.75m Pub is on left.
Open: 11–11 (Sun 12-10.30) ᴌ L 12–2.30 D 7–10
🍽 L 12–2.30 D 7–10 Facilities: Children and dogs welcome Garden Parking: 42 Notes: 🖈 ⊕ 🍷 18

Attractive gardens with a sunny terrace confirm that this village pub is a cherished establishment. There may be a fire burning in the snug, while the cheery dining room is warmed by its rich decor. Choose a small plate (Oak tapas; pressed rabbit and guinea fowl rillettes) or a main meal (slow-roast pork belly on cumin sweet potato; pan-fried smoked haddock on cauliflower and grain mustard purée), all prepared from local produce and beautifully presented. Beers are from the nearby Rebellion Brewery.
Recommended in the area
Cliveden; Boat trips on the Thames; Chiltern Hills

The Ivy House

★★★★ INN

Address: London Road,
CHALFONT ST GILES, HP8 4RS
Tel: 01494 872184
Fax: 01494 872870
Email: enquiries@theivyhouse-bucks.co.uk
Website: www.theivyhouse-bucks.co.uk
Map ref: 3, SU99
Directions: On A413 2m S of Amersham & 1.5m
N of Chalfont St Giles

Open: 12–3 6–11 (Sat 12–11, Sun 12-10.30) ⓑ L 12–2.30 D 6.30–9.30 (Sat and Sun 12–9.30) ⓘ L 12–2.30 D 6.30–9.30 (Sat and Sun 12–9.30) **Rooms:** 5 en suite S £75 D £95 **Facilities:** Children welcome Garden **Parking:** 45 **Notes:** ⓟ ⓦ Free House ♀ 22

Anthony and Jane Mears both grew up in Dorset and loved the county's beautiful old country public houses. When they gave up their business careers eleven years ago it was with the intention of recreating something similar here. Perhaps for that reason a little reluctant to use the word 'gastropub', they do acknowledge that this is what they have created – both are well travelled and have put their love of international food to good use. The pub has a lovely warm atmosphere, resulting from a combination of old beams, open fires, books, brass and armchairs, and, not least, from the personalities of the owners. Selections from the menus include starters such as hot steaming tiger prawns in a coconut curry sauce or Italian crab au gratin. Main dishes include pan-fried sea bass fillets; fresh salmon fillet with home-grown mixed herb and cheddar crust; Thai style prawn salad; ostrich fillets; or chargrilled Gressingham duck with special Ivy House sauce. The menu at the Ivy House changes frequently, as does the range of cask conditioned ales from local and national breweries. An extensive wine list is also available.

Recommended in the area

Chiltern Open Air Museum; Milton's Cottage; Bekonscot Model Village

The Red Lion

Address:	CHENIES, Chorleywood,
	Rickmansworth, WD3 6ED
Tel:	01923 282722
Fax:	01923 283797
Map ref:	3, TQ09

Directions: Between Rickmansworth & Amersham on A404, follow signs for Chenies and Latimer
Open: 11–2.30 5.3–11 Sun 5.30-10.30 ⓛ L 12–2 D 7–10 **Facilities:** Garden **Parking:** 14 **Notes:** 🐕 🛢
Free House ⓨ 10

Michael Norris has just about reached the end of his second decade at this popular hostelry, and under his expert direction the pub has achieved considerable renown. He is keen to stress that this is a pub that does food, not a restaurant that does beer, but that's not to say that the quality and range of food on offer is in any way an afterthought. Michael has put together an extensive menu that should have something to please everyone, with a wide range of snacks, starters and main meals. Among the listings you'll find the ever-popular jacket potatoes; pasta carbonara; and a tasty beef, mustard and cheese pie, plus a number of more exotic dishes that might include Moroccan chicken breast with couscous; pork fillet with prunes; oxtail with root vegetables; and fresh tuna loin with roasted Mediterranean vegetables. Not so much exotic as downright unusual, the hot bacon and Milky Bar in a bap has its fans, too. But even with all this choice, it would be a shame not to try the famous, original Chenies lamb pie. Needless to say, the real ales on offer are kept in perfect condition and there are some good wines to choose from too. The Red Lion is not far outside the M25 at Junction 18 and is well worth making a detour to enjoy its pleasant, country-pub atmosphere – very much the ideal of what pubs used to be like before piped music and fruit machines were invented – and the garden makes for enjoyable alfresco summer lunches.

Recommended in the area

Legoland; Bekonscot Model Village; Rare Breeds Centre

The Crown

Address: Spurt Street, CUDDINGTON, HP18 0BB
Tel: 01844 292222
Email: david@anniebaileys.com
Website: www.thecrowncuddington.co.uk
Map ref: 3, SP71
Directions: Off A418 between Aylesbury and Thame
Open: 12–3 6–11 (all day Sun) ▣ L 12–2.30 D
6.30–10 ▣ L 12–2.30 D 6.30–10 **Facilities:** Children
welcome Garden **Parking:** 12 ⊕ Fullers Brewery ☻ 9

Fans of *Midsomer Murders* might recognise The Crown, which has been used several times as a location for the popular TV series. There's nothing sinister about the place in real life, though. It's a delightful thatched and whitewashed pub at the heart of a picturesque village, and has made a name for itself as a great place to eat. Having successfully run Annie Bailey's bar/brasserie in Cuddington for a number of years, the Berrys turned their attention to improving the nearby Crown, a delightful Grade II listed pub. Customers will find plenty of character inside, with a popular locals' bar and several low-beamed dining areas filled with charming prints and the glow of evening candlelight. The good choice of beers on tap includes Fullers London Pride and Adnams, and the extensive, well-chosen wine list and the eclectic menu all add to the enjoyment of a visit here. Starters might include the Crown fishcake with sweet chilli jam; linguini with prawn, chilli and spring onion; avocado, smoked chicken and pine kernel salad; and roasted red pepper with shaved Parmesan and croutons. On the main course menu you will find such dishes as confit duck on Puy lentil stew; Thai seafood curry with coconut and lime-scented rice; honey-glazed shank of lamb; chargrilled rib-eye steak; and vegetarian alternatives such as the Mediterranean vegetable risotto with pesto. The changing selection of desserts on offer is chalked up on a blackboard menu, and is guaranteed to conclude the eating out experience here in fine style.

Recommended in the area

Waddesdon Manor; Ascott House; Stowe House

The Swan Inn

Address: Village Road, DENHAM, UB9 5BH
Tel: 01895 832085
Fax: 01895 835516
Email: info@swaninndenham.co.uk
Website: www.swaninndenham.co.uk
Map ref: 3, TQ08
Directions: From A40, take the A412. In 200 yds turn
right for Denham; go through village, last pub on left
Open: 11–11 Sun 12-10.30 🍺 L 12–2.30 D 7–10
🍴 L 12–2.30 D 7–10 Facilities: Children welcome
Garden Parking: 12 Notes: ⚲ ⊞ 🍷 18

The pretty, unspoiled village of Denham is home to this wisteria-clad Georgian inn – just minutes away from suburban London and two motorways (M25 and M40), but as secluded and peaceful as the country inns it epitomises. Inside, there's a welcoming bar with a log fire and private dining room, both equally suitable for intimate dinners or business meetings. On the menu are small bites that double as starters and dishes such as pan-fried pigeon breasts with fig and blackberry preserve and thyme jus.
Recommended in the area
Bekonscot Model Village; Milton's Cottage; Chiltern Open Air Museum

The Rising Sun

Address: Little Hampden, GREAT MISSENDEN,
            HP16 9PS
Tel: 01494 488393
Fax: 01494 488788
Email: sunrising@rising-sun.demon.co.uk
Website: www.rising-sun.demon.co.uk
Map ref: 3, SP80
Directions: From A413, N of Gt Missenden, take Rignall
Rd on left signed Princes Risborough 2.5m. Turn right
signed Little Hampden only.
Open: 11.30–3 6.3–10 (Sun 12–3 only) Open BH lunchtime 🍺 L 12–2 D 7–9 🍴 L 12–2 D 7–9
Facilities: Children welcome Garden Parking: 20 Notes: ⊘ on premises ⊞ Free House 🍷 10

This 250-year-old country inn is beautifully located in the Chilterns, surrounded by beech woods and glorious scenery, with a network of footpaths beginning at the front door. It's well-run and welcoming, non-smoking throughout, and has an interesting menu that offers starters which can double as snacks, an extensive à la carte selection and a good range of seafood. Booking advisable.
Recommended in the area
Clivedon; Hughendon Manor; Milton's Cottage

The Dinton Hermit

★ 75% SMALL HOTEL

Address:	Water Lane, FORD,
	Aylesbury HP17 8XH
Tel:	01296 747473
Fax:	01296 748819
Email:	dintonhermit@btconnect.com
Website:	www.dinton-hermit.com
Map ref:	3, ST87

Directions: Off the A418 between Aylesbury & Thame
Open: 12–11 ⛺ L 12–2 D 7–9 ⚲ L 12–2 D 7–9
Rooms: 13 en suite S £80 D £80 **Facilities:** Garden
Parking: 40 ⊕ Free House

Built in 1595, and set back from the lane in an isolated hamlet, this 16th-century stone-built pub is named after John Biggs, clerk to one of the judges who condemned Charles I to death in 1649. So ashamed was he of his part in the execution that he became a hermit, and subsequently a local legend. A tasteful renovation has seen the accommodation extended, ensuring that it's all in keeping with its Grade II listed status. To the rear there's a large, beautifully maintained garden with tables spaced out across its neat lawns. The pub offers a good range of beers, including real ales and a guest ale from a local brewery, together with an interesting menu of dishes that use fresh produce, sourced locally wherever possible. Part of the recent renovation has included converting an old barn into a characterful restaurant, where you can begin your meal with such starters as marinated seared scallops or twice roasted duck leg. Main courses might include beef rossini with carrot and parsnip rosti, foie gras and spinach or roasted turbot fillet with homemade lemon pasta, herb crust and crayfish sauce. Home made desserts on the menu feature such favourites as crumbles, pavlovas and sticky toffee pudding.

Recommended in the area

Rycote Chapel; Waddesdon Manor; Long Crendon Courthouse

The Green Dragon

@ @

Address: 8 Churchway,
HADDENHAM, HP17 8AA
Tel: 01844 291403
Fax: 01844 299532
Email: pete@eatatthedragon.co.uk
Website: www.eatatthedragon.co.uk
Map ref: 3, SP70
Directions: From Thame, take A418 towards Aylesbury,
turning 1st right after entering Haddenham

Open: 12–3 6.3–11 🦽 L 12–2 D 6.30–9.15 🍽 L 12–2 D 6.30–9.15 **Facilities:** Garden
Parking: 18 **Notes:** ⊘ on premises ⊞ Enterprise Inns ♟ 10

Chef-proprietor Paul Berry and partners Sue and Pete Moffat are celebrating their fifth anniversary at the Green Dragon, a 350-year-old inn located close to the green and the parish church, a spot that has attracted many a television crew. The garden offers two large lawned areas offering some shade and a mix of tables and chairs, some distance from the main building. There is also seating under a canopy near to the door. Real ales include the local village beer, and there's a decent selection of wines by the glass. This is a serious dining pub with a great reputation for its food and therefore booking is strongly advised. Ingredients are locally sourced and supplied where possible, with fresh fish from Devon. Menus offer an interesting choice supplemented by daily specials and vegetarians are also well catered for with a selection of dishes. Typically, dishes range from home-made steak and kidney pudding with Wychert ale (the village brew), to fillet of sea bass on red pepper risotto cake with confit garlic prawns. The 'Simply Dinner' menu on Tuesday and Thursday nights is great value offering two courses (starter and main or main and pudding). The full Sunday lunch featuring local meats is another popular option.

Recommended in the area

Buckinghamshire Railway Centre; Waddesdon Manor; Claydon House

The Stag

Address: The Green,
MENTMORE, LU7 0QF
Tel: 01296 668423
Email: reservations@ilmaschio.co.uk
Website: www.ilmaschio.co.uk
Map ref: 3, SP91
Directions: Mentmore is off the A418 between
Aylesbury and Leighton Buzzard
Open: 12–11 ⓑ 12–10.30 (Sun 12–10) ⓘⓞⓘ 12–10.30
(Sun 12–10) **Facilities:** Garden
Notes: ⓟallowed ⓧ in restaurant ⓑ ⓟ 20

The Stag, rumoured to be haunted by a former patron named George, is set in the picturesque and historical (it's mentioned in the Domesday Book) village of Mentmore. The village, the former seat of Lord Roseberry, is home to the well-known Mentmore Towers which has been the set of Hollywood movies such as *Batman Returns*, *Eyes Wide Shut* and *The Thin Red Line*. The Stag has the advantage of both a snug, cosy public bar and an 80 cover (non-smoking) restaurant. Having recently changed hands, the establishment has been extensively refurbished and facilities have been vastly improved. The new owners, an international mix of Italian, Portuguese and Australian (the latter of Formula 1 fame) have rebranded the restaurant to become Il Maschio @ The Stag. The change of ownership has been very well received by locals and newcomers alike. Manuel, the Portuguese owner/chef has formulated a delectable mix of Mediterranean produce to recreate his award-winning menu which includes fresh fish, shellfish and meat products as well as a traditional pizza and fresh pasta menu. In addition to the extensive menu there is also a children's menu which caters superbly for all tastes and offers two and three course meals at fantastic value for money.

Recommended in the area

Ivinghoe Beacon and The Ridgeway; Whipsnade Zoo; Ascott (NT)

St Laurence's Church, West Wycombe.

The George and Dragon Hotel

Address: High Street, WEST WYCOMBE, HP14 3AB
Tel: 01494 464414
Fax: 01494 462432
Email: sue.raines@btconnect.com
Website: www.george-and-dragon.co.uk
Map ref: 3, SU89
Directions: On A40, close to M40
Open: 11–2.30 5.3–11(Sat 11-3, 5.30-11) (Sun 12–3, 6–9.30) ⓛ L 12–2 D 6–9.30 **Facilities:** Children welcome Garden **Parking:** 35 **Notes:** 🖛 ⊕ Enterprise Inns ♟ 8

Visitors from a bygone era are rumoured to haunt the corridors of this historic inn, which, reached through a cobbled archway, comprises a delightful jumble of timber-framed buildings. The range of real ales is excellent, and the menu includes starters such as spicy Cajun chicken wings, herb mushrooms or deep-fried goat's cheese followed by chargrilled steaks and specialities like pigeon and bacon pie, beef Wellington, chicken tikka masala, and bean and wild mushroom goulash.

Recommended in the area

West Wycombe Caves; Cliveden; Hughenden Manor

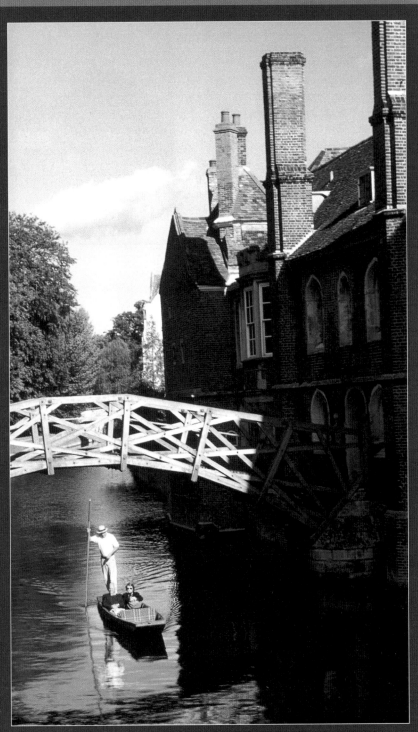

The Mathematical Bridge, Cambridge.

The George Inn at Babraham

Address: High Street, BABRAHAM,
Cambridge, CB22 3AG
Tel: 01223 833800
Email: george@inter-mead.com
Website: www.georgeinnbabraham.co.uk
Map ref: 4, TL55
Directions: Southeast of Cambridge, just off the A11,
the A505 and the A1307
Open: 11.30–3 5.3–11(Open all day summer w/ends)
⮞ L 12–2.15 D 6.30–9 ⦿ L 12–2.15 D 6.30–9
Facilities: Children welcome Garden **Parking:** 41 ⊕ Free House ♀ 8

Following a devastating fire in 2004, it was thought that this famous old inn would be lost forever, but new owner George Wortley has lovingly restored The George into a beautifully furnished and decorated village dining pub. During work on the 18th-century building, George's team of craftsmen incorporated new kitchens, a new dining area and a delightful dining terrace – the perfect place to eat al fresco. The newly-built second dining room, which opens onto the terrace, is also used for conferences, meetings and wedding receptions. The restaurant offers a varied selection of contemporary food ranging from lunchtime treats such as filled ciabattas; home-made soups; home-made fish cakes; and steak and kidney pie, to an evening menu that might include roasted fillet of venison on a wild berry compôte; pan-fried sea bream on a bed of spiced prawn lentils; or tandoori-marinated chicken breast with lime and coriander wild rice and naan bread. A well-chosen wine list ensures bottles that complement the dishes on the menu. There are additional dining tables in the bar, where you can also enjoy a pint of Old Speckled Hen or Abbot Ale. Children are made very welcome with their own thoughtfully prepared menu and special competitions. Dogs are allowed too, with water bowls provided. Special events and themed menus are a regular feature.

Recommended in the area

Audley End House, Duxford Air Museum, Newmarket Races

The Crown

Address:	Bridge Road, BROUGHTON,
	Huntingdon, PE28 3AY
Tel:	01487 824428
Fax:	01487 824912
Email:	simon@thecrownbroughton.co.uk
Website:	www.thecrownbroughton.co.uk
Map ref:	3, TL27
Directions:	Just off A141 Huntingdon–Warboys road.

Open: 12–3 6–11 (all day Sun) 🍴 L 12–2 D 6.30–9
🍽 L 12–2 D 6.30–9 **Facilities:** Children welcome
Garden **Parking:** 25 **Notes:** 🐕 ⊕ Free House 🍷 10

The Crown is an 18th-century country pub set next to the church in a conservation village. When it closed in 2000 around 40 villagers raised the money to buy it and renovate it for reopening in 2001. Now a village-owned tenancy, it is run by chef proprietor Simon Cadge, who offers a good choice of food from a varied menu, and real ales from Greene King, Elgood's and other local breweries. Occasional live music in the spacious garden is hugely popular.

Recommended in the area

Houghton Mill (NT); Hinchingbrook House & Park; Raptor Foundation

The Black Horse

Address:	14 Overend, ELTON,
	nr Peterborough, PE8 6RU
Tel:	01832 280240
Map ref:	3, TL09
Directions:	Off A605 Peterborough–Northampton road

Open: 12–11.30 🍴 L 12–2 D 6–9 🍽 L 12–2 D 6–9
Facilities: Children welcome Garden **Parking:** 30
Notes: 🐕 ⊕ Free House 🍷 14

A genuine village inn with a warm country atmosphere, in  spite of the fact that one past landlord was an assistant to Tom and Albert Pierrepoint, Britain's most famous hangmen, and the building once was a morgue and village jail. Today's clientele is very much alive, and its current landlord is having to expand the car park to meet growing demand. The real ales include Everards Tiger and seasonal Nethergate brews, while superb food features bar snacks (lunchtime only) and full à la carte in the restaurant. During the summer a tapas menu is available if the kitchen is ever closed. Traditional set Sunday lunch menu. The delightful one-acre rear garden overlooks Elton's famous church and rolling open countryside.

Recommended in the area

Peterborough Cathedral; Prebendal Manor House; Elton Hall

The Pheasant Inn

Address: Village Loop Road, KEYSTON, Huntingdon, PE28 0RE
Tel: 01832 710241
Fax: 01832 710340
Email: thepheasant@cyberwave.co.uk
Website: www.huntsbridge.com
Map ref: 3, TL07
Directions: Signed from A14, W of Huntingdon
Open: 12–3 6–11 ⓑ L 12–2 D 6.30–9.30 ⓘⓞⓘ L 12–2 D 6.30–9.30 **Facilities:** Children welcome Garden
Parking: 40 **Notes:** ⊘ on premises ⊕ Huntsbridge Ltd ♟ 16

This is one of four pubs in the Huntsbridge group, owned by Master of Wine John Hoskins and the service is in typical Huntsbridge style – friendly and informal, but efficient. The large bar is a traditional and unspoilt mixture of oak beams, big open fires and simple wooden furniture, with three real ales on offer, and the three dining areas are comfortable and intimate. Chef Jay Scrimshaw has devised an eclectic menu with influences rooted in the south of France.

Recommended in the area

Grafham Water; Boughton House; Rushden Triangular Lodge

The Three Horseshoes

Address: High Street, MADINGLEY, CB3 8AB
Tel: 01954 210221
Fax: 01954 212043
Email: thethreehorseshoes@huntsbridge.co.uk
Website: www.huntsbridge.com
Map ref: 3, TL36
Directions: W of Cambridge off A1303, Nr M11 junc 13
Open: 11.30–3 6–11 (Sun eve 6–8.30) ⓑ L 12–2 D 6.30–9.30 ⓘⓞⓘ L 12–2 D 6.30–9.30 **Facilities:** Garden
Parking: 70 ⊕ Huntsbridge Inns ♟ 20

The Three Horseshoes is a picturesque thatched inn with a busy bar serving Adnams Bitter and Hobson's Choice, and a conservatory-restaurant. Owner/chef, Richard Stokes, is a local from the Fens whose Italian-influenced food and wine list attracts a mixed crowd of locals, business people and visitors. It's best to book at weekends. Imaginative starters include carpaccio of beef with rocket and horseradish crème fraîche, with main courses such as double-baked spinach and ricotta torte, or pizzetta of red onions, plum tomatoes and smoked mozzarella. Finish with cherries in Valpolicella.

Recommended in the area

Cambridge University Botanic Gardens; Imperial War Museum Duxford; Wimpole Hall

The George Inn

Address: High Street, SPALDWICK,
Huntingdon, PE28 0TD
Tel: 01480 890293
Fax: 01480 896847
Map ref: 3, TL17
Directions: 3m W of Huntingdon on A14, junct 18
towards Spaldwick/Stow Longa
Open: 12–11 (Fri-Sat 11–12) ᴪ and ▯◍▮ L 12–2.30
D 6–9.30 **Facilities:** Garden **Parking:** 25 **Notes:** ⊞ ♟ 20

The George has a long history of providing warm and welcoming hospitality to thirsty and hungry visitors. Originally a private residence belonging to the Dartington family, it opened as a coaching inn in 1679 and remains a serene presence beside the manor house and overlooking the village green. These days it is run by The George Partnership of Mark and Louise Smith and Nick Thoday. The fine old building retains a number of its historic features – Heurician wall paintings, the original beams, and fireplaces – all remain intact throughout. The bar is very relaxing, with its comfortable leather sofas, where customers sink back and enjoy good conversation. Cask Marque ales are served here, including Adnams Broadside, Green King IPA and Youngs Special, and there is an extensive wine list. On fine summer days you can take your drinks outside into the beer garden. The lunchtime menu includes bar snacks such as tuscan bean and tomato soup and The George's famous fish pie. There's also a separate award-winning restaurant, located in a beautifully converted barn, where traditional British and Mediterranean dishes are offered from a comprehensive menu. Typical among the starters is baked camembert with rosemary and onion foccacia, while main courses might include home-smoked pork tenderloin with homemade black pudding or crushed celeriac and mustard cream jus. Desserts might include a warm melting valhrona chocolate mousse with pistachio ice-cream. Everything is homemade (including the bread) and all produce is fresh, sourced locally and organic where possible.

Recommended in the area

Grafham Water; Hinchingbrooke Country Park; Hinchingbrooke House

The Bell Inn

★★★ 77% ◉ HOTEL

Address:	Great North Road, STILTON, Peterborough, PE7 3RA
Tel:	01733 241066
Fax:	01733 245173
Email:	reception@thebellstilton.co.uk
Website:	www.thebellstilton.co.uk
Map ref:	3, TL18

Directions: In village centre, just off A1(M) junction 16.
Open: 12–2.30 6–11 (Sun 12–3, 7–10.30 Fri–Sat
5–12) ⓑ L 12–2 D 6.30–9.30 ⓘ L 12–2 D 7–9.30
Rooms: 23 en suite S £75.5 D £99.5 **Facilities:** Garden
Parking: 30 ⊕ Free House ☗ 8

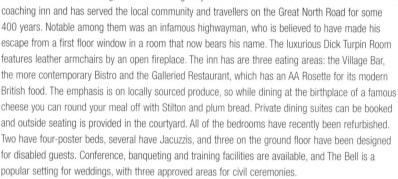

An attractive historic building, The Bell was originally a coaching inn and has served the local community and travellers on the Great North Road for some 400 years. Notable among them was an infamous highwayman, who is believed to have made his escape from a first floor window in a room that now bears his name. The luxurious Dick Turpin Room features leather armchairs by an open fireplace. The inn has are three eating areas: the Village Bar, the more contemporary Bistro and the Galleried Restaurant, which has an AA Rosette for its modern British food. The emphasis is on locally sourced produce, so while dining at the birthplace of a famous cheese you can round your meal off with Stilton and plum bread. Private dining suites can be booked and outside seating is provided in the courtyard. All of the bedrooms have recently been refurbished. Two have four-poster beds, several have Jacuzzis, and three on the ground floor have been designed for disabled guests. Conference, banqueting and training facilities are available, and The Bell is a popular setting for weddings, with three approved areas for civil ceremonies.

Recommended in the area

Peterborough Cathedral; Flag Fen; Imperial War Museum Duxford

The garden of Arley Hall.

The Bhurtpore Inn

Address: Wrenbury Road, ASTON,
Nantwich, CW5 8DQ
Tel: 01270 780917
Email: simonbhurtpore@yahoo.co.uk
Website: www.bhurtpore.co.uk
Map ref: 6, SJ64
Directions: Just off the A530 Nantwich–Whitchurch road
Open: 12–2.30 6.30–11.30 (Sun 12–11.30) ␣ L 12–2
D 6.45–9.30 ␣ L 12–2 D 6.45–9.30 **Facilities:** Garden
Parking: 40 **Notes:** ␣ Free House ␣ 9

An intriguing pub name usually means a colourful history, and The Bhurtpore is named after a city in northern India where a local landowner, Lord Combermere, was involved in a fierce battle in 1825. The present owners' family had run the pub back in the 19th century, and in 1991 they bought it back and turned it into this lively village free house. The pub now offers freshly prepared food, and an exceptional range of Highland malts and real ales from small independent craft brewers. The bottled beer collection totals 150, including one of the largest ranges of Belgian ales in Britain.
Recommended in the area
Blue Planet Aquarium; Mouldsworth Motor Museum; Arley Hall and Gardens

The Pheasant Inn

★★ 81% ⊛ HOTEL
Address: BURWARDSLEY, Nr Tattenhall, CH3 9PF
Tel: 01829 770434
Fax: 01829 771097
Email: info@thepheasantinn.co.uk
Website: www.thepheasantinn.co.uk
Map ref: 6, SJ55
Directions: From Chester take A41 Whitchurch rd, after
4m go left to Burwardsley, signs 'Cheshire Workshops'
Open: 11–11 ␣ L 12–10 D 12–10 **Rooms:** 12 en suite,
S £65 D £85 **Facilities:** Children welcome Garden **Parking:** 40 **Notes:** ␣ Free House ␣ 8

In a beautiful rural setting, with views over the Cheshire plain, this delightful half-timbered country inn is cosy, with reputedly the largest log fire in the county, which makes a great setting for the well-kept ales and sophisticated cooking. Expect dishes such as sizzling monkfish and tiger prawns in sweet chilli jam; steak and ale pie; pan-fried venison; braised lamb shank; and spinach and ricotta cannelloni.
Recommended in the area
Beeston Castle; Cholmondeley Castle Gardens; Oulton Park

Albion Inn

Address: Park Street, CHESTER, CH1 1RN
Tel: 01244 340345
Email: christina.mercer@tesco.net
Website: www.albioninnchester.co.uk
Map ref: 5, SJ46
Directions: City centre, by city walls and Newgate
Open: 12–3 5–11 (Sat 12–3 6–11, Sun 12–2.30
7–10.30) ᕈ L 12–2 D 5–8 **Notes:** ㍿ ⊕ Punch Taverns

A Victorian corner pub with old-fashioned values, the
Albion is dedicated to the Great War (1914–18) and there are four officially listed war memorials in the
pub. Other memorabilia including cast iron fireplaces, enamel signs, William Morris wallpaper, and
a 1928 Steck Duo Art Player Piano set the atmospheric scene. Where possible, food is locally sourced,
free range or organic. Dishes range from boiled gammon; roast turkey; and faggots to curries; pasta;
and casseroles, and the house speciality is Staffordshire Oatcakes. Puddings are traditional and drinks
encompass New World wines, guest beers, malt whiskies and stoneground coffee. Dogs are welcomed
with water and a cold sausage, but strictly no children. Bedrooms available.
Recommended in the area
City Walls; River Dee; Chester Cathedral; Roman Amphitheatre

The Cholmondeley Arms

♦♦♦

Address: CHOLMONDELEY, Malpas, SY14 8HN
Tel: 01829 720300
Fax: 01829 720123
Email: guy@cholmondeleyarms.co.uk
Website: www.cholmondeleyarms.co.uk
Map ref: 6, SJ55
Directions: On A49, between Whitchurch and Tarporley
Open: 11–3 6–11 ᕈ L 12–2.30 D 6.30–10
㍿ L 12–2.30 D 6.30–10 **Rooms:** 6 en suite, S £50
D £70 **Facilities:** Children welcome Garden **Parking:** 60 **Notes:** ㍿ ⊕ Free House ♟ 7

Guy Ross-Lowe was a solicitor until he, his wife Carolyn, and Lord and Lady Cholmondeley, the local
landowners, converted this old school into a 'quintessential English pub', which has won many regional
and national awards. All food is freshly prepared, using local produce wherever possible and the set
menu offers sandwiches, steaks and lunchtime-only snacks. Specials include rack of lamb with
flageolet beans; spinach, pine nut and pesto lasagne; and lobster tail with garlic butter.
Recommended in the area
Cholmondeley Castle Gardens; The Croccy Trail; Beeston Castle

Chetwode Arms

Address: Street Lane, LOWER WHITLEY, WA4 4EN
Tel: 01925 730203
Fax: 01925 730870
Email: info@chetwodearms.com
Website: www.chetwodearms.com
Map ref: 6, SJ67
Directions: Chetwode Arms is on the A49, 2m S from junct 10 of the M56, 6m S of Warrington
Open: 12–11 (winter 12–4, 5.30–11) 🍴 L 12–3 D 6–9 ❯ L 12–3 D 6–9.30 **Facilities:** Garden **Parking:** 60
Notes: 🐕 🍺 Punch Taverns 🍷 12

A 400-year-old former coaching inn adorned with window boxes, the Chetwode Arms is built from Cheshire brick and has an interior as cosy and rambling as you could wish for. There's a tap room, which welcomes walkers and their dogs, a bar room with an open fire, and a warren of small, intimate dining rooms and passageways. Somewhere underground, so it is said, a tunnel leads from the pub to the vicarage, and then on to St Luke's Church, which is believed to be the oldest brick-built church still standing in England. From the main dining room you can step out onto a terrace overlooking the pub's own crown green bowling green, one of the best kept in the country. There, with the wall heated gently by the sun, you can while away the hours with a pint of Adnams Broadside or Jennings Cumberland. The proprietors are English and Austrian, so expect a continental touch to the cooking. Lunchtime snacks feature filled baguettes and paninis, while the menu includes such starters as chilli crab cakes with sweet chilli sauce; duck liver pâté with apricot and fresh figs; and wild boar, apple and calvados sausage with sweet potato crisps. Main courses might include such specials as game pie or king prawn pasta, and there's always a selection of meat and fish cooked on volcanic stone, including steaks, wild duck breasts, venison. lamb, salmon and lobster.

Recommended in the area

Arley Hall and Gardens; Anderton Boat Lift; Norton Priory Museum and Gardens

Little Moreton Hall, Congleton.

The Swettenham Arms

Address:	Swettenham Lane, SWETTENHAM, Congleton, CW12 2LF
Tel:	01477 571284
Fax:	01477 571284
Email:	info@swettenhamarms.co.uk
Website:	www.swettenhamarms.co.uk
Map ref:	6, SJ86

Directions: Off the A535 Holmes Chapel to Alderley Edge road, via Forty Acre Lane.
Open: 12–3 6.30–11 (all day Sun) ⓑ and ⑩ L 12–2.30
D 7–9.30 ⑩ **Facilities:** Children welcome Garden **Parking:** 150 ⑭ Free House ⑨ 8

Tucked away behind the parish church, this lovely 16th-century inn has a fascinating history and a bright future, thanks to the excellent range of real ales and the tasty dishes on the extensive menu. Old English Country Fare includes succulent roasts; baked ham and steak and kidney pudding, with specials such as grey mullet filled with prawn duxelle; beef strogonoff; and supreme of chicken filled with goats cheese and red capsicum. Lighter meals include pastas, chilli and Lancashire hot pot.

Recommended in the area

Jodrell Bank Visitor Centre; Little Moreton Hall (NT); Brereton Heath Country Park

"Sea Thrift growing on the Lizard Peninsula.

Trengilly Wartha Inn

♦♦♦ ◎

Address:	Nancenoy, CONSTANTINE, nr Falmouth TR11 5RP
Tel:	01326 340332
Fax:	01326 340332
Email:	reception@trengilly.co.uk
Website:	www.trengilly.co.uk
Map ref:	1, SW72
Directions:	SW of Falmouth off the A39 or A394 Helston road

Open: 11–3 6.30–11 ♨ L 12–2.15 D 6.30–9.30 ▐◎ 7.30–9.30 Rooms: 8 en suite, D £80
Facilities: Children welcome Garden Parking: 40 Notes: ⌒ ⊕ Free House ♟ 15

Trengilly Wartha means 'settlement above the trees' and the trees in question are in the valley of Polpenwith Creek, an offshoot of the Helford River. The inn is tucked away in the hamlet of Nancenoy, surrounded by six acres of gardens and meadows, including a vine-shaded pergola – perfect for summer dining. There is a small restaurant on the side of the pub with an AA Rosette for its food, and plenty of space in the informal bar area, where a conservatory extension houses the family room. Talented chefs prepare everything from scratch using the best local ingredients. The bar menu offers pub favourites and some more adventurous choices, notably 'Trengilly Classics' such as Pad Thai or Tagliolini Cipriani, while in the restaurant there is a fixed price menu of two or three courses. There's always a good seafood selection, with the catch of the day coming straight from a local boat, and in summer it can sell out early. There are some interesting meat dishes too, and a vegetarian alternative. The inn, a free house, offers a great choice of ales (several served straight from the stillages), over 40 malt whiskies and 150 wines, with 15 available by the glass. Six cottage bedrooms are located in the main building, with two more in the Garden Annexe overlooking the lake.

Recommended in the area

Trebah Gardens; National Seal Sanctuary; Helford River Area of Outstanding Natural Beauty

The Halzephron Inn

Address:	GUNWALLOE, Helston, TR12 7QB
Tel:	01326 240406
Fax:	01326 241442
Email:	halzephroninn@gunwalloe1.fsnet.co.uk
Website:	www.halzephron-inn.co.uk
Map ref:	1, SW62

Directions: 3m S of Helston on A3083, right to Gunwalloe, through village, Inn on left.
Open: 11–2.30 6.30–11 (summer eve 6–11) ⓛ L 12–2 D 7–9 ⑩ L 12–2 D 7–9 **Facilities:** Garden **Parking:** 14
Notes: ⊞ Free House ♟ 6

Ex-teacher and recipient of an AA Inn of the Year award at her previous establishment at Trebarwith, Angela Thomas has been at the Halzephron for 15 years. She ensures a warm welcome, a good choice of real ales, a large selection of malts, and delicious food prepared from fresh local produce. Specials in the bar and bistro-style restaurant include pork, mushroom and rosemary fricassée with rice pilaff; calves' liver and chorizo casserole; and roasted brill on Savoy cabbage and bacon.
Recommended in the area
RNAS Culdrose; Trebah Gardens; Goonhilly Satellite Earth Station

---

The Halfway House Inn

Address:	Fore Street, KINGSAND, Torpoint, PL10 1NA
Tel:	01752 822279
Fax:	01752 823146
Email:	info@halfwayinn.biz
Website:	www.halfwayinn.biz
Map ref:	1, SX45

Directions: Off A38/A374, signs Mount Edcumbe
Open: 12–3 7–11 (all day in summer) ⓛ L 12–2 D 7–9 ⑩ L 12–2 D 7–9 **Facilities:** Children welcome
Notes: ⌂ ⊞ Free House ♟ 10

The Halfway House is just a few steps from the coastal path, among the narrow lanes and colour-washed houses of this quaint fishing village. Licensed since 1850, it has a pleasant stone-walled bar with low-beamed ceilings and a large fireplace. The restaurant serves local produce, notably fresh seafood such as crab; scallops; monkfish tails with peppers and white wine; and fillet of brill with artichokes and bacon.
Recommended in the area
The Eden Project; Dobwalls Adventure Park; Goonhilly Satellite Earth Station

The Pandora Inn

Address: Restronguet Creek, MYLOR BRIDGE,
Falmouth, TR11 5ST
Tel: 01326 372678
Fax: 01326 378958
Website: www.pandorainn.com
Map ref: 1, SW83
Directions: From Truro/Falmouth follow A39, turn left at
Carclew and follow signs to pub.
Open: 10–12 (winter 10.30–11) ⚓ L 12–3 D 6.30–9
🍴 L 12–3 D 7–9 **Facilities:** Children welcome Pontoon
Parking: 30 **Notes:** 🐾 🍺 St Austell Brewery 🍷 9

One of the best known inns in Cornwall, The Pandora is
set by the water in the beautiful surroundings of
Restronguet Creek. Parts of the thatched, white-painted
building date back to the 13th century, and its flagstone floors and low beamed ceilings suggest that
little can have changed since. The atmosphere is splendidly traditional, with lots of snug corners, three
log fires and a collection of maritime memorabilia. The inn is named after the good ship *Pandora*, sent
to Tahiti to capture the *Bounty* mutineers. Unfortunately it was wrecked and the captain court-
marshalled so, forced into early retirement, he bought the inn. A full range of drinks is served,
including fine wines and beers from St Austell Brewery, HSD, Bass and Tribute. Meals are served in the
bars or upstairs in the sail loft restaurant, the Upper Deck. When the sun shines, the tables and chairs
set out on the new pontoon provide an experience akin to walking and eating on water. Food is taken
seriously here, and the lunchtime and evening menus are supplemented by daily specials displayed on
boards. Options range from sandwiches at lunchtime and afternoon teas to fine dining in the
restaurant. Local seafood is a speciality of the house.

Recommended in the area

Trelissick Gardens (NT); National Maritime Museum; Pendennis Castle

The Victory Inn

Address: Victory Hill, ST MAWES, TR2 5PQ
Tel: 01326 270324
Fax: 01326 270238
Email: info@roseland-inn.co.uk
Website: www.victory-inn.co.uk
Map ref: 1, SW83
Directions: Up the Victory Steps adjacent to the Harbour
Open: 11–11 (Fri–Sat 11–12) ৬ L 12–2.15 D 6.30–9
⏹ L 12–2.15 D 6.30–9 Facilities: Children welcome
Notes: ⌁ ⊕ ☺ 6

This friendly fishermen's local, with spectacular harbour views, is named after Nelson's flagship, HMS *Victory*. These days it doubles as a modern award-winning dining pub, offering the freshest of local seafood. The blackboard specials change according to the day's catch, with dishes such as fresh crab salad; lobster thermidor; cod and chips; crab and mushroom omelette; and trio of fish with squid ink risotto. There's also a choice of pub grub and lunchtime snacks. In addition to the range of real ales, there's a decent selection of wines by the glass, plus speciality spirits.

Recommended in the area

The Eden Project; Falmouth Maritime Museum; St Mawes Castle

The Falcon Inn

◆◆◆◆

Address: ST MAWGAN, Nr Newquay, TR8 4EP
Tel: 01637 860225
Fax: 01637 860884
Email: enquiries@thefalconinn-newquay.co.uk
Website: www.thefalconinn-newquay.co.uk
Map ref: 1, SW86
Directions: Northeast of Newquay off A3059 or A39
(follow airport signs); in village, pub is at bottom of hill
Open: 11–3 6–12 (Sun 12–5, 7–11) ৬ L 12–2 D 6–9
⏹ L 12–2 D 6–9 Rooms: 2 en suite, D £78 Facilities: Children welcome Garden Parking: 25
Notes: ⌁ ⊕ St Austell Brewery ☺ 7

St Mawgan, a recent winner of Best Kept Village in Cornwall, is the lovely setting for this unspoilt 16th-century inn, which has log fires in winter and award-winning gardens with children's play area. A range of dishes is offered, from lunchtime snacks to three-course dinners, including creative seafood specials, in a dining room which retains its original Delabole slate floor.

Recommended in the area

Watergate Bay; Eden Project; Crealy Adventure Park

The Springer Spaniel

Address: TREBURLEY, Nr Launceston, PL15 9NS
Tel: 01579 370424
Fax: 01579 370113
Email: springerspaniel@btconnect.com
Website: www.thespringerspaniel.org.uk
Map ref: 1, SX37
Directions: On the A388 halfway between Launceston and Callington
Open: 11–3 6–11 ▆ L 12–2 D 6.30–9 ▐◎▐ L 12–2 D 6.30–9 **Facilities:** Children welcome Garden
Parking: 30 **Notes:** ⊬ ⊕ Free House ♇ 7

Reputedly a pub for the last 200 years, the old creeper-clad walls of The Springer Spaniel conceal a cosy bar with high-backed wooden settles, farmhouse-style chairs and a wood-burning stove to keep the chill out on colder days. The atmosphere is friendly and conversation flows naturally, making it easy for the visitor to join in and discover interesting facts about Cornish rural life from the locals. Ales from Cornish brewers are served – St Austell, Sharps and Skinners – and wines are treated seriously, with a list that features wines of the month. There is a cosy candlelit restaurant, and for better weather a landscaped garden with outdoor seating. The menu changes with the seasons, and specials change by the day, so the food reflects the unique landscape in which it is produced, cooked and served. A recent winter menu from the restaurant included such warming offerings as seafood chowder; pan fried strips of Cornish beef in a creamy Stilton and brandy sauce; venison and game pie; and the vegetarian option of spiced winter vegetable casserole. Bar lunches are no less tempting, with such favourites as steak and kidney pudding; local pork sausages with mash and onion gravy; and chilli or meatballs with spaghetti, both made from organic beef. To round off the meal, desserts might include warm dark chocolate tart; fruit crumble; and ice cream from Langage Farm in Devon.

Recommended in the area

Hidden Valley; Tamar Otter Sanctuary; Launceston Castle

The New Inn

★★ 78% ◉ ◉ HOTEL

Address:	New Grimsby, TRESCO, Isles of Scilly, TR24 0QQ
Tel:	01720 422844
Fax:	01720 423200
Email:	newinn@tresco.co.uk
Website:	www.tresco.co.uk/holidays/new_inn.asp
Map ref:	1, SV81
Directions:	By New Grimsby Quay

Open: 11–11 🍺 L 12–2 D 6–9 ©️ 7–9
Rooms: 16 en suite, D from £150 (B&B for 2) Facilities: Children welcome Garden
Notes: 🍺 Free House 🍷 8

The only pub on Tresco, The New Inn is on most visitors' itineraries, so it's a good idea to make a reservation for a meal here. It stands perched above the harbour of New Grimsby, looking across the narrow channel to Bryher and is the island's social centre, a natural interface between the islanders – gardeners, fishermen, farmers, shopkeepers and estate workers – and visitors. The main bar is panelled with exotic woods that were washed ashore from a passing ship, and here a range of real ales is served, including the local Tresco Tipple. Outside there is a patio area with some of the sub-tropical plants for which the island is famous. Wonderful, fresh locally caught seafood is the speciality of the house, along with tender Tresco-reared beef, and the inn has two AA Rosettes for its food. Special events throughout the year include real ale festivals in May and September, visiting musicians and a Guy Fawkes evening in November. Guests visiting out of season might see the massing of migrant birds, witness whole fields of narcissi flowering while the mainland shivers, or experience the full force of a winter storm from the sanctuary of the cosy bar. Children's facilities are provided, and overnights guests can enjoy spectacular harbour views from some of the rooms.

Recommended in the area

Tresco Abbey Garden; Valhalla Figurehead Collection; sandy beaches

Greenhow Hill, Yorkshire Dales National Park.

Drunken Duck Inn

♦♦♦♦♦ ◉◉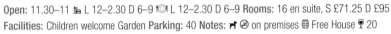

Address: Barngates, AMBLESIDE, LA22 0NG
Tel: 015394 36347
Fax: 015394 36781
Email: info@drunkenduckinn.co.uk
Website: www.drunkenduckinn.co.uk
Map ref: 5, NY30
Directions: From Kendal take A591 to Ambleside, then follow Hawkshead sign. In 2.5m there's an inn sign on right, and it's 1m up hill

Open: 11.30–11 ⓑ L 12–2.30 D 6–9 ⓘⓞⓘ L 12–2.30 D 6–9 **Rooms:** 16 en suite, S £71.25 D £95
Facilities: Children welcome Garden **Parking:** 40 **Notes:** ⌗ ⊘ on premises ⊞ Free House ⓦ 20

This 17th-century inn is surrounded by 60 private acres of rapturously beautiful countryside. In spring, you can barely move for flowers, and all year round there are striking views of fells and lakes. Under the same family ownership since 1977, the Drunken Duck has been refurbished to high standards, with a stylish mix of modern luxury and old world charm. Expect plenty of sofas to lounge in, a pretty residents' garden, and glamorous bedrooms should you feel inclined to stay. The bar, with its antique settles and log fires, serves beers from the inn's own Barngate Brewery. These have been named after much loved dogs: Cracker, Tag Lag and Chester's Strong and Ugly. The candlelit restaurant offers intelligent, modern British cuisine, with the same menu offered at lunch and dinner, supplemented by specials. Start, perhaps, with smoked haddock and pea risotto, or duck and spring onion confit with parmesan tuilles and chilli jam, followed by pan-fried Holker venison fillet with wild mushroom and foie gras croûte; rump of Kendal rough fell lamb with minted pea puree, Lyonnaise potatoes and rosemary jus; or hand-dived seared scallops. Desserts might include saffron scented brûlée with sesame caramel and mango salsa, or you could try the gourmet cheese list, with seven artisan offerings.

Recommended in the area

Lake District Visitor Centre; Armitt Museum; Windmere Steamboat Centre

Derwent Water from Walla Crag.

The Pheasant

★★★ 81% ◉ HOTEL

Address:	BASSENTHWAITE LAKE, Cockermouth, CA13 9YE
Tel:	017687 76234
Fax:	017687 76002
Email:	info@the-pheasant.co.uk
Website:	www.the-pheasant.co.uk
Map ref:	5, NY23
Directions:	On A66 Keswick–Cockermouth road
Open:	11.30–2.30 5.30–10.30 (Sun 6–10.30)

 L 12–2 D – ⏃ L 12.30–2 D 7–9 **Rooms:** 15 en suite, S £80 D £150 **Facilities:** Garden **Parking:** 50 **Notes:** ⌖ ⏀ Free House ⏃ 12

Huntsman John Peel was a regular, and the Cumbrian painter Edward Thompson bartered for beer in the pub – two of his originals hang in the bar. The interior is resplendent with period furnishings, panelled walls, oak settles and beams and food is taken very seriously, with such dishes as roast rack of Cumbrian lamb and honey-glazed guinea fowl. The bar has a selection of 50 malt whiskies.

Recommended in the area

Muncaster Castle; Derwent Water; Rheged Discovery Centre

The Wheatsheaf at Beetham

★★★★ INN

Address: BEETHAM, nr Milnthorpe, LA7 7AL
Tel: 015395 62123
Fax: 015395 64840
Email: info@wheatsheafbeetham.com
Website: www.wheatsheafbeetham.com
Map ref: 6, SD47
Directions: On A6 5m N of M6 junct 35
Open: 11.30–3 5.30–11 (Sun 12–3, 6.30–10.30)
L 12–2 D 6–9 L 12–2 D 6–9 Rooms: 6 en suite,
S £55 D £69.50 Facilities: Garden Parking: 40 Notes: ⊘ on premises ⊕ Free House ♟ 10

A family-owned free house dating from 1609, The Wheatsheaf is very much a dining inn and a perfect base for exploring the Lake District and the Yorkshire Dales. The award-winning menu is served in the tap bar by a real fire, in the lounge bar, or upstairs in the more formal dining room, where candlelight and fresh flowers contribute to the sense of occasion. The menu has a long list of starters and light dishes that would also make a perfect bar snack, and main courses are separated into 'simple' and 'special' categories. Simple dishes might include steak, mushroom and local ale pie; sausage and mash; or slowly braised lamb, while more elaborate concoctions have recently included halibut loin with a sauté of hot buttered garlic prawns; slow roasted half of duck in honey and coriander with black cherry sauce; and wild mushroom, tomato and goat's cheese bread-and-butter pudding with sweet chilli oil. All dishes are home-made using only the freshest and finest of locally-sourced ingredients. The cellar is well stocked with local ales and a good choice of wines, including 11 by the glass. The AA has recently awarded a four-star rating to the newly refurbished accommodation. All the rooms have TVs, tea- and coffee-making facilities and toiletries, and some rooms have DVD players. The Wheatsheaf also has three rooms for conferences, training courses, receptions and private meals.

Recommended in the area

Levens Hall; Lakeland Wildlife Oasis; Leighton Hall

Sunset across Eskdale in the Lake District National Park.

The Boot Inn

Address: BOOT, Eskdale Valley, CA19 1TG
Tel: 019467 23224
Fax: 019467 23337
Email: enquiries@bootinn.co.uk
Website: www.bootinn.co.uk
Map ref: 5, NY10
Directions: From A595 follow signs Eskdale, then Boot
Open: 11–11 ▣/◉ L 11–3 D 6–9 **Facilities:** Children
welcome Garden **Parking:** 30 **Notes:** ⌁ ⊞ Hartleys ♇ 8

Whether you are in the bar with its crackling log fire, in the light and airy conservatory, or in the dining room, which dates back to 1578, you are assured of a very warm welcome by Francis, Lesley and the friendly staff at The Boot Inn. At the end of an energetic day, enjoy a drink in the bar, the snug or the Green room and plan a day amidst some of the best scenery and walking areas in England. Traditional games are available in the bar, as well as pool and a plasma screen TV. There is also a good selection of real ales, a comprehensive wine list and some good malt whiskies. Nine bedrooms are also available, all comfortably furnished with lovely views and tea- and coffee-making facilities.

Recommended in the area

Muncaster Castle; La'al (Little) Ratty Steam Train; Whitehaven Rum Story

Hare & Hounds Country Inn

Address: BOWLAND BRIDGE,
Grange-over-Sands,   LA11 6NN
Tel: 015395 68333
Fax: 015395 68777
Map ref: 6, SD48
Directions: From M6 junct 36 take A590, turning left
after 3m to stay on the A590, then right after 3m onto
A5074, after 4m sharp left and next left after 1m
Open: 11–11 ⓑ L 12–2.30 D 6–9 ⓞ L 12–2.30 D 6–9
Facilities: Children welcome Garden **Parking:** 80
Notes: ⊞ Free House ♇ 10

Formerly a coaching inn, dating back to the 17th century, the Hare & Hounds is beautifully located
in the hamlet of Bowland Bridge in the spectacular Winster Valley, with superb views of the nearby
Cartmel Fells. Just a short drive west on minor roads is Windermere. Inside, the pub has plenty
of character, with its flagstone floors, stone walls and exposed oak beams, and to enhance the
traditional atmosphere, open fires warm the ancient pews in inclement weather. The bar serves
a number of well-kept real ales, including Jennings and Black Sheep, and a dozen wines are available
by the glass. From the full menu you can choose starters like smoked salmon and crab cakes with dill
and mustard mayonnaise; and button mushrooms grilled with Welsh rarebit. Main course offerings
might include roast duck with honey, ginger and bitter orange sauce; salmon and broccoli 'en croute'
with orange and chervil hollandaise; or shank of lamb with rosemary, roasted garlic. Fresh mussels are
cooked in one of three sauces according to your preference, and a choice of sauces is also available
to accompany the succulent chargrilled steaks. Children have their own menu, or they can have child
portions of dishes from the adult menu, and on fine days, they will appreciate the play area and
swings in the lovely garden.

Recommended in the area

Windermere and Bowness; Holker Hall & Gardens; Levens Hall

Sun Hotel & 16th Century Inn

Address: CONISTON, LA21 8HQ
Tel: 015394 41248
Fax: 015394 41219
Email: thesun@hotelconiston.com
Website: www.thesunconiston.com
Map ref: 5, SD39
Directions: From the A591 at Ambleside take A593 to Coniston. Pub is signed from the bridge in the village.
Open: 12–11 🍺 L 12–2.30 D 6–9 🍽 L 12–2.30 D 6–9
Facilities: Garden **Parking:** 20 **Notes:** 🐕 ⊕ 🍷 7

The Sun, a 16th-century inn with a hotel attached, is set on a hill leading up to the Old Man of Coniston. A lovely Lakeland building, it retains its stone walls and floors, beams and an old range in the fireplace, and was Donald Campbell's base during his final water speed record. The menus offer a good choice of food and there are great views from the conservatory and large garden.
Recommended in the area
Coniston Water boat trips in Steam Yacht Gondola; Grizedale Forest Park; Brantwood

The Shepherd's Arms Hotel

Address: ENNERDALE BRIDGE,
Lake District National Park, CA23 3AR
Tel: 01946 861249
Fax: 01946 861249
Email: shepherdsarms@btconnect.com
Website: www.shepherdsarmshotel.co.uk
Map ref: 5, NY01
Directions: SW of Cockermouth off A5086 Egremont rd
Open: 11–2 6–11 (all day Apr–Oct) 🍺 L 12.15–1.45 D 6.15–8.45 🍽 L 12.15–1.45 D 6.15–8.45
Facilities: Children welcome Garden **Parking:** 8
Notes: 🐕 ⊕ Free House

On one of the loveliest stretches of Wainwright's Coast to Coast footpath, this informal free house is a favourite with walkers. There are a selection of real ales, and during colder months, open fires warm the bar, which is a venue for local musicians. A nicely varied menu has dishes like breaded haddock or local sirloin steak and plenty for vegetarians, such as nut and mushroom fettuccine.
Recommended in the area
Florence Mine Heritage Centre; The Rum Story; Clints Quarry Nature Reserve

The Highland Drove Inn and Kyloes Restaurant

Address: GREAT SALKELD, Penrith, CA11 9NA
Tel: 01768 898349
Fax: 01768 898708
Email: highlanddroveinn@btinternet.com
Website: www.highland-drove.co.uk
Map ref: 6, NY53
Directions: E from Penrith on A686 then N on B6412.
Open: 12–3 6–11 (Sat 12–11) ♿ L 12–2 D 6.30–9
🍽 L 12–2 D 6.30–9 Facilities: Children welcome
Garden Parking: 6 Notes: 🐾 🛢 Free House 🍷 14

Dating back 300 years, this one-time droving pub is in the heart of the stunning Eden Valley. Traditional local dishes are featured on the menus, and the daily specials reflect what's in season. There's always sea bass, brill and wild salmon, sharing the menu with innovative chicken dishes and succulent, properly matured steaks from herds reared in Cumbria.

Recommended in the area

Wetheriggs Country Pottery; Brougham Castle; Acorn Bank Garden

The Queens Head Hotel

★★   71% ® HOTEL
Address: Main Street, HAWKSHEAD, LA22 0NS
Tel: 015394 36271
Fax: 015394 36722
Email: enquiries@queensheadhotel.co.uk
Website: www.queensheadhotel.co.uk
Map ref: 5, SD39
Directions: 8m N of Newby Bridge off A590
Open: 11–11 ♿/🍽 L 12–2.30 D 6.15–9.30 Rooms:
14 (12 en suite), Dbl en suite from £45 (£37.50 private
bathroom) Facilities: Children welcome Garden Parking: 14 🛢 Frederic Robinson Ltd 🍷 11

In the heart of the village where Wordsworth went to school and Beatrix Potter created Peter Rabbit, this handsome Elizabethan establishment has flagstone floors, oak timbers and open fires. Close to Esthwaite Water, between Lake Windermere and Coniston Water, this makes a good base for exploring the Lake District. Food, served in the lounge or the dining room, features fresh local produce. Of the bedrooms, some are contemporary, while others have romantic four-poster beds.

Recommended in the area

Hilltop; Brantwood; Grizedale Forest Park

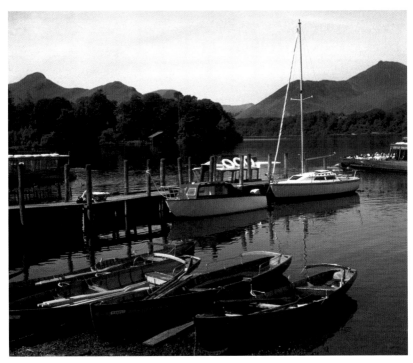

Derwent Water.

The Horse and Farrier Inn

Address: Threlkeld Village, KESWICK, CA12 4SQ
Tel: 017687 79688
Fax: 017687 79823
Email: info@horseandfarrier.com
Website: www.horseandfarrier.com
Map ref: 5, NY22
Directions: Off A66 E of Keswick, in centre of village.
Open: 8am–12am ⓑ L 12–2 D 6–9 ⓘ L 12–2 D 6–9
Facilities: Children welcome Garden **Parking:** 60
Notes: ⓣ ⊕ Jennings Brothers Plc ⓟ 15

An old stone-built inn with a long garden, The Horse and Farrier is in a beautiful village with views of Skiddaw to the west and Helvellyn to the south. Wonderful walks in the vicinity include the former line of the Keswick to Threlkeld railway. Real ales from Cumbrian brewer Jennings are served in bars with hunting prints and log fires, and regular diners are a testament to the quality of the food offered in the bar or beamed restaurant. The guest bedrooms and adjacent cottage all have amazing views. Dogs are permitted.

Recommended in the area

Theatre by the Lake; Rookin House Adventure Centre; Keswick Golf Club

Three Shires Inn

★★ 71% HOTEL

Address:	LITTLE LANGDALE, Ambleside, LA22 9NZ
Tel:	015394 37215
Fax:	015394 37127
Email:	enquiries@threeshiresinn.co.uk
Website:	www.threeshiresinn.co.uk
Map ref:	5, NY30

Directions: Turn off A593, m W of Ambleside signed Wrynose Pass. take 1st left, then 1m up lane
Open: 11–11 (Dec–Jan 12–3, 8–10.30) ▟ L 12–2
D 6–8.45 ▝◎▘ 6–8.30 Rooms: 10 en suite, D £76 Facilities: Children welcome Garden
Parking: 20 Notes: ⊘ on premises ⊕ Free House

This 19th-century hotel stands in the beautiful and unspoilt valley of Little Langdale, close to the Three Shires Stone where the old counties of Cumberland and Westmorland once joined Lancashire. The Cumbrian slate and stone building was erected in the 1880s, when it provided a much-needed resting place for travellers on the journey over the high passes of Hardknott and Wrynose. Today, with the same family at the helm since 1983, it offers a warm welcome in cosy, completely smoke-free surroundings. The interior combines beams and exposed brickwork with a floral country-house style of decor and on fine days visitors can dine outside and enjoy the fine views. In addition to the list of 40 wines and 50 malt whiskies, real ales from local breweries include Jennings Best, Cumberland Ale, Black Sheep, Hawkshead Bitters and Coniston Ales. The lunchtime menu includes a selection of sandwiches and baguettes, soup, ploughman's and hot dishes, including a home made 'pie of the day'. In the evening you can feast on such starters as prawns marinated with chilli and lemon grass, with mango sauce; or grilled goat's cheese with orange glaze and roasted peppers. These can be followed by a selection of fish, vegetarian options and meat dishes, perhaps local venison with port and stilton sauce and peppered strawberries.

Recommended in the area

Greenburn Mine; Hardknott Roman Fort; Rydal Mount

There are many gift and curiosity shops in Kendal.

The Fat Lamb Country Inn

★★ 67% HOTEL

Address: Crossbank, RAVENSTONEDALE, Kirkby Stephen, CA17 4LL

Tel: 015396 23242

Fax: 015396 23285

Email: fatlamb@cumbria.com

Website: www.fatlamb.co.uk

Map ref: 6, NY70

Directions: On A683 Sedbergh–Kirkby Stephen road

Open: 11–2 6–11 ⓑ L 12–2 D 6–9 🍴 L 12–2 D 6–9

Rooms: 12 en suite, S £52 D £84 **Facilities:** Children welcome Garden **Parking:** 60

Notes: ⌁ ⊕ Free House

A country inn that's serious about the countryside. Proprietor Paul Bonsall owns acres of wetlands behind his hotel and has created a haven for a wide variety of wildlife. Bar snacks and meals are an option, or there's a fixed-price menu in the restaurant, featuring traditional farmhouse fare and modern delights such as smoked local trout with red onion relish, and savoury pancakes.

Recommended in the area

Lake District National Park; Yorkshire Dales National Park; Settle and Carlisle Railway

King's Head

★★★ INN

Address: RAVENSTONEDALE,
             Kirkby Stephen, CA17 4NH
Tel: 015396 23284
Email: enquiries@kings-head.net
Website: www.kings-head.net
Map ref: 6, NY70
Directions: Ravenstonedale is 7m from M6 junct 38
via A685; 6m from Kirkby Stephen
Open: 11–3 6–11 (Fri–Sat all day spring and summer)
🍺 L 12–2 D 6–9 ○ L 12–2 D 6–9 **Rooms:** 3 (2 en suite), S £45 D £60 **Facilities:** Children welcome Garden **Parking:** 10 **Notes:** 🐕 ⊕ Free House ♟ 6

One of the oldest buildings in Ravenstonedale, dating from 1627, this fine old inn is in an unspoilt village in the upper Eden Valley – part of the old county of Westmorland – in an area of outstanding natural beauty between two national parks. In January 2005, it was devastated by Cumbria's worst floods in living memory. During the four months' closure for extensive refurbishment, the owners took the opportunity to discreetly modernise the interior, without compromising its old-world charm. The main bar and snug, for example, still feel very welcoming, especially when you're enjoying a pint of Black Sheep or Dent ale by the log fire. The 50-seat candlelit restaurant has one of the largest collections of whisky jugs in the north of England on display. Here you can choose from extensive lunchtime and evening menus and frequently changing specials, all based on local produce. You might start with the rich Cumberland paté, followed by Ravenstonedale salmon with garlic butter, or perhaps a stir-fry, a pasta dish or one of the char-grilled steaks. Outside in the riverside beer garden you can enjoy the antics of local red squirrels using the aerial runs and feeding stations provided for their support. Bedrooms here are equipped with televisions and tea and coffee-making facilities.

Recommended in the area

Lake District National Park; Yorkshire Dales National Park; Ullswater Steamers cruises

Queen's Head Inn

♦♦♦♦

Address:	TIRRIL, Penrith, CA10 2JF
Tel:	01768 863219
Fax:	01768 863243
Email:	bookings@queensheadinn.co.uk
Website:	www.queensheadinn.co.uk
Map ref:	6, NY52
Directions:	On B5320 Penrith–Pooley Bridge road

Open: 12–3 6–11(all day Fri–Sun and daily Apr–Oct)
🛏 L 12–2 D 6–9.30 🍽 L 12–2 D 6–9.30 Rooms: 7,
S £40 D £70 Facilities: Children welcome Parking: 60 Notes: 🐕 ⊕ Free House 🍷 10

Poet William Wordsworth was once the landlord of this 18th-century free house. Today's owner, Chris Tomlinson, has set up Tirril's micro-brewery next door which produces three beers, the best bitter named after John Bewsher, who bought the pub from Wordsworth. Home of the Cumbrian Beer and Sausage Festival (Aug), and full of beams, flagstones, open fires and memorabilia, this is a pleasant place to enjoy good home-made food such as shoulder of Lakeland lamb or fresh Ullswater trout.

Recommended in the area

Wetheriggs Pottery; steamer cruises on Ullswater; Rheged Discovery Centre

Queens Head Hotel

♦♦♦♦

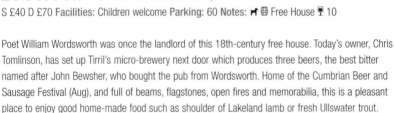

Address:	Townhead, TROUTBECK,
	Windermere, LA23 1PW
Tel:	015394 32174
Fax:	015394 31938
Email:	enquiries@queensheadhotel.com
Website:	www.queensheadhotel.com
Map ref:	6, NY40
Directions:	N of Windermere, on A592 beyond

Troutbeck turning.
Open: 11–11 (Sun 12–10.30) 🛏 L 12–2 D 6.30–9 🍽 L 12–2 D 6.30–9 Rooms: 16 en suite,
S £67.50 D £100 Facilities: Children welcome Parking: 100 ⊕ Free House 🍷

A classic, thriving 17th-century coaching inn, with stunning views across the Garburn Pass, this pub has a reputation for fine food with varied menus, ranging from simple braised dishes to imaginative seafood options. You could start with risotto of crab and Parmesan served with chive salad, followed by shank of Lakeland lamb braised in red wine and rosemary, then the delicious sticky toffee pudding.

Recommended in the area

Brockhole National Park Visitor Centre; The World of Beatrix Potter; Lake Windermere

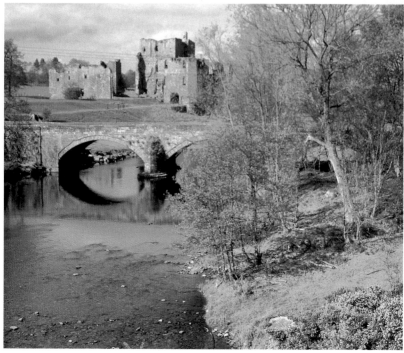

Brougham Castle near Penrith, Lake District National Park.

The Yanwath Gate Inn

Address: YANWATH, Penrith, CA10 2LF
Tel: 01768 862386
Fax: 01768 899892
Email: enquiries@yanwathgate.com
Website: www.yanwathgate.com
Map ref: 6, NY52
Directions: From M6 junct 40, take A66 into Penrith,
then turn rt on A6; cross river and go rt on B5320
Open: 12–11 🍺 L 12–2.30 D 6–9 🍽 L 12–2.30
D 6–9.30 **Facilities:** Children welcome Garden
Parking: 25 **Notes:** 🐕 ⊘ on premises ⊕ Free House ♟ 9

This inn has been offering hospitality in the North Lakes since 1683 and today the busy kitchen is the driving force, offering classic and modern cuisine using fresh local produce. Only Cumbrian ales are served here – Hesket Newmarket, Tirril or Jennings bitter. Fish is delivered fresh every morning and bread is baked on site. Start, perhaps, with tian of black pudding and haggis, with a poached egg and Cumbrian ham, before locally-reared roast beef with chilli roast potatoes and wild mushroom fricassee.
Recommended in the area
Rheged; Brougham Hall; steamer cruises on Ullswater

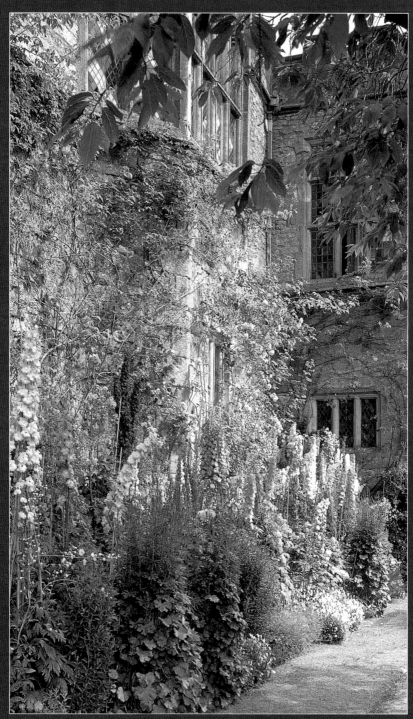

The garden of Haddon House, Peak District National Park..

The Monsal Head Hotel

★★ 75% HOTEL

Address: Monsal Head, BAKEWELL, DE45 1NL
Tel: 01629 640250
Fax: 01629 640815
Email: enquiries@monsalhead.com
Website: www.monsalhead.com
Map ref: 7, SK26
Directions: 3m from Bakewell, off A6 Buxton road,
taking B6465 via Ashford. Follow Monsal Head signs
Open: 11.30–11(Sun 12–10.30) ᴸ L 12–9.30 D –
|◎| L 12–9.30 D 7–9.30 **Rooms:** 7 en suite, S £40 D £40 **Facilities:** Children welcome Garden
Parking: 20 **Notes:** 🐕 🍺 Free House ♟ 15

In the heart of the Peak District, with superb views over hills and dales, this delightful real ale pub has
flagstone floors, a welcoming fire in winter and a range of cask ales. The menu serves the bar and
restaurant, with a flexible choice of snacks such as marinated salmon or oven-baked goat's cheese
and more filling options like pork loin cutlet served with apple mash and black pudding.

Recommended in the area

Chatsworth House; Haddon Hall; Peak District National Park

Yorkshire Bridge Inn

★★ 72% HOTEL

Address: Ashopton Road, BAMFORD,
               Hope Valley, S33 0AZ
Tel: 01433 651361
Fax: 01433 651361
Email: info@yorkshire-bridge.co.uk
Website: www.yorkshire-bridge.co.uk
Map ref: 7, SK28
Directions: South of A57 onto A6013, pub 1m on right
Open: 10–11 ᴸ L 12–2 D 6–9 |◎| L 12–2 D 6–9
Rooms: 14 en suite, S £50 D £68 **Facilities:** Children welcome Garden **Parking:** 40
Notes: 🐕 🍺 Free House

The inn takes its name from the old packhorse bridge across the River Derwent and makes a great
base for exploring the Peak District. The bars are cosy and welcoming, with plentiful beams, and
on fine summer days you can take a drink or meal outside in the courtyard or spacious beer garden.
The accommodation includes three family rooms. Well behaved dogs are welcome.

Recommended in the area

Ladybower Reservoir; Peak District National Park; Chatsworth House

The Waltzing Weasel Inn

♦♦♦

Address: New Mills Road, BIRCH VALE,
              High Peak, SK22 1BT
Tel: 01663 743402
Fax: 01663 743402
Email: w-weasel@zen.co.uk
Website: www.w-weasel.co.uk
Map ref: 7, SK08
Directions: From A6 take A6015 towards Hayfield
Open: 12–11 (Sun 12–10.30) ⓘ L 12–9 D 7–9
ⓘ L 12–2 D 6–9 Rooms: 8 en suite, S £48 D £75
Facilities: Garden Parking: 42 Notes: ⓘ Free House ⓘ 10

Set amid rolling countryside and old stone walls to the
east of Stockport, this inn offers hearty sustenence
to hikers and motorists alike. Soup, stews, casseroles, game or fresh meat pie are all on the menu,
and the fish and seafood are among the very best around. Enjoy a sloe gin or malt by the open fire.
Recommended in the area
Kinder Scout; Blue John Cavern; Ladybower Reservoir

Bentley Brook Inn

★★ 69% HOTEL

Address: FENNY BENTLEY, Ashbourne, DE6 1LF
Tel: 01335 350278
Fax: 01335 350422
Email: all@bentleybrookinn.co.uk
Website: www.bentleybrookinn.co.uk
Map ref: 7, SK14
Directions: At junct A515/B5056 2m N of Ashbourne
Open: 11–12 ⓘ L 12–9 D 12–9 ⓘ L 12–2.30 D 7–9
Rooms: 10 (9 en suite), S £52.5 D £76
Facilities: Children welcome Garden Parking: 100 Notes: ⓘ ⓘ

This fine old building, within the Peak District National Park, has plenty of charm and character, and
dates back to the 16th century, when it was a farmhouse. Beer connoisseurs will relish the real ales
by Leatherbritches, the Bentley Brook's on-site brewery. The kitchen uses local produce wherever
possible to make its sausages, black pudding, dry cured bacon, oatcakes and bread rolls, and produce
such dishes as Derbyshire lamb hotpot; steak and ale pie; and vegetarian nut roast.
Recommended in the area
Cromford Mill; Middleton Top Engine House; Alton Towers

The Chequers Inn

◆◆◆◆ ◉

Address:	Froggatt Edge, FROGGATT, Calver, Hope Valley, S32 3ZJ
Tel:	01433 630231
Fax:	01433 631072
Email:	info@chequers-froggatt.com
Website:	www.chequers-froggatt.com
Map ref:	7, SK27
Directions:	On the A625 0.5m N of Calver

Open: 12–2 6–9.30 (all day Sat and Sun) ⅃ L 12–2
D 6–9.30 **Rooms:** 5 en suite, from S £70 D £70 **Facilities:** Garden **Parking:** 45
Notes: ⊘ on premises ⊞ Free House ♟ 9

Originally four stone-built 16th-century cottages, this country inn is set on the steep banks of Froggatt Edge, with its westward panorama of the Peak District National Park. Wonderful walks in the area include a wild woodland path leading directly to the Edge from the inn's own garden, which overlooks Hope Valley. Also recommended is a stroll through the pretty village of Froggatt. Relics of former days at the inn include the horse-mounting blocks and old stables, now used to store logs for the winter fires. The smart interior has a bistro feel with rag-washed yellow walls, bare floorboards and Windsor chairs. The menu offers impressive modern gastro-pub fare and the accurately cooked dishes, with an AA rosette for their quality, represent great value for money. The menu features interesting starters such as smoked duck with caramelised kumquats and redcurrant dressing, or glazed goat's cheese with roasted vegetables, and main courses might include saddle of rabbit with creamed leeks and red wine jus; braised lamb shank with rosemary mash and redcurrant sauce; or local speciality sausage on buttered mash with shallot gravy. At lunchtime, the menu is supplemented by hearty sandwiches, pies, battered fish and casseroles. Cosy rooms have either double, twin or four-poster beds.

Recommended in the area

Chatsworth House; Haddon Hall; Eyam

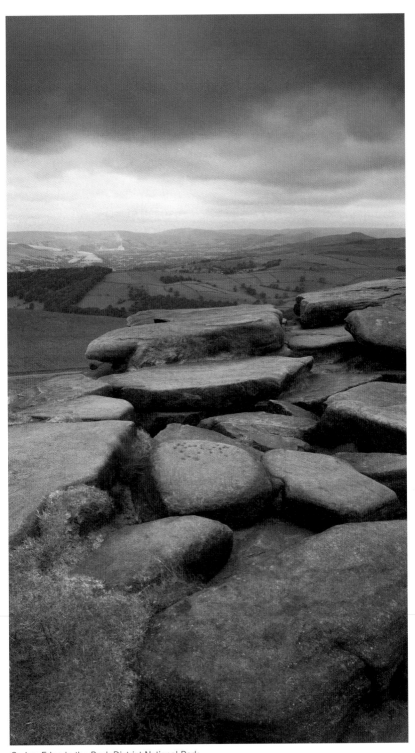

Curbar Edge in the Peak District National Park.

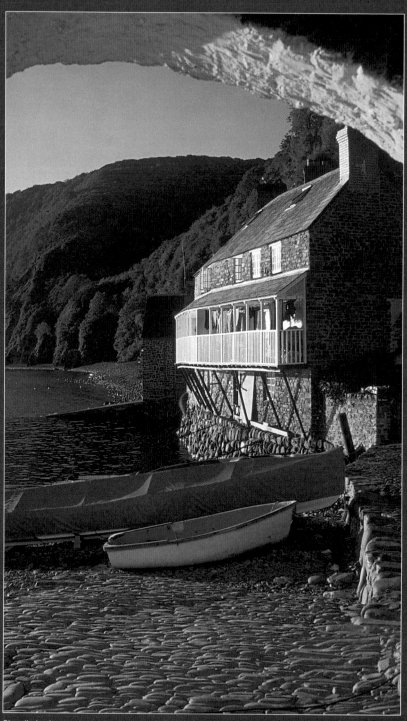

Clovelly harbour.

The Masons Arms

★ ★   78% ◉ HOTEL

Address:	BRANSCOMBE, EX12 3DJ
Tel:	01297 680300
Fax:	01297 680500
Email:	reception@masonsarms.co.uk
Website:	www.masonsarms.co.uk
Map ref:	2, SY18

Directions: Turn off A3052 towards Branscombe,
go down hill and hotel is at bottom

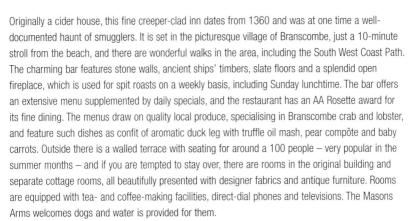

Open: 11–11 (times vary, please phone) 🍴 L 12–2
D 7–9 🍽 D 7–9 **Rooms:** 20 en suite, S £75 D £75 **Facilities:** Children welcome Garden
Parking: 40 **Notes:** 🐾 ⊕ Free House 🍷 14

Originally a cider house, this fine creeper-clad inn dates from 1360 and was at one time a well-documented haunt of smugglers. It is set in the picturesque village of Branscombe, just a 10-minute stroll from the beach, and there are wonderful walks in the area, including the South West Coast Path. The charming bar features stone walls, ancient ships' timbers, slate floors and a splendid open fireplace, which is used for spit roasts on a weekly basis, including Sunday lunchtime. The bar offers an extensive menu supplemented by daily specials, and the restaurant has an AA Rosette award for its fine dining. The menus draw on quality local produce, specialising in Branscombe crab and lobster, and feature such dishes as confit of aromatic duck leg with truffle oil mash, pear compôte and baby carrots. Outside there is a walled terrace with seating for around a 100 people – very popular in the summer months – and if you are tempted to stay over, there are rooms in the original building and separate cottage rooms, all beautifully presented with designer fabrics and antique furniture. Rooms are equipped with tea- and coffee-making facilities, direct-dial phones and televisions. The Masons Arms welcomes dogs and water is provided for them.

Recommended in the area

Old Bakery, Manor Mill and Forge (NT); Jurassic Coast World Heritage Site; Donkey Sanctuary

The marina at Exmouth.

The Five Bells Inn

Address: CLYST HYDON, Cullompton, EX15 2NT
Tel: 01884 277288
Email: info@fivebellsclysthydon.co.uk
Website: www.fivebellsclysthydon.co.uk
Map ref: 2, ST00
Directions: Off M5 at junct 28, then B3181 towards Broadclyst; follow signs for Clyst Hydon
Open: 11.30–3 6.30–11 (winter 11.30–3, 7–11, Sun 12–3, 7–10.30) L 11.30–2 D 7–9 L 11.30–2 D 7–9 **Facilities:** Children welcome Garden **Parking:** 40
Notes: Free House 8

This attractive thatched pub, a farmhouse in the 16th century, actually became a pub early in the 20th century and takes its name from the five bells in the village church tower. It has a reputation for cheerful hospitality and good food, and among beers on offer are Cotleigh Tawny Ale, Otter Bitter and O'Hanlon's. Light meals can be eaten in the bar or garden, with country views, while the restaurant is among four areas that serve a selection of grills, specials, vegetarian and fish dishes.

Recommended in the area

Exeter; Grand Western Canal Country Park; South Devon Coast

The New Inn

♦♦♦♦

Address:	COLEFORD, Crediton, EX17 5BZ
Tel:	01363 84242
Fax:	01363 85044
Email:	enquiries@thenewinncoleford.co.uk
Website:	www.thenewinncoleford.co.uk
Map ref:	2, SS70

Directions: From Exeter take A377, 1.5m after Crediton turn left for Coleford, continue for 1.5m

Open: 12–3 6–11 (Sun 7–10.30) 🍴 L 12–2 D 7–10

🍽 L 12–2 D 7–10 Rooms: 7 en suite, S £60 D £75 Facilities: Children welcome Garden

Parking: 50 Notes: 🛢 Free House ♟ 8

This charming pub, set deep in the heart of Devon and dating back to the 13th century, epitomises the village inn. The pretty whitewashed exterior beneath a thatched roof gives way inside to a treasure trove of old world mementoes such as horse brasses, tankards and plates. There are fires to warm yourself by in colder months, as well as a glorious terraced garden for alfresco dining in the sun. The final touch is Captain, the pea-green resident parrot, always ready to welcome guests in his own inimitable way. A good range of real ales, wines and malts are available. The team, headed by owners Simon and Melissa Renshaw, are passionate about using local produce and supporting local growers. The modern menu relies on simple dishes cooked well: perhaps smoked bacon and liver pâté with green salad to start, followed by brill fillet stuffed with prawns and cheese. There are also imaginative options for vegetarians: goat's cheese, spinach and tomato pancake; or an elegantly simple bowl of tagliatelle with lemon, cream and parsley sauce. The accommodation is spacious and stylish, with coordinating colour schemes in restful tones, and some of the rooms overlook the village stream. Each has a television, tea- and coffee-making facilities and Internet connection.

Recommended in the area

Castle Drogo (NT); Exeter Cathedral; Dartmoor National Park

The Tuckers Arms

Address: DALWOOD, Axminster, EX13 7EG
Tel: 01404 881342
Fax: 01404 881138
Email: davidbeck@tuckersarms.freeserve.co.uk
Website: www.tuckersarms.co.uk
Map ref: 2, ST20
Directions: Off A35 between Honiton and Axminster
Open: 12–3 6.30–11 (Sun 12–10.30) ♨ L 12–2
D 7–8.30 ⑩ L 12–2 D 7–9 Facilities: Garden
Notes: ⊞ Free House ♆ 8

In easy reach of Exeter, Honiton and the Jurassic Coast World Heritage Site, this is a typical Devon longhouse, reputedly dating back about 800 years. The cosy interior features low beams, flagstone floors and inglenook fireplaces. The blackboard menus frequently list game, fresh fish and locally caught crab, with the range changing daily according to market availability. Main courses could include rack of lamb; beef steak terayaki; supreme of chicken, filled with Stilton and served with port wine sauce; or halibut and prawns with parsley and lemon butter.

Recommended in the area

Seaton Tramway; Burrow Hill Farm Gardens; Pecorama Pleasure Gardens

Royal Castle Hotel

★★★ 75% HOTEL
Address: 11 The Quay, DARTMOUTH, TQ6 9PS
Tel: 01803 833033
Fax: 01803 835445
Email: enquiry@royalcastle.co.uk
Website: www.royalcastle.co.uk
Map ref: 2, SX85
Directions: Centre of Dartmouth, overlooking the river.
Open: 11–11 ♨ L 11.30–6.30 D 6.30–10 ⑩ L 12–2
D 7–9.30 Rooms: 25 en suite, S £85 D £155
Facilities: Children welcome Parking: 14 Notes: ⌲ ⊞ Free House ♆ 12

In 1782 two merchants' houses were combined to become this celebrated inn (then called the Castle) and since then it's hosted a string of royals (in 1877 the then Prince of Wales and sons; the current Prince of Wales and Prince Andrew), sailors (Chay Blythe, Sir Francis Chichester) and film stars (Cary Grant; Gregory Peck; Donald Sutherland, while filming *Ordeal by Innocence* here). The fine restaurant specialises in local produce and seafood, with snacks and traditional beers in the bar.

Recommended in the area

Woodland Leisure Park; Dartmouth Castle; Paignton and Dartmouth Steam Railway

The Nobody Inn

Address:	DODDISCOMBSLEIGH, Exeter, EX6 7PS
Tel:	01647 252394
Fax:	01647 252978
Email:	info@nobodyinn.co.uk
Website:	www.nobodyinn.co.uk
Map ref:	2, SX88

Directions: 3m SW of Exeter Racecourse on A38
Open: 12–2.30 6–11 (Sun 7–10.30) 🍺 L 12–2 D 7–10
🍽 D 7.30–9 Facilities: Garden Parking: 50
Notes: 🛢 Free House 🍷 20

Dating from around 1591, this inn has a curious history, including having served as the village's unofficial church house. Apparently it became The Nobody Inn when a deceased landlord's burial took place without him actually in his coffin. Today it's a very popular inn where you will be spoilt for choice in the unusual local ales, 240 whiskies, 600 wines, and 40 local cheeses. Starters include the house speciality, Nobody soup, and crab crumble, followed, perhaps, by sautéed lamb's liver with thyme; fillet of beef with creamy tarragon sauce; or herb-crumbled marlin with lightly spiced pepper courgette.

Recommended in the area

Exeter Cathedral; Crealy Adventure Park; Royal Albert Memorial Museum and Art Gallery

The Hoops Inn and Country Hotel

★ ★ ★ 71% 🏵 HOTEL

Address:	Clovelly, HORNS CROSS,
	Bideford, EX39 5DL
Tel:	01237 451222
Fax:	01237 451247
Email:	sales@hoopsinn.co.uk
Website:	www.hoopsinn.co.uk
Map ref:	1, SS32

Directions: On the A39 between Bideford and Clovelly
Open: 8–11 🍺 L 12–9.30 D 6–9.30 🍽 L 12–3 D 6–9.30 Rooms: 13 en suite, S £65 D £95
Facilities: Children welcome Garden Parking: 100 Notes: 🐾 🛢 Free House 🍷 20

Set in 2½ acres of grounds, this thatch-roofed, cob-walled 13th-century smugglers' inn combines olde worlde charm with a great range of real ales and modern British cooking. Fresh local produce goes into specials such as moules marinière, goat's cheese crostini and classic fish stew.

Recommended in the area

North Devon Maritime Museum; Dartington Crystal; RHS Rosemoor

The Harris Arms

Address:	Portgate, LEWDOWN, EX20 4PZ
Tel:	01566 783331
Fax:	01566 783359
Email:	whiteman@powernet.co.uk
Website:	www.theharrisarms.co.uk
Map ref:	1, SX48
Directions:	Off A30 between Lifton and Lewdown

Open: 12–3 6–11 ⅃ L 12–2 D 6.30–9 ⅃◎⅃ L 12–2
D 6.30–9 Facilities: Children welcome Garden
Parking: 30 Notes: ⅃ ⊕ Free House ⅃ 18

Owners Rowena and Andy Whiteman, Licensees of the
Year 2006, have invested a great deal of time and energy
into establishing the pub's reputation as a place for
discerning diners. Having run vineyards in France and
New Zealand, their wine list is rather special, with many wines from small and ecologically sound
vineyards. Honest food with substance and style, is prepared from locally sourced ingredients.

Recommended in the area

Dartmoor National Park; Lydford Gorge; Dingles Steam Village

Castle Inn

Address:	LYDFORD, EX20 4BH
Tel:	01822 820242
Fax:	01822 820454
Website:	www.castleinnlydford.co.uk
Map ref:	2, SX58
Directions:	Off A386 S of Okehampton

Open: 11–11 (Sun 12–10.30) ⅃ L 12–2
D 6.30–9 ⅃◎⅃ L 12–2 D 6.30–9 Parking: 10
Notes: ⅃ ⊕ Heavitree ⅃ 13

This pretty village pub has one of the loveliest beer gardens in the country, just a short walk from the
impressive Lydford Gorge. The interior oozes atmosphere, with its slate floors, low, lamp-lit beams,
decorative plates and huge ancient fireplace. Owners Richard and Sarah Davies offer Fullers, Otter and
Wadworth cask ales, and freshly prepared dishes, with fresh fish being the house speciality. Expect
starters like warm goat's cheese salad with Parma ham, to be followed, perhaps, by fillet of salmon
with coriander dressed noodles and lemon-butter sauce; with sticky toffee or bread-and-butter
pudding to finish. The shrub-filled garden is great for summer dining.

Recommended in the area

Lydford Gorge; Lydford Castle; Museum of Dartmoor Life

Dartmoor Inn

Address:	LYDFORD, Okehampton, EX20 4AY
Tel:	01822 820221
Fax:	01822 820494
Email:	karen@dartmoorinn.co.uk
Website:	www.dartmoorinn.com
Map ref:	2, SX58
Directions:	On A386 S of Okehampton

Open: 11.30–3 6.30–11 (6–11 in summer)
🍽 L 12–2.15 D 6.30–9.15 🍴 L 12–2.15 D 6.30–9.15
Facilities: Children welcome Garden **Parking:** 35
Notes: 🐾 ⊘ on premises ⊞ Free House 🍷 6

In a pretty village on the edge of Dartmoor, this inn is almost certainly referred to in Charles Kingsley's novel *Westward Ho!* Rustic decor and log fires in winter make the bar an inviting place for a pint of Dartmoor Best, Otter or St Austell HSD. Dishes of character include steamed scallops with oriental dressing or mixed grill of sea fish with garlic and parsley butter.

Recommended in the area

Lydford Castle and Gorge; Finch Foundry; Launceston Steam Railway

Rising Sun Hotel

★★ 69% ◉ ◉ HOTEL

Address:	Harbourside, LYNMOUTH, EX35 6EG
Tel:	01598 753223
Fax:	01598 753480
Email:	risingsunlynmouth@easynet.co.uk
Website:	www.risingsunlynmouth.co.uk
Map ref:	2, SS74
Directions:	19m W of Minehead off A39

Open: 11–11 🍽 L 12–4 D 7–9 🍴 L 12–2 D 7–9
Rooms: 16 en suite, S £59 D £78 **Facilities:** Garden
Notes: ⊞ Free House 🍷

Beneath the Countisbury Cliffs, the highest in England, the Rising Sun has uneven oak floors, crooked ceilings and thick walls, and has inspired literary romance: part of that wild Exmoor love story *Lorna Doone* was written here, and Shelley honeymooned in the garden cottage. With sea and moor nearby, game and seafood are plentiful on the menu. Start with hare and pearl barley terrine, or fennel tarte Tatin, followed by wild boar braised in Cognac, or trio of local game birds on blue poppy seed mash.

Recommended in the area

Exmoor National Park; Woolacombe Beach; Dunster Castle

Noss Mayo.

The Ship Inn

Address: NOSS MAYO, Plymouth, PL8 1EW
Tel: 01752 872387
Fax: 01752 873294
Email: ship@nossmayo.com
Website: www.nossmayo.com
Map ref: 2, SX54
Directions: 5m S of Yealmpton on River Yealm estuary
Open: 11–11 ⓑ L 12–9.30 **Facilities:** Children welcome
Garden **Parking:** 10 **Notes:** ⌀ ⊗ on premises ⌗ Free
House ⦿ 10

The Ship is a waterside free house that has been beautifully renovated using reclaimed materials, including English oak and local stone, in a style that is simple and properly pub-like. The inn's tidal location is superb, making it a popular port of call for yachting enthusiasts (who can tie their boat up right outside) as well as walkers. The daily changing menu of home-made dishes majors on local produce, notably fish, and regional and local beers include Tamar, Jail Ale and Butcombe Blonde. Outside, there is a waterside garden with great views. Dogs are allowed, but only downstairs.

Recommended in the area

Dartmoor National Park; Plymouth; South Devon Coastal Path

The Fox & Goose

Address: PARRACOMBE, EX31 4PE
Tel: 01598 763239
Fax: 01598 763621
Website: www.foxandgoose-parracombe.co.uk
Map ref: 2, SS64
Directions: The Fox is 1m from the A39 between
Blackmoor Gate (2m) and Lynton (6m). Signposted to
Parracombe, with a 'Fox & Goose' sign on approach
Open: 12–3 6–11 🅱/🍽 L 12–2 D 6–9
Facilities: Garden Parking: 15 Notes: 🐾 🍺 Free House ♀ 10

Set in the heart of an unspoilt Exmoor village, this charming free house was originally no more than
a couple of tiny thatched cottages serving the local farming community. It remains a relaxing place,
where drinkers are welcomed with a selection of local ales including Cotleigh Barn Owl, Exmoor Ale
and various guest beers. An extensive wine list has also been introduced, compiled with the help
of local merchants. The inn enjoys a sound reputation for good food, with meals served in the bar
as well as the non-smoking restaurant and, in nice weather, on the paved courtyard overlooking the
river. There's a wide selection of dishes to suit all tastes, based on produce from surrounding farms
and the Devon coast. The blackboard menus change daily, and may include rustic pâtés, venison, lamb
or fillet steak, rich casseroles or hearty pies. Seafood lovers won't be disappointed with a selection
that is brought in daily from local boats. The choice encompasses seasonal crab and lobster, local
mussels, and dishes such as cod fillet with tiger prawns; skate wing with caper salsa; bouillabaisse;
or wild sea bass with stir-fried vegetables. There is also a vegetarian menu, featuring such dishes
as mixed vegetable tagine with cous cous or mushroom stroganoff. To fill that last little space, there's
a nice selection of tempting home-made puddings, which might include a fondue of dark chocolate
melted with Cointreau, with fruit and marshmallows; or hot lemon sponge with clotted cream.

Recommended in the area

Watermouth Castle and Family Theme Park; Combe Martin Wildlife and Dinosaur Park; Exmoor Zoo

Jack in the Green Inn

Address: London Road, ROCKBEARE,
Nr Exeter, EX5 2EE
Tel: 01404 822240
Fax: 01404 823445
Email: info@jackinthegreen.uk.com
Website: www.jackinthegreen.uk.com
Map ref: 2, SY09
Directions: On A30, 3m E of M5 junct 29
Open: 11–2.30 6–11 (Sun 12–10.30) ▙ L 11–2
D 6–9.30 ▥ L 11–2 D 6–9.30 Facilities: Children
welcome Garden Parking: 120 Notes: ⊕ Free House ♟ 12

There has been an inn on this site for several centuries,
but since Paul Parnell took over some 14 years ago,
it has become a beacon of good food in a contemporary and relaxed atmosphere, earning it two
AA Rosettes. The inn is set in four acres of grounds and within its whitewashed walls is a lounge
bar furnished with comfy seating and dark wood tables, and a smart restaurant. The courtyard features
herb beds, hanging baskets and country views. The simple philosophy here is to serve real food to real
people, with a firm commitment from the kitchen to sourcing the best and freshest local produce and
preparing it to a consistently high standard. Typical dishes on the bar menu range from venison
sausages with spiced red cabbage and mash to tomato risotto with chorizo and basil; in the restaurant
you will find dishes such as chicken breast with chestnuts, smoked bacon, shitake mushrooms and
a juniper and Madeira jus; or pan-fried salmon with cucumber, dill and sauce mousseline. The inn is
a free house, serving Cotleigh Tawny Ale, Hardy Country, Otter Ale and Yellowhammer and a list of
nearly 100 wines. Dogs are allowed, with water provided outside and a field for walking them.

Recommended in the area

Bicton Park; Escot Park; Crealy Adventure Park

The Victoria Inn

Address: Fore Street, SALCOMBE, TQ8 8BU
Tel: 01548 842604
Fax: 01548 844201
Email: info@victoriainnsalcombe.co.uk
Website: www.victoriainnsalcombe.co.uk
Map ref: 2, SX73
Directions: centre of Salcombe, overlooking estuary. Salcombe is SW of Torquay via A379 and A381
Open: 11–11 (may close 3–6pm during winter)
L 12–2.30 D 6–9 L – D 7–9 **Facilities:** Children welcome Garden **Notes:** St Austell Brewery 9

The Victoria's chef/landlord, Andy Cannon, is seeing his commitment to using Devon ingredients in his cooking emulated in a big way. Since Andy and his kitchen team won the top award in owner St Austell Brewery's Signature Dish Challenge 2004, the brewery is actively encouraging its entire chain of 156 pubs to work towards the same goal. The dish in question is a delicious chowder starter of handpicked Salcombe white crabmeat, prawns and other shellfish with white wine, fresh dill and Devon double cream. It's hardly surprising that fish and shellfish feature prominently on the menu – the fishing boats that bring in the catch can be seen in the picturesque harbour from the first-floor restaurant. Dishes might include pan-fried turbot wrapped in smoked bacon; seared fillet of sea bass; and fresh white crabmeat platter. Meat-eaters will find much to tempt them here too, such as braised local pheasant accompanied by a rich damson and port sauce with creamed potato and root vegetable mash; a slow-roasted half shoulder of Devon lamb; or free-range chicken and crispy bacon salad. Vegetarians will find an alternative to suit them, such as open wild mushroom lasagne. During the day, a good range of hearty and interesting open sandwiches is also available, and it's always worth checking out the daily specials on the blackboard.

Recommended in the area

Sorley Tunnel Adventure Worlds; Woodlands Leisure Park; South West Coast Path

The Tower Inn

Address:	Church Road, SLAPTON,
	Kingsbridge, TQ7 2PN
Tel:	01548 580216
Email:	towerinn@slapton.org
Website:	www.thetowerinn.com
Map ref:	2, SX84

Directions: Off A379 S of Dartmouth, turn left at
Slapton Sands
Open: 12–3 6–11 (Sun 7–10.30; closed Sun and Mon
evening in winter) ⓑ L 12–2.30 D 6–9.30 ⓘⓞⓘ L 12–2.30
D 7–9.30 Facilities: Children welcome Garden Parking: 6
Notes: ⛨ ⊕ Free House ⓨ 8

The Tower is a 14th-century inn set in the historic village of Slapton in Devon's lovely South Hams region. Its name comes from the ruined tower overlooking the pub's walled garden, which is all that remains of the Collegiate Chantry of St Mary, founded by Guy de Brian in 1373. Indeed, the inn may have been the college's guesthouse, beginning a centuries old tradition of hospitality. The approach to the inn is by a narrow lane and through the porch into a fascinating series of interconnecting rooms, with stone walls, beams, pillars and pews, flagstone floors, scrubbed oak tables and log fires. There's an excellent range of traditional beers, augmented by local cider and mulled wine in winter, and the wine list includes Old and New World wines. Food is available at lunchtime, ranging from sandwiches to full meals, and a separate evening menu is served by candlelight. You might start with a platter of locally smoked seafood, then try the slow-cooked lamb shank, or a leek and gruyère filo parcel with tomato and basil sauce. Desserts might include treacle orange tart, or summer pudding with local ice cream, with a platter of West Country cheeses as an alternative. The bedrooms, in a self-contained wing, have tea and coffee making facilities and TV. Dogs are allowed (water and biscuits provided).

Recommended in the area

Slapton Sands; Slapton Ley Nature Reserve; Cookworthy Museum of Rural Life

The Kings Arms Inn

♦♦♦♦

Address: STOCKLAND, Nr Honiton, EX14 9BS
Tel: 01404 881361
Fax: 01404 881732
Email: info@kingsarms.net
Website: www.kingsarms.net
Map ref: 2, ST20
Directions: 6m NE of Honiton off A30 towards Chard
Open: 12–3 6.30–11.30 ▄ L 12–2 D 6.30–9 ▖◎▐ L
12–2 D 6.30–9 Rooms: 3 en suite, S £45 D £70
Facilities: Children welcome Garden Parking: 45 Notes: 🐾 ⊞ Free House 🍷 15

Tucked away in the Blackdown Hills, this Grade II listed, thatched and whitewashed inn dates from the 16th century and has an impressive flagstone entrance, a medieval oak screen and an original bread oven. Local real ales are served and a good choice of food is offered, including exotic choices such as ostrich and squirrel fish. More cautious diners will be glad to find dishes such as steak and kidney pie; tournedos Rossini; slow-roast belly of pork; salmon hollandaise; and plenty of vegetarian options.

Recommended in the area

Cricket St Thomas Wildlife Park; Jurassic Coast World Heritage Site; Beer Quarry Caves

The Tradesman's Arms

Address: STOKENHAM, Kingsbridge, TQ7 2SZ
Tel: 01548 580313
Fax: 01548 580313
Email: nick@thetradesmansarms.com
Website: www.thetradesmansarms.com
Map ref: 2, SX84
Directions: Just off A379 Kingsbridge–Dartmouth road
Open: 11–3 6–11 (Sun 12–10.30) ▄ L 12–2.30
D 6.30–9.30 ▖◎▐ L 12–2.30 D 6.30–9.30
Facilities: Garden Parking: 14 Notes: 🐾 ⊞ Free House 🍷 18

This part-thatched free house dates from 1390 and forms the centrepiece of a picturesque village that was given to Anne of Cleves by Henry VIII in 1539. Incorporating the former brewhouse and three cottages, the pub is named after the tradesmen who used to call in while working in the area, and is unpretentious and simply furnished. Real ales include Brakspear and South Hams (brewed nearby), while the menu focuses on dishes made from fresh local produce, including prawn and avocado salad; smoked salmon with dill mayonnaise; rack of Loddiswell lamb; and steak and ale pie.

Recommended in the area

Cookworthy Museum of Rural Life; Coleton Fishacre (NT); Overbeck's Museum and Garden (NT)

Totnes.

The Durant Arms

◆◆◆◆

Address: Ashprington, TOTNES, TQ9 7UP
Tel: 01803 732240
Email: info@thedurantarms.com
Website: www.thedurantarms.com
Map ref: 2, SX86
Directions: From Totnes take A381 Kingsbridge road, after 1m turn left for Ashprington
Open: 11.30–2.30 6.30–11 ⓫ L 12–2.30 D 7–9.15
🍽 L 12–2 D 7–9.15 **Rooms:** 7 en suite, S £45 D £75
Facilities: Children welcome (except overnight) Garden **Parking:** 8 **Notes:** ⊕ Free House ⏐ 8

A locally renowned dining pub set in a pretty South Hams village, the Durant Arms dates from the 18th century and was originally the counting house for the neighbouring 500-acre Sharpham Estate. Sharpham wines and cheese are among the culinary delights, offered alongside a choice of real ales and dishes cooked to order, using local produce where possible. The bedrooms are individually designed and furnished to a very high standard.

Recommended in the area

Sharpham Vineyard & Cheese Dairy; Elizabethan town of Totnes; River Dart

The Digger's Rest

Address: WOODBURY SALTERTON, EX5 1PQ
Tel: 01395 232375
Fax: 01395 232711
Email: bar@diggersrest.co.uk
Website: www.diggersrest.co.uk
Map ref: 2, SY08
Directions: E of Exeter. From M5 junct 30, take A376 Exmouth road, turn left onto A3052, towards Newton Poppleford and Sidmouth, then right to Woodbury Salterton
Open: 11–3 6–11 (all day Sat and Sun) ⓑ L 12–2 D 7–9.30 ⓘ L 12–2 D 6.30–9.30 **Facilities:** Children welcome Garden **Parking:** 30 **Notes:** ⓜ Free House ⓟ 10

Originally a Devon cider house, this picturesque country inn is noted for traditionally drawn Otter ales, for its home-cooked food and for its relaxed, welcoming atmosphere. The thick 500-year-old walls consist of stone and cob with heavy beams beneath a thatched roof. Inside, soft furnishings, soft lighting and West Country art works contrast with antique furniture and a refurbished skittle alley. The patio garden provides the perfect setting for alfresco drinking and dining, and is especially attractive when lit up at night. A single menu is offered in the bar and non-smoking restaurant. Weekly changing dishes could include pan-fried scallops with bacon, served with dressed leaves; crab and ginger salad with lemon confit; warm roasted Mediterranean vegetable crostini; chargrilled lamb cutlets with caramelised red onions and yoghurt and mint dressing; Devon free-range chicken breast, pan-fried with Muscat wine and black pudding; slow cooked lamb shanks in a rich red wine and tomato sauce; and penne pasta with mushroom, parmesan, garlic and cream sauce. A passion fruit crème brûlée; or warm raspberry and cinnamon torte can sweetly round off the dining experience.

It would be a shame to have to rush through such a meal, but for travellers in a hurry, who might not have time for the cooked-to-order meals to arrive, the Digger's Rest will take orders by email on the day you want to eat there (email must be received by 11am for lunch, 11.30am for other times) and guarantee to have your meal served within 15 minutes of your specified time of arrival. It's a thoughtful service that epitomises the care and attention that's the hallmark of this fine establishment.

Recommended in the area

Crealy Adventure Park; Bicton Park Botanical Gardens; The World of Country Life

DORSET

Lyme Regis harbour.

Shave Cross Inn

Address: Shave Cross, Marshwood Vale,
BRIDPORT, DT6 6HW
Tel: 01308 868358
Fax: 01308 867064
Email: roy.warburton@virgin.net
Website: www.theshavecrossinn.co.uk
Map ref: 2, SY49
Directions: From Bridport take B3162, in 2m turn left
signed Broadoak/Shave Cross, then Marshwood
Open: 11–3 6–11 (all day Tue–Sun in summer and on
BH Mons) ⓑ L 12–2.30 D 5–9.30 ⓘ L 12–2.30 D 7–9.30 **Facilities:** Children welcome Garden
Parking: 30 **Notes:** 🚭 ⊕ Free House ♟ 8

With its thatched roof and ancient cob and flint walls, the friendly family-run Shave Cross looks every
inch the typical Dorset pub, and it's tucked away down narrow lanes in the heart of the beautiful
Marshwood Vale. Dating from the 13th century, it was once a stopping point for pilgrims and monks
on their way to the church of St Wite in nearby Whitchurch Canonicorum, and it was here at the inn
that the monks had their tonsures shaved – hence the name. In the bar, with timeworn blue lias
flagstones on the floor, is the perfect inglenook fireplace for smoking hams. The restaurant has some
wonderful old beams, combining with the elegantly set tables and stylish decor to create a particularly
inviting atmosphere. The kitchen uses fresh local produce wherever possible, and since the chef
is from Tobago, a Caribbean influence is plain to see on a menu. This might manifest itself in a lively
jerk chicken salad with plantain, bacon and aioli; or perhaps roast Creole duck with cherry compote.
Traditional British tastes are met too, particularly at lunchtime, when you might find freshly battered
haddock and chips, rump steak, ploughman's, and fresh crab sandwiches on the menu. The inn is
home to a thatched skittle alley that is reputed to be the oldest in the country.

Recommended in the area

Chesil Beach; Jurassic Coast World Heritage Site; Lyme Regis

The old lifeboat station (now a museum) Poole Quay

The Cock & Bottle

Address: EAST MORDEN, Wareham, BH20 7DL
Tel: 01929 459238
Map ref: 2, SY99
Directions: From A35 W of Poole turn right onto
B3075, pub is 0.5m on left
Open: 11–3 6–11 (Sun 12–3, 7–10.30) ⓫ L 12–2
D 6–9 ⓘ L 12–2 D 6–9 **Facilities:** Children welcome
Garden Parking: 40 **Notes:** 🐕 ⊕ Hall & Woodhouse ⓨ 6

From the outside, the brick facades of this pub conceal
the fact that it is a cob-walled Dorset longhouse, built some 400 years ago – the brick skin was added
around 1800. Inside it is as rustic and charming as one could hope for, with a plethora of nooks and
crannies around the log fires. Outside, the pub has a paddock where in summer vintage car rallies are
occasionally hosted. In addition to the popular locals' bar, there's a cosy lounge bar and an attractive
restaurant extension. The kitchen produces an eclectic mix of traditional and inventive cooking, using
local produce where possible: confit of potted pheasant could be followed by steamed sea bass fillets
with Poole Bay mussel and saffron broth.

Recommended in the area

Monkey World; Hardy's Cottage; Bovington Tank Museum

The Acorn Inn

♦♦♦♦

Address:	EVERSHOT, Dorchester, DT2 0JW
Tel:	01935 83228
Fax:	01935 83707
Email:	stay@acorn-inn.co.uk
Website:	www.acorn-inn.co.uk
Map ref:	2, ST50

Directions: Off the A37 Yeovil–Dorchester road, turning right for Evershot

Open: 11–11 ⓑ L 12–2 D 7–9 ⏁ L 12–2 D 7–9

Rooms: 10 en suite, S £75 D £100 Facilities: Children welcome Garden Parking: 40

Notes: 🐾 ⊕ Free House ⏧ 11

Thomas Hardy immortalised this 16th-century stone-built inn as the Sow and Acorn in *Tess of the d'Urbervilles*, and the carefully restored building stands in the pretty village of Evershot (Hardy's Evershead), amid a designated Area of Outstanding Natural Beauty. It is thought that the notorious 'Hanging Judge' Jeffreys used the Grand Hall – now the stylish Hardy Restaurant – as a court house, while a skittle alley occupies the former stables. There are two oak-panelled bars, one with a flagstone floor and the other tiled, and log fires blaze in carved Hamstone fireplaces. Meals and drinks can be taken outside in the lawned gardens. Several of the bedrooms feature interesting four-poster beds, and two rooms are suitable for families. Rooms are equipped with satellite television and facilities for making hot drinks. Most of the inn's food is sourced within a 15-mile radius. Bar meals include hearty soups, open sandwiches and steak and ale pie, and go down well with a pint of Draymans ale. Typical dishes in the restaurant include a starter of pan-fried pigeon breasts with butternut squash and sage risotto, drizzled with red wine jus, and such main courses as roast fillet of beef, poached in red wine with thyme and garlic. Scallops, seabass and bream also feature among a decent selection of fish.

Recommended in the area

Mapperton House and Gardens; Jurassic Coast World Heritage Site; Dorchester

The Cricketers

◆◆◆◆◆

Address:	IWERNE COURTNEY OR SHROTON,
	Blandford Forum, DT11 8QD
Tel:	01258 860421
Fax:	01258 861800
Map ref:	2, ST81

Directions: Off the A350 Shaftesbury road, north of
Blandford Forum, signed from Shroton
Open: 11.30–2.30 6.30–11 (winter Sun eve 7–11)
🅱 L 12–2 D 6.30–9 ⏃ L 12–2 D 6.30–9
Rooms: 1 en suite, S £40–45 D £70–75 **Facilities:** Children welcome Garden **Parking:** 19
Notes: ⊕ Free House ⏦ 10

Built at the beginning of the 20th century, The Cricketers is as classically English as cricket itself, and
is, appropriately, between the local cricket pitch and the village green. The cricket theme is perpetuated
inside with a collection of memorabilia celebrating the sport on display within the bar – even the hand
pumps for the real ales are shaped like cricket bats. Above all, though, this is a welcoming local pub,
comprising a main bar, the said sports bar and a den, all light and airy rooms that lead through to the
restaurant at the rear. This in turn overlooks a lovely garden that is well stocked with trees and flowers.
In fine weather, there's nothing customers like more than to eat outside where there is seating for
approximately 100. The pub is popular with hikers too, who are lured in from Wessex Way which runs
conveniently through the garden. They can slake their thirst with one of the well-kept real ales on offer
– Ringwood 49er, Greene King IPA, Tanglefoot, Wadworth 6X – and fill up from the extensive menu,
which serves both the bar and restaurant. It offers a good choice of interesting dishes featuring
unusual combinations, typical options including beetroot risotto with pecans and feta cheese, and fillet
of sea bass grilled on Oriental stir-fry vegetables with soy.

Recommended in the area

Cranbourne Chase; Shaftesbury Abbey Museum and Garden; Sherborne Castle

The Vale of Marshwood, Pilsdon.

The Bottle Inn

Address: MARSHWOOD, Bridport, DT6 5QJ
Tel: 01297 678254
Fax: 01297 678739
Email: thebottleinn@msn.com
Website: www.thebottleinn.co.uk
Map ref: 2, SY39
Directions: On the B3165 Crewkerne–Lyme Regis road.
Open: 12–3 6.30–11 ᾧ L 12–2 D 6.30–9
Facilities: Children welcome Garden **Parking:** 40
Notes: ⊕ Free House ♀ 7

The thatched Bottle Inn was first mentioned as an ale house back in the 17th century, and was the first pub in the area during the 18th century to serve bottled beer rather than ale from the jug – hence the name. Standing on the edge of the glorious Marshwood Vale, its rustic interior has simple wooden settles, scrubbed tables and, in winter, a blazing fire. Taking the organic food theme to its furthest reaches, the pub is home to the annual World Stinging-Nettle Eating Championships. Recent additions to the menu have included local pork tenderloin; Highland chicken; and aubergine in oregano batter.
Recommended in the area
Wildlife Park at Cricket St Thomas; Mapperton House and Garden; Pecorama

Barnard Castle bridge.

Romaldkirk church, Teesdale.

Rose and Crown

★★ ◎◎ HOTEL

Address: ROMALDKIRK, Barnard Castle, DL12 9EB
Tel: 01833 650213
Fax: 01833 650828
Email: hotel@rose-and-crown.co.uk
Website: www.rose-and-crown.co.uk
Map ref: 7, NY92
Directions: 6m NW from Barnard Castle on B6277
Open: 11.30–3 5.30–11 ⓫ L 12–1.30 D 6.30–9.30
⦿ L 12–1.30 D 7.30–9 **Rooms:** 12 en suite, S £80
D £130 **Facilities:** Children welcome **Parking:** 24 **Notes:** ↠ ⊕ Free House ⓦ 10

Dating back to 1733, this inn stands in the middle of three greens, still bearing the ancient stocks and water pump, in a very picturesque village. Inside it's all polished wood panelling, old beams, gleaming brasses and fresh flowers. Substantial, interesting lunches are available in the bar, while a restaurant dinner might consist of farmhouse ham with fresh figs to start, followed by parsnip and honey soup then roast Teesdale fell lamb with kidney casserole and woodland mushrooms with Madeira jus.

Recommended in the area

Bowes Museum; Barnard Castle; Egglestone Abbey

91

ESSEX

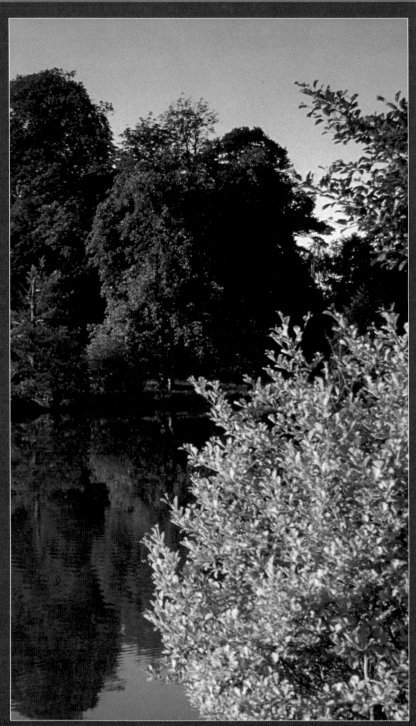

Weald Country Park.

Axe & Compasses

Address: High St, ARKESDEN, CB11 4EX
Tel: 01799 550272
Fax: 01799 550906
Email: naja@sakernet.com
Website: www.axeandcompasses.co.uk
Map ref: 3, TL43
Directions: From M11 junct 10, take A505 E, then A1301 and B1383 S to Newport; take B1038 towards Buntingford then right for Arkesden
Open: 11.30–2.30 6–11 ⓑ L 12–2 D 6.45–9.30
🍽 L 12–2 D 6.45–9.30 **Facilities:** Garden **Parking:** 18 **Notes:** ⊕ Greene King ⍾

Picture postcard perfect, this historic inn is located in the narrow main street of a captivating village. A stream called Wicken Water runs alongside, criss-crossed by footbridges leading to white, cream and pink colour-washed thatched cottages. The central section of the inn – the thatched part – dates from approximately 1650, but the building has since been extended to utilise the old stable block, which accommodated horses until the 1920s, and into a 19th-century addition that now houses the public bar. The beamed interior is full of character and includes the welcoming bar, a comfortable and softly lit restaurant, and a cosy lounge furnished with antiques, and displaying horse brasses and old agricultural implements. During winter there may well be a warming fire blazing in the hearth, and in summer there is further seating outside on the patio. Beer lovers will enjoy the real ales on tap, which include Greene King IPA, Abbot Ale and Old Speckled Hen. For those who prefer the juice of the vine, there is a wine list that's split almost evenly between France and the rest of the world. The restaurant offers a full carte, while an extensive blackboard menu is available in either the lounge or bar. Dishes range from an authentic moussaka on the bar menu to a restaurant dish of beef fillet served with pâté on a Madeira and red wine sauce with horseradish mash quenelles.

Recommended in the area

Audley End House and Gardens; Imperial War Museum Duxford; Mountfitchet Castle

The Green Dragon at Young's End

Address:	Upper London Road, Young's End, BRAINTREE, CM77 8QN
Tel:	01245 361030
Fax:	01245 362575
Email:	info@greendragonbraintree.co.uk
Website:	www.greendragonbraintree.co.uk
Map ref:	4, TL72

Directions: M11 junct 8, take A120 towards Colchester. At Braintree bypass take A131 S towards Chelmsford, exit at Youngs End on Great Leighs bypass
Open: 12–3 5.30–11 (Sun and BHs 12–11) ♨ L 12–2.15 D 6–9.30 ⭐ L 12–2.15 D 6–9.30
Facilities: Garden **Parking:** 40 **Notes:** ⊞ Greene King ♀ 10

This quietly situated country pub on the old A131 is the closest eating establishment to the new Great Leighs Racecourse. The theme of the Green Dragon is 'reassuringly traditional', and awards for the well-kept cask ales and high standards of hygiene testify to the landlord's commitment to quality. Among those traditional ales are Greene King IPA, Abbot Ale, Ruddles County and Old Speckled Hen. Wine drinkers, too, have a choice of 10 wines by the glass. The pub has been in the same family for over 21 years, and they pride themselves on running a good-value, family-friendly establishment. Cosy bars lead through to the Barn and first floor Hayloft restaurant areas, with their plain brick walls and old beams. If you prefer to sit outside, there is a large garden and a patio with heaters. The same good choice of light snacks, starters, main courses and puddings is offered throughout the place. Seafood is a particular strength, including the likes of mussels in white wine; Loch Duart salmon; and seafood platter. Other typical dishes are rack of venison with cranberries, roast saddle of rabbit, and Essex rib-eye steaks. An ever-changing daily special board adds to the variety.

Recommended in the area

Working Silk Mill; Paycocke's (NT); RHS Garden Hyde Hall

The Cricketers

Address: CLAVERING, Saffron Walden, CB11 4QT
Tel: 01799 550442
Fax: 01799 550882
Email: cricketers@lineone.net
Website: www.thecricketers.co.uk
Map ref: 3, TL43
Directions: From M11 junct 10, take A505 E, then A1301 and B1383 S to Newport; take B1038 towards Buntingford
Open: 10.30–11 🍺 L 12–2 D 7–10 🍽 L 12–2 D 7–10
Facilities: Children welcome Garden **Parking:** 100 **Notes:** ⊘ on premises ⊞ Free House ♚ 10

This is the pub where celebrity chef Jamie Oliver learned his craft, and it is still run by his parents, Trevor and Sally. Not surprisingly, the food is a highlight of a visit, but the lovely 16th-century pub is a great place to pop in for a drink too, with real ales such as Adnams Broadside and Bitter, Tetley Bitter and Green King IPA. As the name suggests, the pub stands near the village cricket pitch, and cricket memorabilia decorates the bar and restaurant. To get back to the food, the seasonally changing menus reflect a strong Italian influence and fresh fish is featured daily. Fish-lovers should try to come on Tuesday, though, when seafood takes prominence, based on what looks good at the market. The menu is individually priced in the bar, and fixed price in the restaurant. Typical dishes might include starters such as lightly spiced boneless quail, roasted and served on a courgette, ruby chard and fresh Asian salad; butternut squash and coriander soup with home made bread; or chicken liver parfait. Main courses from a recent menu included grilled halibut with fresh crabmeat and a sun-blushed tomato and shellfish bisque sauce; medallions of local venison with a parsnip and celeriac puree and a rich port wine jus; and lasagne of Mediterranean vegetables and pine nuts, layered with fresh pasta and a rich blue cheese sauce. Desserts are equally irresistible.

Recommended in the area

Audley End House and Gardens; Imperial War Museum Duxford; Mountfitchet Castle

Bell Inn & Hill House

Address:	High Road,
	HORNDON ON THE HILL, SS17 8LD
Tel:	01375 642463
Fax:	01375 361611
Email:	info@bell-inn.co.uk
Website:	www.bell-inn.co.uk
Map ref:	4, TQ68

Directions: Off M25 junct 30/31 signed Thurrock.
Lakeside A13, then B1007 to Horndon
Open: 11–2.30 5.30–11 (Sun 12–4, 7–10.30)
L 12–1.45 D 6.45–9.45 L 12–1.45 D 6.45–9.45 Facilities: Children welcome Garden
Parking: 50 Notes: Free House 16

When the present family acquired this coaching inn in 1938 it had no running water or electricity.
Today there are plenty of mod cons, but the restoration has retained such features as the courtyard
balcony where luggage was lifted from coach roofs. There's a good range of real ales, a lengthy wine
list, and dishes such as poached leg of lamb with olive polenta are among the intriguing food options.
Recommended in the area
Tilbury Fort; Hadleigh Castle; Southend Museum, Planetarium and Discovery Centre

The Mistley Thorn

Address:	High Street, Mistley,
	MANNINGTREE, CO11 1HE
Tel:	01206 392821
Fax:	01206 390122
Email:	info@mistleythorn.com
Website:	www.mistleythorn.com
Map ref:	4, TM13

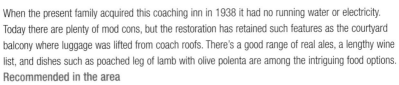

Directions: Leave the A12 at Hadleigh and follow signs
to East Berholt and Maningtree/Mistrey.
Open: 12–11 L 12–2.30 D 7–10 L 12–2.30
D 7–9.30 Facilities: Children welcome Parking: 6 Notes: on premises Free House 10

Reopened early in 2004 after a complete refurbishment, this is believed to be the first completely
non-smoking pub in Essex. Under the ownership of award-winning chef Sherri Singleton, who also
runs the Mistley Kitchen cookery school, the menu's emphasis is on locally sourced produce with
a leaning towards fresh seafood. Imaginative dishes include seared Isle of Skye diver scallops with
organic leaves; Colchester native oysters stew; and venison steak with roasted vegetables.
Recommended in the area
Mistley Towers; Harwich Redoubt Fort; Beth Chatto Gardens

The Cricketers' Arms

◆◆◆◆

Address:	Rickling Green,
	SAFFRON WALDEN, CB11 3YG
Tel:	01799 543210
Fax:	01799 543512
Email:	reservations@cricketers.demon.co.uk
Website:	www.thecricketersarms.com
Map ref:	4, TL53

Directions: From M11 junct 8, take A120 west, go
north to Stansted Mountfitchet and then take the B1383
to Quendon. Pub 300yds on left, opposite cricket ground.
Open: 12–11 🍴 L 12–2.30 D 7–9.30 🍽️ L 12–2.30 D 7–9.30 Rooms: 9 en suite, S £65 D £95
Facilities: Children welcome Garden Parking: 40 Notes: ⊞ Free House 🍷 8

Built as a terrace of timber-framed cottages, this historic inn is set in a beautiful village on the Essex
Cambridgeshire border, overlooking the cricket green. The cricketing connection began in the 1880s
when Rickling Green became the venue for London society cricket matches. Associations with the
England team and the county game continue to this day. Refurbishment has brought a stripped-back
contemporary style to a traditional setting, with big leather sofas against a backdrop of exposed beams
and stone floors. A pretty Japanese terrace garden provides an attractive alternative on fine days.
One comprehensive modern menu serves all three dining areas, which comprise two country
restaurants and a further dining and conference room. Jennings and Greene King ales are served on
tap, and a series of guest ales is available under the Punch microbrewery programme. The bedrooms
offer free-to-view satellite TV, DVD and telephones, and there's a luxurious honeymoon suite with
views of the village green. A choice of full English or continental breakfast is served in the restaurant,
with newspapers to hand. The inn has its own on-call taxi service to Stansted Airport.

Recommended in the area

Saffron Walden; Hedingham Castle; Audley End House and Gardens

River Windrush, Bourton-on-the Water.

Cirencester House, divided from the town by a semicircular yew hedge.

The Crown of Crucis

★★★ 73% HOTEL

Address: Ampney Crucis, AMPNEY CRUCIS, GL7 5RS
Tel: 01285 851806
Fax: 01285 851735
Email: info@thecrownofcrucis.co.uk
Website: www.thecrownofcrucis.co.uk
Map ref: 3, SP00
Directions: On A417 to Lechlade, 2m E of Cirencester
Open: 10.30–11 🍴 L 12–10 D 12–10 ᵗⓄᴵ L 12–2.30
D 7–9.30 **Rooms:** 25 en suite, S £65 D £75
Facilities: Children welcome Garden **Parking:** 70 **Notes:** 🐾 ⊕ Free House ♇ 10

A beautiful South Cotswolds village not far from Cirencester is the setting for this 16th-century inn, overlooking the village cricket green, with the Ampney Brook running by. An extensive menu is offered alongside the real ales in the beamed bar, supplemented by blackboard specials. Alternatively you can dine more formally in the restaurant, where an innovative menu is prepared by a team of young chefs. Seats are available outside in the Mediterranean courtyard or riverside garden.

Recommended in the area

Cotswold Water Park; Corinium Museum; Westonbirt The National Arboretum

The Kilkeney Inn

Address: Kilkeney, ANDOVERSFORD,
Cheltenham, GL54 4LN
Tel: 01242 820341
Fax: 01242 820133
Website: www.kilkeneyinn.co.uk
Map ref: 3, SP01
Directions: On A436 1m W of Andoversford
Open: 11–3 5–11 ᑲ L 12–2 D 7–9.30 ⏛ L 12–2
D 7–9.30 **Facilities:** Garden **Parking:** 50 ⏛ Free House ⏛ 9

The rolling Cotswold landscape stretches away from this charming country dining pub, located on the main road outside Andoversford. Well worth the drive out from Cheltenham, the best views of the Cotswolds are from the front of the pub and the mature garden that was originally six individual plots belonging to the old terrace of stone cottages. Real ales available are Hook Norton Best and St Austells Tribute, and these are joined by various guest ales. The lunch menu ranges from filled ciabattas; herb sausages in Yorkshire pudding; and warm chicken Caesar salad; to the Kilkeney special, a slow-roast shoulder of lamb with smashed root vegetables in a rich red wine and mint glaze. In the evening, try a starter of warm tartlet of crayfish tails, leeks and pink peppercorns, bound with a white wine sauce; or goat's cheese stuffed with onion marmalade wrapped in filo pastry, with a sweet pimento dressing. To follow, the main courses might include strips of chicken breast in tomatoes, black olives and thyme, topped with parmesan; home made beef, onion and mushroom pie with Stilton and Guinness; or fillet of sea bass on buttered leeks and creamy mash, topped with crispy parma ham. Puddings are equally enticing, and might include warm cherries with meringue and ice cream; pineapple and coconut brûlée; home made bread-and-butter pudding; or double chocolate biscuit cake. There's also a good cheese selection for those who don't have a sweet tooth. All of the dishes are freshly prepared and cooked to order, and it's advisable to make a reservation.

Recommended in the area

Chelteham; Gloucester and Warwick Railway; Cotswold Farm Park

Ashleworth Manor House.

The Queens Arms

Address: The Village, ASHLEWORTH, GL19 4HT
Tel: 01452 700395
Map ref: 2, SO82
Directions: From Gloucester go N on A417 for 5m.
At Hartpury, turn right to Ashleworth; 100yds past village.
Open: 12–2.30 7–11 ♿ L 12–2 D 7–9 🍴 L 12–2 D
7–9 **Facilities:** Garden **Parking:** 50 **Notes:** ⊘ on
premises 🍺 Free House 🍷 12

South African-born Tony Burreddu and his Zimbabwean
wife Gill ran an award-winning Durban steakhouse before coming to England in 1995, inspecting 250
pubs before settling on The Queens Arms. They believe the building dates from the 16th century, and
although the Victorians left their mark, the original beams and iron fireplaces remain, and with the help
of antique furniture, Persian rugs, art-deco mirrors and old cooking utensils, the interior is a treat. Two
separate rooms make up the dining area, with regular pub food from a blackboard menu, and specials
that might include roasted local partridge with black pudding mash, port and juniper sauce; pan-fried
Gressingham duck breast with black cherry and kirsch sauce; and a couple of South African dishes.
Recommended in the area
Ashleworth Tithe Barn; Gloucester Docks and Museum; Slimbridge Wildfowl & Wetlands Trust

The Kings Head Inn

◆◆◆◆

Address:	The Green, BLEDINGTON, OX7 6XQ
Tel:	01608 658365
Fax:	01608 658902
Email:	kingshead@orr-ewing.com
Website:	www.kingsheadinn.net
Map ref:	3, SP22

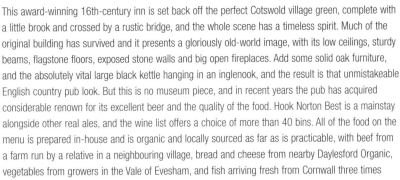

Directions: 4m SE of Stow-on-the-Wold; go E on A36, then turn right onto B4450 Chipping Norton road

Open: 11.30–3 6–11 (weekends and BHs open from 12)

🍽 L 12–2 D 7–9.00 🍴 L 12–2 D 7–9.00 (Fri-Sat until 9.30) **Rooms:** 12 en suite, from S £55 D £70

Facilities: Garden **Parking:** 35 **Notes:** ⊞ Free House ♟ 8

This award-winning 16th-century inn is set back off the perfect Cotswold village green, complete with a little brook and crossed by a rustic bridge, and the whole scene has a timeless spirit. Much of the original building has survived and it presents a gloriously old-world image, with its low ceilings, sturdy beams, flagstone floors, exposed stone walls and big open fireplaces. Add some solid oak furniture, and the absolutely vital large black kettle hanging in an inglenook, and the result is that unmistakeable English country pub look. But this is no museum piece, and in recent years the pub has acquired considerable renown for its excellent beer and the quality of the food. Hook Norton Best is a mainstay alongside other real ales, and the wine list offers a choice of more than 40 bins. All of the food on the menu is prepared in-house and is organic and locally sourced as far as is practicable, with beef from a farm run by a relative in a neighbouring village, bread and cheese from nearby Daylesford Organic, vegetables from growers in the Vale of Evesham, and fish arriving fresh from Cornwall three times

a week. A meal could begin with tiger prawns cooked in lemongrass, ginger and garlic; home made duck spring roll with sweet chilli sauce; or chargrilled courgette, watercress and cous cous salad with harissa dressing. This might be followed by grilled mustard and herb chicken breast with purple sprouting broccoli and chorizo parmentier potatoes; chargrilled tuna steak with ginger and leek salad; or spicy green vegetable curry, with turmeric rice, naan and coriander yoghurt. Hopefully, there'll be room to finish off with a white peach or strawberry crème brûlée; chocolate caramel brownie with vanilla ice cream; lemon meringue tartlet; or a selection from the British cheeses, including Shropshire Blue and Cotswold Organic Brie.

Recommended in the area

Blenheim Palace; Cotswold Wildlife Park; Hook Norton Brewery

Eight Bells Inn

Address: Church Street, CHIPPING
CAMPDEN, GL55 6JG
Tel: 01386 840371
Fax: 01386 841669
Email: neilhargreaves@bellinn.fsnet.co.uk
Website: www.eightbellsinn.co.uk
Map ref: 3, SP13
Directions: Off A44, about half-way between
Stow-on-the-Wold and Evesham, via B4081
Open: 12–11 (every day) ᴸ L 12–2.30 D 6.30–9.30
⦿ L 12–2.30 D 6.30–9.30 **Facilities:** Children welcome Garden
Notes: ⊁ ⊗ on premises ⊞ Free House ♟ 8

This beautiful 14th-century Cotswold stone inn was built to house stonemasons working on the nearby church and to store the eight church bells. There is an atmospheric bar and a candlelit dining room with oak beams, open fires and a priest's hole. Traditional ales and ciders are served and there's a daily-changing menu of freshly prepared local food. Outside is a terrace and courtyard garden.
Recommended in the area
The Cotswold Way; Hidcote Manor (NT); Stratford-upon-Avon

The Tunnel House Inn

Address: COATES, Cirencester, GL7 6PW
Tel: 01285 770280
Fax: 01285 770120
Email: info@tunnelhouse.com
Website: www.tunnelhouse.com
Map ref: 2, SO90
Directions: From Cirencester A433 Tetbury road, in 2m
turn right towards Coates; signs to Canal Tunnel and Inn
Open: 11–3 6–11 (all day Fri–Sun) ᴸ L 12–2.15
D 6.45–9.15 **Facilities:** Children welcome Garden
Parking: 50 **Notes:** ⊁ ⊞

The Tunnel House stands down a very bumpy track by Sapperton Tunnel on the Thames and Severn Canal, and once provided accommodation for canal construction workers. It was rebuilt in 1957 after a fire, and the bar has some oddities, including an upside-down table on the ceiling. The monthly changing menu offers simple dishes such as local sausages with mash and red onion marmalade; ham, egg and chips; home-made lasagne; and caramelised onion, goat's cheese and thyme tart.
Recommended in the area
Westonbirt Arboretum; Cotswold Water Park; World of Mechanical Music

The fan-vaulted ceilings of Gloucester Cathedral's cloisters.

The Green Dragon Inn

♦♦♦♦

Address:	Cockleford, COWLEY, Cheltenham, GL53 9NW
Tel:	01242 870271
Fax:	01242 870171
Website:	www.green-dragon-inn.co.uk
Map ref:	2, SO91
Directions:	5m S of Cheltenham, off A435

Open: 11–11 (Sun 12–10.30) 🍴 L 12–2.30 D 6–10
Rooms: 9 en suite, S £65 D £85 Suite: £140
Facilities: Children welcome Garden Parking: 100 Notes: 🐕 ⊕ Free House ♟ 9

Dating from the 17th century, the Green Dragon is at the heart of the picturesque Cotswolds and is a popular retreat for those who appreciate good food, fine wine and real ales. The menu includes lunchtime sandwiches, children's favourites, and starters/light meals such as smoked halibut on Thai marinated vegetable tagliatelle or Caesar salad. The Daily specials board might include local Cockleford trout with garlic and caper butter or pave of venison on sweet potato mash with a wild mushroom sauce.

Recommended in the area

Holst Birthplace Museum; Gloucester Cathedral; Witcombe Roman Villa

Plough Inn

♦♦♦♦

Address: FORD, Nr Temple Guiting, GL54 5RU
Tel: 01386 584215
Fax: 01386 584042
Email: info@theploughinnatford.co.uk
Website: www.theploughinnatford.co.uk
Map ref: 2, ST87
Directions: 4m NW of Stow-on-the-Wold on B4077 Tewkesbury road
Open: 11am–12pm (Fri–Sat 11am–1am) ᴪ L 12–2
D 6.30–9 ⑩ L 11.30–2 D 6.30–9 **Rooms:** 3 en suite, S £40 D £70 **Facilities:** Children welcome
Garden **Parking:** 50 **Notes:** ⊞ Donnington ♒ 7

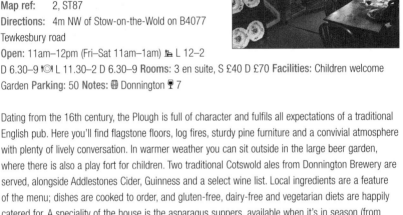

Dating from the 16th century, the Plough is full of character and fulfils all expectations of a traditional English pub. Here you'll find flagstone floors, log fires, sturdy pine furniture and a convivial atmosphere with plenty of lively conversation. In warmer weather you can sit outside in the large beer garden, where there is also a play fort for children. Two traditional Cotswold ales from Donnington Brewery are served, alongside Addlestones Cider, Guinness and a select wine list. Local ingredients are a feature of the menu; dishes are cooked to order, and gluten-free, dairy-free and vegetarian diets are happily catered for. A speciality of the house is the asparagus suppers, available when it's in season (from April to early June), and the Plough's race-day breakfasts are very popular with race-goers on their way to Cheltenham Racecourse. Sunday roasts are also a great favourite, and booking for the dining room is particularly recommended at weekends. It's location make the inn an ideal base for exploring the beautiful Cotswolds and surrounding places such as Oxford, Stratford-upon-Avon and Gloucester, and accommodation is provided in the Tallot, a quaint old building converted from a hayloft and stables. Two of the rooms are suitable for family occupation, with an additional single bed in the room.

Recommended in the area

Cotswold Farm Park; Sudeley Castle; Hailes Abbey (NT)

The Inn at Fossebridge

Address: FOSSEBRIDGE, nr Cheltenham, GL54 3JS
Tel: 01285 720721
Fax: 01285 720793
Email: info@fossebridgeinn.co.uk
Website: www.fossebridgeinn.co.uk
Map ref: 3, SP01
Directions: On A429, 7m NE of Cirencester; pub on left
Open: 12–12 (Sun 12–11.30) 🍺 L 12–3 D 6–10
🍽 L 12–3 D 6–10 Facilities: Children welcome Garden
Parking: 40 Notes: 🐕 ⊕ Free House 🍷 8

This Coln Valley inn enjoys wonderful Cotswold views. The building today is mostly Regency, but the Bridge bar and restaurant, located in the oldest part of the building, dates back to the 15th century and has a friendly and informal ambience. Exposed beams, stone walls, flagstone floors and open fires provide the setting for a pint of Bass, Youngs or Hook Norton, or a meal based on lots of local produce. Try simple smoked salmon and scrambled eggs, or home made cheese-and-bacon beefburgers, then slow roast lamb shank with root vegetables. Finish with poached pear with chocolate sauce.

Recommended in the area

Chedworth Roman Villa (NT); World of Mechanical Music; Holst Birthplace Museum

The White Horse

🌸

Address: Cirencester Road, FRAMPTON MANSELL,
            Stroud, GL6 8HZ
Tel: 01285 760960
Email: emmawhitehorse@aol.com
Map ref: 2, SO90
Directions: 6m W of Cirencester on A419 Stroud road
Open: 11–3 6–11 🍺 L 12–2.30 D 7–9.45 🍽 L
12–2.30 D 7–9.45 Facilities: Children welcome Garden
Parking: 40 Notes: 🐕 ⊕ Free House 🍷 8

The White Horse is a smart dining pub with an atmosphere amenable both for a quiet drink (Uley Bitter, Hook Norton Best, and Arkells Summer Ale) or a great meal out, with a large sofa and comfy chairs in the bar. Recently completely refurbished, the restaurant has new chairs, bright decor, contemporary artwork and linen tablecloths. There's a fixed-price menu as well as the carte, and the food has a growing reputation. Fresh seafood from a large seawater tank is a strong point, along with dishes such as Toulouse sausage with sweet potato mash.

Recommended in the area

Corinium Museum; Cotswold Water Park;; Miserden Park

The Weighbridge Inn

Address: MINCHINHAMPTON, GL6 9AL
Tel: 01453 832520
Fax: 01453 835903
Email: enquiries@2in1pub.co.uk
Website: www.2in1pub.co.uk
Map ref: 2, SO80
Directions: S of Stroud off A46; turn onto B4014
Nailsworth–Avening road
Open: 12–11 (Sun 12–10.30) ⓑ/⚫ L 12–9.30 D
12–9.30 **Facilities:** Children welcome Garden
Parking: 50 **Notes:** ⛵ ⓦ ⚑ 16

This lovely 17th-century free house is steeped in history. It stands amid pretty Cotswold countryside beside the old packhorse trail to Bristol, now a quiet footpath and bridleway, and continues to satisfy the appetites of walkers, motorists and locals. The building has been carefully renovated, but the original features remain unspoilt. The bars are cosy, and food is a highlight. Try the famous 2-in-1 pies that were invented here, with a choice of fillings that include meats, vegetarian and seafood.

Recommended in the area

Painswick Rococo Garden; Owlpen Manor; Prinknash Abbey and Pottery

The Britannia

Address: Cossack Square, NAILSWORTH, GL6 0DG
Tel: 01453 832501
Fax: 01453 832010
Email: pheasantpluckers2003@yahoo.co.uk
Website: www.foodclub-uk.com
Map ref: 2, ST89
Directions: In town centre
Open: 11–11 ⓑ L 11–2.45 D 5.30–10 ⚫ L 11–2.45
D 5.30–10 **Facilities:** Children welcome Garden
Parking: 100 **Notes:** ⛵ ⓦ Free House ⚑ 12

This impressive 17th-century manor house occupies a delightful position on the southern side of Nailsworth's Cossack Square. The open plan interior is bright and uncluttered with low ceilings, a blue slate floor and cosy fires, while outside there's a pretty garden with plenty of tables, chairs and umbrellas. Inside or out, a pint of well-kept London Pride or Abbot Ale is sure to go down well. The wine list is also worthy of attention. Modern British and continental food is offered on the brasserie-style menu, with ingredients from local suppliers and Smithfield Market.

Recommended in the area

Chavenage; Owlpen Manor; Woodchester Park (NT)

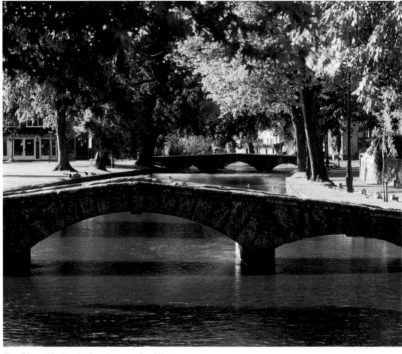

The River Windrush, Bourton-on-the-Water.

Tipputs Inn

Address:	Bath Road, NAILSWORTH, GL6 0QE
Tel:	01453 832466
Fax:	01453 832010
Email:	pheasantpluckers2003@yahoo.co.uk
Website:	www.foodclub-uk.com
Map ref:	2, ST89
Directions:	On A46, 0.5m S of Nailsworth

Open: 11–11 🍺 L 11–10 D 11–10 🍽 L 11–10
D 11–10 **Facilities:** Children welcome Garden
Parking: 75 **Notes:** 🐾 🍺 Free House 🍷 12

An impeccably stylish pub-restaurant in a 17th-century
building of Cotswold stone, with stripped floors, clean-
lined furniture and giant candelabra. Tipputs is owned
by Nick Beardsley and Christophe Coquoin, who started
out as chefs together 12 years ago. The menu takes in brunch, lunchtime quickies, and a full selection
of starters, mains and puddings. Real ales include Greene King IPA, Ruddles Country and Abbot Ale.
Recommended in the area
Chavenage; Owlpen Manor; Woodchester Park (NT)

The Puesdown Inn

♦♦♦♦ ⑨⑩

Address:	Compton Abdale, NORTHLEACH, Cheltenham, GL54 4DN
Tel:	01451 860262
Fax:	01451 861262
Email:	inn4food@btopenworld.com
Website:	www.puesdown.cotswoldinns.com
Map ref:	3, SP11
Directions:	About 10m SE of Cheltenham on A40

Open: 11–3 6–11 (all day Fri–Sun and Jul–Aug)
🛏 L 12–3 D 6–10.30 ⏹ L 12–3 D 6.30–10.30 Rooms: 3 en suite, S £50 D £85 Facilities: Garden
Parking: 80 Notes: 🚭 ♿ Free House 🍷 15

Said to date from 1236, this former coaching inn takes its name from an ancient English phrase meaning 'windy ridge', which seems apposite given its position 800 feet above sea level on the old Salt Way between Cheltenham and Burford. It is a very attractive building of Cotswold stone, lovingly refurbished by proprietors John and Maggie Armstrong. Outside, the patio and large garden offer stunning views over the surrounding countryside, and a path running alongside leads to the pretty village of Hazleton. The inn has an outstanding reputation for its food. The lunchtime menu offers light meals such as griddled organic salmon with shore clams, while dishes from the restaurant take in griddled calves' liver with pancetta, mash and brown onions; or marinated monkfish with gingered noodles, coconut vegetables and mango and lime salsa. Traditional beers include Hook Norton Best Bitter, Hooky Dark, Old Hooky and Haymaker. The bedrooms are are all located on the ground floor with direct access to the car park, and are equipped with showers, televisions, hairdryers, mineral water and tea- and coffee-making facilities. Special events at the inn include regular Jazz in the Week nights and cookery demonstrations.

Recommended in the area

Chedworth Roman Villa (NT); World of Mechanical Music; Cotswold Way

The Falcon Inn

Address: New Street, PAINSWICK, GL6 6UN
Tel: 01452 814222
Fax: 01452 813377
Email: bleninns@clara.net
Website: www.falconinn.com
Map ref: 2, SO80
Directions: On A46 in centre of Painswick
Open: 11–11 Sun 12–10.30 ⓑ L 12–2.30 D 7–9.30
⌖ L 12–2.30 D 7–9.30 **Facilities:** Children welcome
Garden **Parking:** 35 **Notes:** ⌖ ⊕ Free House ♉ 10

Dating from 1554, The Falcon is set in a conservation village and has the world's oldest known bowling green. For three centuries the building served as a courthouse, but today its friendly service extends to a drying room for walkers' gear. Inside you'll find stone floors, wood panelling and open fires, and former stables converted into a function room. The inn is a free house serving real ales and 10 wines by the glass, and has a good reputation for its food. Accommodation is provided in 12 en suite rooms, two for families.

Recommended in the area

Painswick Rococo Gardens; Prinknash Abbey; Gloucester Docks and National Waterway Museum

The Butchers Arms

Address: SHEEPSCOMBE, Nr Painswick, GL6 7RH
Tel: 01452 812113
Fax: 01452 814358
Email: bleninns@clara.net
Website: www.cotswoldinns.co.uk
Map ref: 2, SO81
Directions: N of Stroud between A46 and B4070
Open: 11.30–2.30 6–11.30 ⓑ L 12–2.30 D 7–9.30
⌖ L 12–2.30 D 7–9.30 **Facilities:** Children welcome
Garden **Parking:** 16 **Notes:** ⌖ ⊕ Free House ♉ 10

The building dates from around 1670 and is believed to have been used to hang and butcher the deer that were hunted by Henry VIII in the Sheepscombe Valley. The inn's sign, depicting a butcher sipping a pint of beer with a pig tied to his leg, is one of the most photographed in the country. Laurie Lee was once a regular customer, and the pub is in the heart of '*Cider with Rosie* country'. A varied menu is offered, and real ales include Otter Ale, Moles, Wye Valley and Dorothy Goodbodys Summer Ale. Dogs are welcome.

Recommended in the area

Painswick Rococo Gardens; Prinknash Abbey; Gloucester Docks and National Waterway Museum

The Bakers Arms

Address: SOMERFORD KEYNES, Cirencester, GL7 6DN
Tel: 01285 861298
Fax: 01453 832010
Email: pheasantpluckers2003@yahoo.co.uk
Website: www.foodclub-uk.com
Map ref: 3, SU09
Directions: 2m S of Cirencester; follow signs for Cotwold Water Park
Open: 11am–12pm L 11–3 D 6–10 L 11–3 D 6–10 **Facilities:** Children welcome Garden **Parking:** 60 **Notes:** Free House 12

Within the Cotswold Water Park, this beautiful 15th-century stone pub, with low-beamed ceilings and inglenook fireplaces, stands in mature gardens ideal for alfresco dining, and the nearby Thames Path and Cotswold Way make it popular with walkers. Food is a serious business here, with a balanced, imaginative selection of meals such as Old Spot sausage and mash; steak and kidney pie with bacon dumplings; and hoi sin duck leg with stir-fried noodles and bean sprouts.

Recommended in the area

Cotswold Water Park; Swindon and Cricklade Railway; Corinium Museum

Bear of Rodborough Hotel

★★★ 73% HOTEL
Address: Rodborough Common, STROUD, GL5 5DE
Tel: 01453 878522
Fax: 01453 872523
Email: info@bearofrodborough.co.uk
Website: www.cotswold-inns-hotels.co.uk/bear
Map ref: 2, SO80
Directions: From M5 junct 13 take A419 E; follow signs Stonehouse then Rodborough
Open: 10.30–11 L 12–2.30 D 6.30–10 D 7–9.30
Rooms: 46 en suite, **Facilities:** Children welcome Garden **Parking:** 90
Notes: Free House 6

Built in the 17th century, the inn, with a Yorkstone terrace and walled croquet lawn, stands high above Stroud in acres of National Trust parkland. There are open fires and comfortable seating, traditional ales and an extensive menu. There's live jazz throughout the summer, quiz nights in winter, and a Real Ale Festival at Easter. The restaurant offers contemporary British food.

Recommended in the area

Rodborough Common (NT); Gloucester Cathedral; Painswick Rococo Garden

The Shambles, Stroud.

Rose & Crown Inn

Address: The Cross, Nympsfield, STROUD, GL10 3TU
Tel: 01453 860240
Fax: 01453 861564
Email: gadros@aol.com
Website: www.roseandcrown-nympsfield.com
Map ref: 2, SO80

Directions: From M5 junct 13, take A419 towards Stroud, then B4066 S. Nympsfield is just off B4066.
Open: 12–11 ▒ L 12–9.30 D 6–9.30 ▒ L 12–9.30 D 6–9.30 **Facilities:** Children welcome Garden
Parking: 20 **Notes:** ▒ ⊕ Free House ▓ 7

Mellow old stone hung with colourful hanging baskets and a cosy interior with exposed stone walls, wood panelling and open fireplaces are the hallmarks of this grand 400-year-old pub in the centre of Nympsfield. Traditional bar food is available, while the restaurant offers good English dishes. Starters might include a twice baked goats cheese soufflé, or chicken liver parfait, followed by main courses such as salmon en croûte, faggots in onion gravy and whatever game is in season.

Recommended in the area

Woodchester Park (NT); Owlpen Manor; Cotswold Way

Horse & Groom Inn

Address: UPPER ODDINGTON,
Moreton-in-Marsh, GL56 0XH
Tel: 01451 830584
Email: info@horseandgroom.uk.com
Website: www.horseandgroom.uk.com
Map ref: 3, SP22
Directions: 1.5m S of Stow-on-the-Wold, just off A436
Open: 12–3 5.30–11 (Sun 12–3 5.30–10.30)
🍴 L 12–2 D 6.30–9.30 🍽 L 12–2 D 6.30–9.30
Facilities: Children welcome Garden **Parking:** 50
Notes: 🛢 Free House 🍷 25

Located in a pretty Cotswold conservation village just a short distance from Stow-on-the-Wold, this immaculate 16th-century building features beams, flagstone and English oak floors, and open log fires in winter. A privately owned free house, it offers a good selection of local and guest ales, with the likes of Wye Valley Best, Butty Bach, Barley Mole and Hereford Pale Ale, and the wine list has no fewer than 25 wines available by the glass. In warmer weather the terrace garden is the perfect place for dining outside, with tables overlooking dry stone walls and pretty stone-built cottages. The head chef, Jason Brewster, uses fresh local ingredients in his quest to create the best pub food in the Cotswolds. Where possible, vegetables are bought from the market garden in the village and other top quality produce includes Hereford Beef and Cotswold lamb. Bread is freshly baked here daily, and the puddings are all home made. Typical dishes from the specials board include seared calves' liver with bubble-and-squeak mash and crispy bacon; and poached smoked haddock with rarebit sauce. A recent standard menu included starters of local game terrine wrapped in smoked bacon; home-smoked potted salmon; and cream of leek and potato soup. Main courses included roast breast of Adlestrop pheasant; slow-cooked pot roasted belly of pork with blue cheese sauce; and succulent Hereford steaks.

Recommended in the area

Dyrham Park; Hidcote Gardens; Snowshill Manor organic garden

Stroudwater canal and church at Stonehouse

The Old Fleece

Address: Bath Road, Rooksmoor,
            WOODCHESTER, GL5 5NB
Tel: 01453 872582
Fax: 01453 832010
Email: pheasantpluckers2003@yahoo.co.uk
Website: www.foodclub-uk.com
Map ref: 2, SO80
Directions: 2m S of Stroud on the A46
Open: 11–11 ⓑ L 11–2.45 D 5.30–10 ⒪ L 11–2.45
D 5.30–10 **Facilities:** Children welcome Garden
Parking: 40 **Notes:** ⚐ ⊕ Pheasant Pluckers Ltd ⓨ 12

This is a delightful coaching inn, dating back to the 18th century and built of Cotswold stone with a traditional stone roof. The interior has had a complete makeover in the last couple of years, and the atmosphere has been enhanced with wooden floors, wood panelling and exposed stone. Predominantly French chefs prepare quality, freshly produced dishes and ingredients are sourced locally or directly. Main courses such as venison fillet with rich chocolate and balsamic sauce set the style.

Recommended in the area

Woodchester Park (NT); Owlpen Manor; Cotswold Way

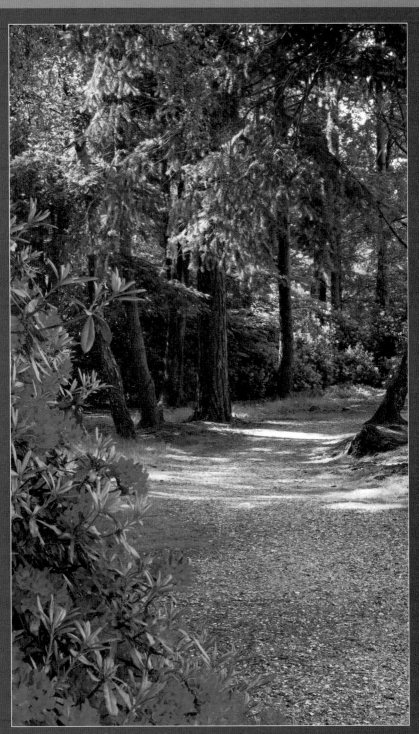

A pathway in the New Forest.

The Globe on the Lake

Address: The Soke, Broad Street,
ALRESFORD, SO24 9DB
Tel: 01962 732294
Fax: 01962 732221
Email: duveen-conway@supanet.com
Website: theglobeonthelake.co.uk
Map ref: 3, SU53
Directions: From M3 junct 9 or 10, follow signs for
Petersfield to join A31. New Alresford is just off A31
via the B3047

Open: 11–3 6–11 (all day Sat and Sun in summer) L 12–2 D 6.30–9 ❤ L 12–2 D 6.30–9
Facilities: Children welcome Garden **Notes:** ⊕ Unique Pub Co Ltd ♟ 6 6

A little way east of the ancient city of Winchester, and just off the northern edge of the South Downs National Park, Alresford is an attractive, rather sedate little town on the River Itchen – famous for its watercress beds. The Globe on the Lake is a 17th-century coaching inn with well-kept gardens, which, as the name suggests, lead down to a reed-fringed lake – not just any old lake, but one which started life 900 years ago as Bishop de Lucy's fish pond. The weir remains an outstanding piece of medieval engineering in an otherwise purely Georgian setting. Daily specials and tapas can be enjoyed in the relaxed and welcoming bar, with its selection of local beers and warming log fires in winter. In summer, try the garden room or – if the weather allows – a table out on the terrace. The dining room is more formal with à la carte dining. Fresh local produce dictates a daily change of menu which can include light starters like roast red peppers stuffed with spinach and goat's cheese, and more substantial main courses such as Meon Valley pork and leek sausages; Alresford watercress flan; or oven-roasted partridge. A generous pudding list ranges from old favourites such as bread-and-butter pudding to the compelling peach and port trifle with mascarpone.

Recommended in the area

Mid-Hants Railway (Watercress Line); Avington Park; Hinton Ampner Gardens (NT)

The Wellington Arms

Address:	Baughurst Road,
	BAUGHURST, RG26 5LP
Tel:	0118 982 0110
Email:	info@thewellingtonarms.com
Website:	www.thewellingtonarms.com
Map ref:	3, SU56

Directions: From M4 junct 12 follow signs to Newbury along A4. At rdbt take left turn to Aldermaston. At rdbt at top of hill take 2nd exit, at T-junc turn left, pub 1m on left

Open: ⸙ L 12–2.30 (Wed–Sun) D 6.30–9.30 (Tues–Sat)

Facilities: Garden **Parking:** 30 **Notes:** ⊘ on premises ⊞ Punch Taverns ⸷ 10

An exceptionally pretty whitewashed building, The Wellington Arms is set in its own large garden surrounded by fields and woodland. New owners Jason King and Simon Page have been operating a boutique catering company for the last six years. Jason has worked for Paul Bocuse in Melbourne and Lyon, and for Terence Conran in London, and was at the helm of the very successful La Bodega restaurant in Hong Kong for six years. This is Jason and Simon's first venture in the pub trade and they have already made their mark with their impressive menus, including a very good-value lunch. The board is chalked up daily: favourites include twice-baked goats cheese soufflé with wilted spinach and toasted pinenuts and veal t-bone with roast pumpkin mash and sage butter. Further evidence of a commitment to quality are the pub's three Langstroth beehives, 35 free-range rare breed chickens, home-grown vegetables and herbs, home-made jams, chutneys and pickles, hand-cut chips and careful sourcing of produce – organically grown within a five-mile radius. Fish is delivered direct from the market in Brixham, and the beef comes from the Orkney Islands. From Australia come a range of botanical soaps, hand cream and special herbal teas, all exclusively available at The Wellington. The pub can comfortably seat 30 people and is available for private functions.

Recommended in the area

The Vyne (NT); Basing House; Roman Silchester;

The Sun Inn

Address: Sun Hill, BENTWORTH, Alton, GU34 5JT
Tel: 01420 562338
Map ref: 3, SU64
Directions: 5m N of Alton. Leave Alton on the A339
Basingstoke road, then follow signs to Bentworth
Open: 12–3 6–11 (Sun 12–10.30) 🍴♥︎🍺 L 12–2 D
7–9.30 **Facilities:** Children welcome Garden
Parking: 2 (ample road parking) **Notes:** 🐴🌐 Free House 🍷

Bentworth is a sleepy village tucked deep in the heart of
the beautiful Hampshire countryside, but this doesn't make it hard to get to, and the M3 (junction 6)
is conveniently just 8 miles to the north. There are several country lanes leading into the village, and
depending on which way you are travelling, this delightful flower-decked pub, located down a narrow
lane on the edge of the village, is either the first building on your way in or the last one on your way
out – and it always seems to come as a surprise, no matter how often you happen across it. The
building is actually a conversion of two former cottages, which have been opened up to create three
interconnecting rooms, each with authentic brick or wood floors. Lots of pews, settles and scrubbed
pine tables add to the relaxed atmosphere, and the place is especially inviting in the evening when the
candles on the tables are lit. All of the food offered here is home made, and this includes no less than
14 varieties of soup (Moroccan chickpea and spinach; pea and ham; smoked bacon and Cheddar).
The menu is hearty and traditional, and main courses might include gigantic Yorkshire puddings with
various fillings; classic liver and bacon, served with mashed potatoes; braised steak in red wine and
mushroom sauce; or game dishes. There are delicious home made desserts to round off the meal.
This is a thriving free house, which offers eight real ales on hand pump, including Cheriton Brewhouse
Pots Ale, Ringwood's Best and Old Thumper, all from Hampshire breweries, plus Brakspear Bitter and
Fuller's London Pride.

Recommended in the area

Gilbert White's House and The Oates Museum; Jane Austen's House; Mid-Hants Railway

Romsey Abbey.

The Bell Inn

★★★ 70% ❀ HOTEL

Address:	BROOK, nr Lyndhurst, SO43 7HE
Tel:	023 80812214
Fax:	023 80813958
Email:	bell@bramshaw.co.uk
Website:	www.bellinnbramshaw.co.uk
Map ref:	3, SU21

Directions: From M27 junct 1 (Cadnam) take B3078 signed Brook; inn is 0.5m on right

Open: 11–11 (Sun 12–11) ♨ L 12–9.30

†◎ D 7.30–9.30 **Rooms:** 25 en suite, S £70 D £90 **Facilities:** Children welcome Garden **Parking:** 60 **Notes:** ⊕ Free House

The Crosthwaite-Eyre family has owned the Bell since 1782. A handsome brick building, it has many period features, notably the imposing inglenook fireplace in the bar and the beamed bedrooms. The menu offers a rich variety of fish, poultry, meat and game, with starters such as chorizo, tomato and feta salad. Main courses might include breast of duck with sweet potato purée and redcurrant jus.

Recommended in the area

New Forest National Park; National Motor Museum; Paulton's Park

The Hampshire Arms

Address: Pankridge Street,
           CRONDALL, GU10 5QU
Tel: 01252 850418
Fax: 01252 850418
Email: dining@thehampshirearms.co.uk
Website: www.thehampshirearms.co.uk
Map ref: 3, SU74
Directions: From M3 junct 5 take A287 S towards
Farnham. Follow signs to Crondall on right
Open: 11–3 6–11.30 (all day Sat, Sun 12–10.30)
L 12–2.30 D – L 12–2.30 D 6.30–9.30
Facilities: Children welcome Garden Parking: 30
Notes: ⊘ on premises Greene King 10

Alan Piesse, the proprietor here since February 2005,
had spent 25 years working all over the world in the oil industry, and the boredom of retirement
prompted him to take on this pub, along with partner Tim Dyer. The building has a long and interesting
history. It began life as two cottages, became a courthouse, then a post office and a bakery, and this
has endowed it with lots of character. Open fires, bare beams, hop bines and candlelight now combine
to create a delightfully welcoming atmosphere. Brasserie menus are offered, with lunchtime treats
such as sandwiches, baguettes and paninis as well as more substantial fare that night include mussels
Marinière or home-baked ham with fried eggs and sauteed new potatoes. Some of the evening menu
dishes are available at lunchtime, too, and these might include a rich lamb stew; linguine with fresh
market fish in a creamy sauce; local pork and herb sausages with garlic mash and rich gravy; or the
'Hampshire Arms very special fish pie'. The desserts selection entices with traditional tarte Tatin;
crème brulée; and a selection of sorbets and ice creams.

Recommended in the area

Birdworld; Stratfield Saye House and Wellington Country Park; Mid-Hants Railway

Beaulieu River, Ipley.

Star Inn

★★★★ ⊛⊛ INN

Address: EAST TYTHERLEY, Nr Romsey, SO51 0LW
Tel/Fax: 01794 340225
Email: info@starinn-uk.com
Website: www.starinn-uk.com
Map ref: 3, SU22
Directions: 5m N of Romsey off A3057; L on B3084 for
Dunbridge, L to Awbridge, Kent's Oak; 1m beyond Lockerley
Open: 11–3 6–11 ⓑ/ⓘ L 12–2.30 D 7–9 **Rooms:** 3 en
suite, S £60 D £90 **Facilities:** Children welcome Garden
Parking: 60 **Notes:** ⌁ ⓐ Free House ⓨ 8

In the heart of the Test Valley, in the smallest village in
Hampshire, this 16th-century inn is next to the village
cricket green. It has an inviting atmosphere, with leather
sofas and tub chairs, and a pretty courtyard garden. Classic dishes with a contemporary touch, using
local ingredients, come from a daily menu, accompanied by traditional real ales, local cider and wines.
Recommended in the area
Mottisfont Abbey and Gardens; Broadlands; New Forest National Park

The Bugle

Address: High Street, HAMBLE, SO31 4HA
Tel: 023 8045 3000
Fax: 023 8045 3051
Email: manager@buglehamble.co.uk
Website: www.buglehamble.co.uk
Map ref: 3, SU40
Directions: Leave M27 at junct 8 and follow signs to Hamble. In village centre turn right at mini rdbt down one-way cobbled street, and pub is at the end
Open: 11–11 (Fri–Sat 11–12) 🍽 L 12–2.30 D 6–9.30
🍴 L 12–2.30 D 6.30–9.30 (Sat & Sun food all day)
Facilities: Children welcome Garden **Notes:** 🐾 🛢 🍷 8

Restored using traditional materials and methods, The Bugle has reclaimed its place at the heart of village life. The historic waterside pub, in a village famous as a yachting centre, sparked a successful rescue campaign among the villagers when demolition threatened as part of the proposals for a new housing development. The saved Grade II listed building features natural flagstone floors, exposed beams and brickwork, a solid oak bar and real open fires. In addition to the restaurant area, a private dining room, the Captain's Table, is available upstairs, accommodating up to 12 guests. Alternatively, the terrace area outside is a great place for lunch and a drink in warmer weather. The seasonal menu is based on fresh, top quality ingredients, using local produce wherever possible, with bar and restaurant meals served alongside well-kept real ales, wines and speciality rums. The menu offers a good range of bar bites such as home-made soup with crusty bread; salt and pepper ribs with sweet chilli dip; and a half pint of prawns with Marie rose sauce. There are lunchtime sandwiches, too, all served with parsnip

crisps. For something a bit more substantial, the 'Classics' section offers beer battered fish and chips with minted mushy peas; wild mushroom and pea risotto; char-grilled Angus steak burger; and sirloin steak with Béarnaise sauce. Fresh seafood and other home-made dishes are offered from the daily specials board, and a tempting range of desserts might include Pimms and lemonade jelly and lemon tart with crème Chantilly and raspberrry coulis. At weekends, The Bugle's brunches, all day breakfasts and traditional roasts are popular, and once a month the Wine Club offers an evening of wine tastings and a two-course meal. Dogs are allowed, except in the restaurant.

Recommended in the area

Hamble River boat trips; Royal Victoria Country Park; Netley Abbey

The Black Swan

Address: High Street, MONXTON, SP11 8AW
Tel: 01264 710260
Fax: 01264 710961
Map ref: 3, SU34
Directions: Just W of Andover off A303, signs Monxton
Open: 12–11 🍺 L 12–2 D 6–9.30 🍽 L 12–2 D 6–9.30
Facilities: Children welcome Garden **Parking:** 40
Notes: 🐾 ⊕ Enterprise Inns 🍷 9

Passing through Monxton it is as if time hasn't touched
the village, and a mixture of thatched and clay tiled buildings, some dating back to the 16th century, create a wonderful backdrop to this popular destination inn. The inn itself dates from at least 1662, and the non-smoking restaurant was once the stables. This restaurant is rapidly earning itself a well-deserved reputation for its fine food, with quality and simplicity of flavours being the bywords in the kitchen. The menu is predominantly French/English with some New World influences, and the dishes change regularly. All the ingredients are locally sourced to ensure freshness and quality. Watch out for the monthly seafood nights.

Recommended in the area

Museum of Army Flying; Hawk Conservancy; Finkley Down Farm Park

The Bush

Address: OVINGTON, Alresford, SO24 0RE
Tel: 01962 732764
Fax: 01962 735130
Email: thebushinn@wadworth.co.uk
Website: www.wadworth.co.uk
Map ref: 3, SU53
Directions: A31 from Winchester, E towards Alton and Farnham, approx 6m turn left to Ovington. 0.5m to pub
Open: 11–3 6–11 (Sun 12–3, 7–10.30) 🍺 L 12–2
D 6.30–9.30 🍽 **Facilities:** Garden **Parking:** 40
Notes: 🐾 ⊕ Wadworth 🍷 12

Tucked away down a meandering lane on the Pilgrim's Way, this is a delightful rose-covered pub with the River Itchen running along the bottom of its pretty garden, and a gentle riverside stroll will set you up in readiness for a lingering meal. Log fires and plenty of old wood furnishings continue the natural theme inside, where you can expect to find simple dishes cooked with flair. The menu makes good use of local produce, changing regularly according to availability.

Recommended in the area

Avington Park; Winchester Cathedral; Mid-Hants Railway

Thatched cottages in the village of Rockbourne.

The Rose & Thistle

Address: ROCKBOURNE, Fordingbridge, SP6 3NL
Tel: 01725 518236
Email: enquiries@roseandthistle.co.uk
Website: www.roseandthistle.co.uk
Map ref: 3, SU11
Directions: S of Salisbury, off A354 Blandford Forum rd or A338 Fordingbridge rd. Follow signs for Rockbourne
Open: 11–3 6–11 (Sun Oct–Apr closes at 8)
⓵ L 12–2.30 D 6.30–9.30 ⑥ L 12–2.30 D 6.30–9.30
Facilities: Children welcome Garden **Parking:** 28
Notes: ⊕ Free House ⚑ 18

Two long, low whitewashed cottages, dating from the 16th century, were converted nearly 200 years ago to create this downland village pub, still full of charming original features. The low-beamed bar and dining area are furnished with country-house fabrics, polished oak tables and chairs, cushioned settles and carved benches. Here fine fresh food is cooked to order, including fish and such dishes as pork fillet with confit of apricots, and rack of lamb with caramelised orange and mint sauce.

Recommended in the area

Rockbourne Rooman Villa; Breamore House and Countryside Museum; New Forest National Park

The Plough Inn

Address: Main Road, SPARSHOLT,
Nr Winchester, SO21 2NW
Tel: 01962 776353
Fax: 01962 776400
Map ref: 3, SU43
Directions: NW of Winchester; from city centre take
B3049 Stockbridge road and look for a left turn to
Sparsholt; inn reached in 1m.
Open: 11–3 6–11 (Sun 12–3, 6–10.30) 🛏 L 12–2
D 6–9 🍴 L 12–2 D 6–9 **Facilities:** Children welcome
Garden **Parking:** 90 **Notes:** 🐕 ⊘ on premises 🍺
Wadworth 🍷 14

Set in beautiful countryside, just a stone's throw from
Winchester, this inn is a great place to refresh yourself
after a walk in the nearby Farley Mount Country Park. Owners Richard and Kathryn Crawford have
a simple philosophy: to serve customers with good quality food and drink in a friendly atmosphere.
The Plough was built about 200 years ago as a coach house for Sparsholt Manor, but within 50 years
it had already become an alehouse. Since then it has been much extended, yet from the inside it all
blends together very well, helped by the farmhouse-style furniture and the adornment with agricultural
implements, stone jars and dried hops. The Wadworth brewery supplies all of the real ales, and there's
a good wine selection. The left-hand dining area is served by a blackboard menu offering such light
dishes as feta and spinach filo parcels with a Thai pesto dressing or a beef, ale and mushroom pie
with vegetables. To the right, a separate board offers meals that reflect a more serious approach –
perhaps breast of chicken filled with mushrooms on a garlic and bacon sauce; lamb shank with
braised red cabbage and rosemary jus; and several fish dishes. Booking is always advisable.

Recommended in the area

Winchester Cathedral; Mottisfont Abbey (NT); Sir Harold Hillier Gardens and Arboretum

HEREFORDSHIRE

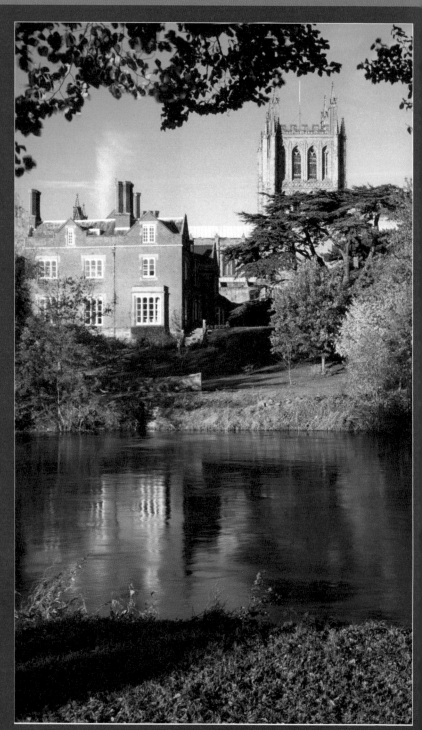

The River Wye at Hereford.

Ross-on-Wye.

The Penny Farthing Inn

Address: ASTON CREWS, Ross-on-Wye, HR9 7LW
Tel: 01989 750366
Fax: 01989 750922
Map ref: 2, SO62
Directions: 5m E of Ross-on-Wye, off A40 Gloucester
road, then B4222
Open: 12–3 6.30–11(all day Fri-Sun and May-Sept)
🅿 L 12–2 D 6–9 ⏀ L 12–2 D 6–9 Facilities: Children
welcome Garden Parking: 50 Notes: 🐎 ⊕

With beautiful views of the Malvern Hills, the Black Hills and the Forest of Dean, this old coaching inn
has lots of nooks and crannies filled with oak beams, antiques and saddlery, and some parts of the
building are over 300 years old. Food has an interesting mix of Mediterranean and other international
influences, and a great variety of seafood, including mussels, monkfish, sea bass, swordfish, tuna,
barramundi, salmon, trout and others, feature regularly on the menu. Specials might include dishes
such as Mediterranean seafood salad with balsamic; Thai fishcakes with date and lime chutney; and
barramundi steak with fresh ginger and coriander butter.

Recommended in the area

Birds of Prey Centre; Forest of Dean; Goodrich Castle

The Riverside Inn

Address:	AYMESTREY, nr Leominster, HR6 9ST
Tel:	01568 708440
Fax:	01568 709058
Email:	theriverside@btinternet.com
Website:	www.theriversideinn.org
Map ref:	2, SO46

Directions: From A49 at Leominster, go W on A44, then N on A4110 through Mortimer's Cross
Open: 11–3 6–11 (all day in summer) ⓛ L 12.30–2.15 D 7–9.15 ⓛ L 12–2.15 D 7–9.15 Facilities: Children welcome Garden Parking: 40 Notes: 🐕 ⓦ Free House ♟ 7

Alongside the lovely River Lugg, overlooking a fine old stone bridge, this delightful black-and-white inn is surrounded by wooded hills and peaceful meadowland. Anglers will certainly appreciate the mile of private fly fishing for brown trout and grayling on the river here. It is located halfway along the Mortimer Way, making it great for walkers, too, and there are a number of circular walks in the vicinity. Walking packages are offered at the inn, with accommodation and free transport provided to and from the start/finish points. The interior of the building, with its low beams and log fires, provides a relaxing atmosphere, reflecting the 400 years of hospitality that have been carried out on this spot. Richard and Liz Gresko are the current hosts, who take a serious approach to the food they offer. Locally-grown produce is used wherever possible, including vegetables, salads and herbs from their own gardens, and home made preserves. The type of cuisine here is best described as English, but with a new and interesting twist. Real ales and ciders from local brewers match bar food specialities such as home-made steak and kidney pudding, while the restaurant menu might include a roasted haunch of local venison on sweet and sour red cabbage. On a pleasant summer's day, there's nothing nicer than to sit outside in the terraced and landscaped garden, watching the river flow by.

Recommended in the area

Hergest Croft Gardens; Berrington Hall, Ashton; Croft Castle

Stockton Cross Inn

Address: KIMBOLTON,
Leominster, HR6 0HD
Tel: 01568 612509
Email: info@stocktoncrossinn.co.uk
Website: www.stocktoncrossinn.co.uk
Map ref: 2, SO56
Directions: On A4112, off A49 just N of Leominster
Open: 12–3 7–11 ⓱/🍴 L 12–2 D 7–9
Facilities: Garden **Parking:** 30 **Notes:** 🐕 (on leash)
⊕ Free House

Stockton Cross is a 16th-century drovers' inn, its picturesque black and white exterior regularly
photographed by tourists and for calendars and chocolate boxes. Its peace and beauty are belied
by the historical fact that alleged witches were once hanged here. Owners Mike Bentley and Samatha
Rosenberg along with head chef Will Hayward have a serious interest in good food. They source much
of their produce locally to provide an interesting and varied menu. There is also a pretty country
garden with umbrellas and two trees for shade.

Recommended in the area

Hergest Croft Gardens; Croft Castle; Berrington Hall (NT)

The Moody Cow

Address: Upton Bishop, ROSS-ON-WYE, HR9 7TT
Tel: 01989 780470
Website: www.moodycow.co.uk
Map ref: 2, SO52
Directions: On B4221 4m E of Ross-on-Wye,
following signs M50 then Upton Bishop, or off M50
junct 3, signed Newent
Open: 12–2.30 6–11 (Sun 12–3) ⓱ L 12–2 D 7–9
🍴 L 12–2 D 7–9 **Facilities:** Children welcome Garden
Parking: 40 **Notes:** 🐕 ⊕ Free House ♟ 7

Popular with tourists and locals alike, this lovely country pub is located at Crow Hill near Upton Bishop.
A major attraction here is the home-cooked food served in the bistro-style Fresco dining room, the
converted barn restaurant, or the bar, where squashy sofas are arranged round the fire. The pub is run
by chef proprietor James Lloyd and his wife Debbie, together with their carefully selected team. The
same menu is offered throughout and everything is made on the premises, including the bread and ice
cream. There's also a great selection of beers, and wines from around the world.

Recommended in the area

Birds of Prey Centre; Forest of Dean; Wye Valley

The Lough Pool Inn at Sellack

Address: SELLACK, Ross-on-Wye, HR9 6LX
Tel: 01989 730236
Fax: 01989 730548
Map ref: 2, SO52
Directions: 4m NW of Ross-on-Wye via A49 Hereford road. Take road signed Sellack/Hoarwithy
Open: 11.30–3 6.30–11 (Sun 11–3, 6.30–10.30)
L 12–3 D 7–9.15 L 12–3 D 7–9.15
Facilities: Children welcome Garden **Parking:** 40
Notes: Free House 10

First, the pronunciation – it's Luff Pool. This is an unspoilt country pub that occupies a 16th-century black and white Herefordshire cottage, which was once the home of the village blacksmith and butcher, and it is located beside the eponymous Lough Pool, home to magnificent weeping willows and wild ducks, within an area of outstanding natural beauty. There are flagstone floors, old beams and cosy fires, and at the rear is a dining room with rustic tables and chairs. Outside there's a peaceful garden and lovely walks to the River Wye right from the door. David and Janice Birch previously ran a successful rural pub in Dorset and they've really made their mark here, with people coming from as far as Cardiff and Cheltenham for a meal. They are passionate about the superb local produce and, together with their new Head Chef, James Miller, offer seasonal menus featuring hand-reared middle white pork, Hereford and rare breed beef, Marches lamb, free-range poultry, game from local estates, fruit and vegetables from nearby farms, garden herbs, clotted cream and local cheeses. The Lough Pool serves expertly-chosen wines from specialist local merchants and these are served alongside real ales, local ciders, perry and varieties of pure apple juice from the county's orchards.

Recommended in the area

Goodrich Castle; Wye Valley Butterfly Farm; Hereford Cathedral and the Mappa Mundi

The Saracens Head Inn

◆◆◆◆

Address: SYMONDS YAT [EAST], HR9 6JL
Tel: 01600 890435
Fax: 01600 890034
Email: contact@saracensheadinn.co.uk
Website: www.saracensheadinn.co.uk
Map ref: 2, SO51
Directions: From A40 Ross-on-Wye to Monmouth road, take B4432, signed Symonds Yat
Open: 11–11 ♿ L 12–2.30 D 6.30–9.30 ⏹ L 12–2.30 D 6.30–9.30 **Rooms:** 11 en suite, S £45 D £70 **Facilities:** Children welcome Garden **Parking:** 38
Notes: 🐕 🍺 Free House 🍷 7

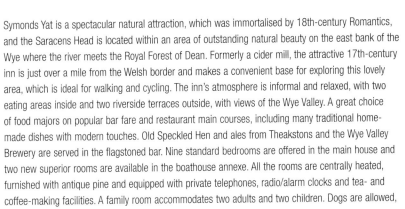

Symonds Yat is a spectacular natural attraction, which was immortalised by 18th-century Romantics, and the Saracens Head is located within an area of outstanding natural beauty on the east bank of the Wye where the river meets the Royal Forest of Dean. Formerly a cider mill, the attractive 17th-century inn is just over a mile from the Welsh border and makes a convenient base for exploring this lovely area, which is ideal for walking and cycling. The inn's atmosphere is informal and relaxed, with two eating areas inside and two riverside terraces outside, with views of the Wye Valley. A great choice of food majors on popular bar fare and restaurant main courses, including many traditional home-made dishes with modern touches. Old Speckled Hen and ales from Theakstons and the Wye Valley Brewery are served in the flagstoned bar. Nine standard bedrooms are offered in the main house and two new superior rooms are available in the boathouse annexe. All the rooms are centrally heated, furnished with antique pine and equipped with private telephones, radio/alarm clocks and tea- and coffee-making facilities. A family room accommodates two adults and two children. Dogs are allowed, with water bowls provided.

Recommended in the area

Goodrich Castle; Symonds Yat Rock; Forest of Dean

The garden at Hatfield House.

The Bricklayers Arms

Address: Hogpits Bottom, FLAUNDEN, Nr Hemel
             Hempstead, HP3 0PH
Tel: 01442 833322
Fax: 01442 834841
Email: goodfood@bricklayersarms.com
Website: www.bricklayersarms.com
Map ref: 4, TL00
Directions: M25 junct 18, then A404 Amersham road,
and turn right at Chenies for Flaunden
Open: 12–11.30 ⓛ L 12–2.30 D 6–9.30 ⓘ L 12–2.30
D 6.30–9.30 Facilities: Children welcome Garden Parking: 50 Notes: ⌖ ⊕ Free House ⓟ 14

This award-winning country pub, owned and managed by Alvin and Sally Michaels, has become a foodie destination thanks to its happy pairing of British traditions and French classics. Tucked away in deepest rural Hertfordshire, it's popular with walkers, locals, and all those who seek a sunny and secluded garden to relax in during the summer months. Rambling and ivy-covered on the outside, its immaculate interior provides the expected low beams, exposed brickwork, candlelight and open fires. The French influence comes from chef Claude Paillet, who trained in Paris at the three Michelin-starred Pierre Gagnaire restaurant. His passion for food is reflected in a menu that marries hearty British cooking with French sophistication, and he shows great respect for the traditions of this old English pub. A meal here might start with brochette of tiger prawns on a rosemary stick or a selection of their home-smoked fish with corriander butter and tomato chutney. Continue, perhaps, with best end of lamb with pea flan and rosemary and Madeira jus; quail stuffed with mushrooms; or pan-fried sea bass with a creamy Chardonnay, red pepper, shallot and basil sauce. Be sure to check out the dessert menu, which might include a Tarte Tatin; rhubarb and raspberry franjipane; chocolate and banana bavarois; or sticky toffee pudding.

Recommended in the area

Chenies Manor House; Berkhamsted Castle; Ashridge Estate (NT);

Alford Arms

Address: Frithsden, HEMEL HEMPSTEAD, HP1 3DD
Tel: 01442 864480
Fax: 01442 876893
Email: info@alfordarmsfrithsden.co.uk
Website: www.alfordarmsfrithsden.co.uk
Map ref: 3, TL00
Directions: From Hemel Hempstead, take A4146 for
2m to Water End; take 2nd left. In 1m turn left at T-junct,
then right after 0.75m. Pub is 100yds on right
Open: 11–11 (Sun 12–10.30) ℔ L 12–2.30 D 7–10
🍽 L 12–2.30 D 7–10 Facilities: Children welcome Garden Parking: 25 Notes: 🐕 ⊕ ♥ 18

Set in an unspoilt hamlet, surrounded by National Trust woodland, the Alford Arms is a pretty Victorian
pub. Despite the traditional trappings – wood floors, quarry tiles, log fires, old furniture and pictures –
it has a light modern feel, and the lively warm atmosphere sets the mood for relaxed yet professional
service. The seasonal menus of modern British style cooking produce dishes such as pan-fried sea
bass with roast aubergine; pan-fried calves' liver; and chargrilled rib-eye steak.

Recommended in the area

Berkhamsted Castle; Walter Rothschild Zoological Museum; Whipsnade Wild Animal Park

The Fox and Hounds

Address: 2 High Street, HUNSDON, SG12 8NH
Tel: 01279 843999
Fax: 01279 841092
Email: info@foxandhounds-hunsdon.co.uk
Website: www.foxandhounds-hunsdon.co.uk
Map ref: 3, TL41
Directions: From M11 junct 7, take A414, skirting
Harlow, towards Ware, turn right to Stanstead Abbots,
then take B180 to Hunsdon.
Open: 12–4 6–11 ℔ L 12–3 D 6–10.30 🍽 L 12–3
D 7–10 Facilities: Children welcome Garden Parking: 40 Notes: ⊘ on premises ⊕ Free House ♥ 7

The pub is set in a pretty village surrounded by Hertfordshire countryside. It has recently been
revamped with a comfy, laid-back bar featuring a log fire, leather sofas and local ales. There's a large
separate dining room and an outside terrace in the large garden. Chef owner James Rix, who trained
under some of the industry's top chefs, has quickly made a name for himself at this family-run
establishment, with a seasonal menu that changes twice a day. Dogs are permitted.

Recommended in the area

Henry Moore Foundation; Paradise Wildlife Park; Lee Valley Park

Carvings in chalk in the Royston Caves depict St Catherine and the crucifixtion.

The Cabinet Free House and Restaurant

Address: High Street, Reed, ROYSTON, SG8 8AH
Tel: 01763 848366
Fax: 01763 849407
Email: thecabinet@btconnect.com
Website: www.thecabinetatreed.co.uk
Map ref: 3, TL34
Directions: 2m S of Royston just off the A10
Open: 12–3 6–11 (all day Sat–Sun in summer) ㅑ L
12–2.30 D 6–10 ㅑ L 12–2.30 D 6–10 **Facilities:** Children welcome Garden **Parking:** 40 **Notes:** ㅑ
🕮 ☗ 50

Touching lofty heights – at the highest point between the UK and the Urals – this 16th-century pub
has been transformed into foodie heaven, with interesting French, British and transatlantic inspirations
showing in such dishes as gambas à la plancha (tiger prawns, garlic butter and lemon); Breckland
duck breast with honey-roast root vegetables and ginger jus; and Tahitian vanilla bean crème brûlée.
Recommended in the area
Fowlmere RSPB Nature Reserve; Imperial War Museum Duxford; Knebworth House

Compton Bay.

The New Inn

Address: Mill Lane, SHALFLEET, PO30 4NS
Tel: 01983 531314
Fax: 01983 531314
Email: info@thenew-inn.co.uk
Website: www.thenew-inn.co.uk
Map ref: 3, SZ48
Directions: About 7m W of Newport, on A3054 Yarmouth road
Open: 11–3 6–11 ⓑ L 12–2.30 D 6–9.30 🍴 L 12–2.30 D 6–9.30 **Facilities:** Garden **Parking:** 20
Notes: 🐕 ⊘ on premises ⊞ Enterprise Inns ♟ 6

One of the island's best known dining pubs and a great favourite with the yachting community, the New Inn is located at the foot of the picturesque Newtown Estuary and National Trust nature reserve. Local walks from the doorstep, including a three-mile or easier 40-minute hike, are recommended, taking in lovely views from Shalfeet Quay and the Newtown Estuary mudflats. When it comes to inns, the term 'new' is relative, and this New Inn has a great feeling of history about it, with inglenook fireplaces, low beams and flagstone floors. It was, in fact, new in 1743, when it replaced an older inn that had been destroyed in a fire. Where food is concerned, the pub has an outstanding reputation for local seafood and other seasonal produce. The standard menu includes a long list of sandwiches and baguettes, traditional pub favourites and seafood specialities, including lobster salad and the gigantic Seafood Royale (for two), and the specials board features local produce such as Rowridge duck and locally made sausages. Real ales include Interbrew Bass, Goddards Special Bitter, Greene King IPA and Marston's Pedigree, and one of the island's most extensive wine lists has six available by the glass. Outside, there is a raised sun deck, perfect for catching the rays in better weather. Dogs are permitted and water is provided. The New Inn has a sister inn, the Horse and Groom, at Ningwood.

Recommended in the area

Afton and Compton Downs (NT); Carisbrooke Castle; Dinosaur Farm Museum

KENT

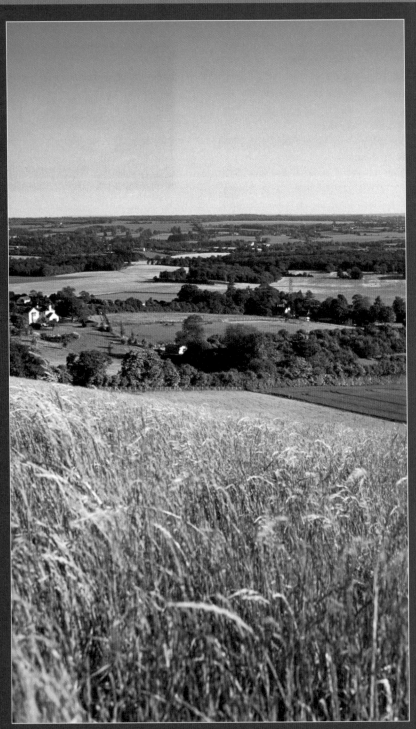

The Kent countryside.

The White Horse Inn

Address: 53 High Street, Bridge,
            CANTERBURY, CT4 5LA
Tel: 01227 832814
Fax: 01227 832814
Website: www.whitehorsebridge.co.uk
Map ref: 4, TR15
Directions: 3m S of Canterbury, just off A2
Open: 11–3 6–11 (Sun 12–5) L 12–2 D 6.30–9
L 12–2 D 7–9 Facilities: Children welcome Garden
Parking: 20 Notes: ⊘ on premises 10

Originally a coach staging post on the main Dover to Canterbury road, this medieval building is still
welcoming modern-day travellers. There is a strong emphasis on food here, and a proud commitment
to local suppliers. Choose between the blackboard bar menu, or more formal dining in the restaurant.
Meals can also be taken outside in the pretty garden, with its large grassed area and mature trees,
or inside by the big log fire. Fullers, Greene King and Shepherd Neame are among the real ales served
in the bar and there are up to 10 wines available by the glass.

Recommended in the area
Canterbury; Howletts Wild Animal Park; North Downs Way

Griffins Head

Address: CHILLENDEN, Canterbury, CT3 1PS
Tel: 01304 840325
Fax: 01304 841290
Map ref: 4, TR25
Directions: From Canterbury take A2 Dover road, then
turn left onto B2046; later turn right for Chillenden
Open: 10.30–11 L 12–2 D 7–9.30 L 12–2
D 7–9.30 Facilities: Garden Parking: 25
Notes: Shepherd Neame 10

Dating from 1286, this Kentish Wealden hall has great historical character, with beamed bars and
inglenook fireplaces. Fine Kentish ales from Shepherd Neame and home-made food have helped the
old inn to make its mark with visitors as well as locals, among them Kent's cricketing fraternity. The
menu is typically English and specialises in game from local estates in season and locally caught fish
where possible. Outside there's a very pretty garden where drinkers can linger at their leisure, and
a bat and trap pitch (an ancient relative of cricket, still popular in Kent). A vintage car club meets here
on the first Sunday of every month.

Recommended in the area
Canterbury; Wingham Bird Park; Howletts Wild Animal Park

Castle Inn

Address: CHIDDINGSTONE, TN8 7AH
Tel: 01892 870247
Fax: 01892 871420
Email: info@castleinn.co.uk
Website: www.castleinn.co.uk
Map ref: 4, TQ54
Directions: 1.5m S of B2027 between Tonbridge and Edenbridge
Open: 11–11 ⓑ L 11–9.30 ⓘ L 12–2 D 7.30–9.30
Facilities: Children welcome Garden Notes: 🐾 ⊕ Free House ♟ 10

The first recorded mention of this mellow brick building was made in 1420, when it was a private house, and it appears that ale wasn't sold here until about 1730. It is as attractive on the outside as internally, where nooks and crannies, period furniture and curios give it an inviting ambience, and the Castle is a popular choice as a movie location. Film appearances include *Elizabeth R*, *Room with a View*, *The Life of Hogarth* and *The Wicked Lady*. Chiddingstone is unusual in that, apart from the church and the castle, the entire village is owned by the National Trust. Meals are served informally in the heavily beamed saloon bar, while the restaurant provides full table service and a much more extensive selection. A recent dinner menu included a starter of Isle of Lewis mussels and Dutch clams in a mild curry sauce, and such main courses as chargrilled local venison on rosemary mash, with red onion marmalade with wild berries. There is much to excite the wine lover in a list running to over 100 bins, and the whisky drinker can choose between around 30 malts. The range of real ales includes Larkins Traditional, brewed in the village by Bob Dockerty. Behind the inn is a vine covered courtyard garden with its own bar, and beyond that a bridge leading to pretty garden with a lawn and flowerbeds. Dogs are welcomed with water and chews.

Recommended in the area

Penshurst Place and Gardens; Hever Castle and Gardens; Groombridge Place Gardens

The Great House

Address: Gills Green, HAWKHURST, TN18 5EJ
Tel: 01580 753119
Fax: 01622 851881
Email: info@thegreathouse.net
Website: www.thegreathouse.net
Map ref: 4, TQ73
Directions: Just off A229 between Cranbrook and Hawkhurst
Open: 11–11 (Sun 12–10.30) 🍺 L 12–9.30
🍴 L 12–9.30 **Facilities:** Children welcome Garden
Farm Shop/Deli Market **Parking:** 80 **Notes:** ⊘ on premises ⊕ Free House 🍷 13

The Great House, dating from the 16th century, is a wonderfully atmospheric pub, full of character, but very much more comfortable now than it might have been during its days as a smugglers inn. There are three dining areas to choose from and the more recent addition of an Orangery, which is licensed for civil marriage ceremonies. This in turn leads out onto a Mediterranean-style terrace, overlooking the lovely garden, with its mature trees and shrubs and an attractive Kentish lych gate. Herbs for the kitchen are also grown here in an aromatic herb garden. The Great House attracts a lot of custom for its food, and its informal brasserie-style menu offers a lot of interest. Deli boards include platters of charcuterie, cheeses, fish and antipasti, and there are also stone baked pizzas and toasted paninis. Starters might include Mediterranean fish soup; crispy vegetable basket with rocket and pesto dressing; and the signature dish of fresh scallops, which you could follow with such main courses as oven roasted salmon fillet with creamy cabbage, smoked bacon and hollandaise sauce; pan-fried wood pigeon with red onion marmalade; lamb and mint burger with goat's cheese melt and beetroot salsa; and slow cooked venison casserole. The wine list features 70 choices, three of which come from the nearby Tenderden vineyard.

Recommended in the area

Bedgebury National Pinetum; Bodiam Castle; Sissinghurst Castle Garden (NT)

The Bottle House Inn

Address: Coldharbour Road, PENSHURST,
Tonbridge, TN11 8ET
Tel: 01892 870306
Fax: 01892 871094
Email: info@thebottlehouseinnpenshurst.co.uk
Website: www.thebottlehouseinnpenshurst.co.uk
Map ref: 4, TQ54
Directions: From Tunbridge Wells take A264 W then
B2188 N
Open: 11–11 (Sun 11–10.30pm) 🍺 L 12–10 D 12–10
🍽 L 12–10 D 12–10 **Facilities:** Children welcome Garden **Parking:** 36 **Notes:** 🐕 🌐 Free House 🍷 8

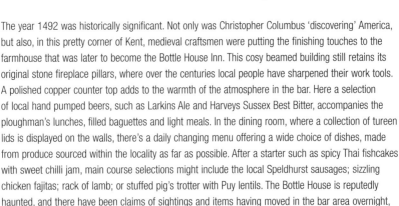

The year 1492 was historically significant. Not only was Christopher Columbus 'discovering' America, but also, in this pretty corner of Kent, medieval craftsmen were putting the finishing touches to the farmhouse that was later to become the Bottle House Inn. This cosy beamed building still retains its original stone fireplace pillars, where over the centuries local people have sharpened their work tools. A polished copper counter top adds to the warmth of the atmosphere in the bar. Here a selection of local hand pumped beers, such as Larkins Ale and Harveys Sussex Best Bitter, accompanies the ploughman's lunches, filled baguettes and light meals. In the dining room, where a collection of tureen lids is displayed on the walls, there's a daily changing menu offering a wide choice of dishes, made from produce sourced within the locality as far as possible. After a starter such as spicy Thai fishcakes with sweet chilli jam, main course selections might include the local Speldhurst sausages; sizzling chicken fajitas; rack of lamb; or stuffed pig's trotter with Puy lentils. The Bottle House is reputedly haunted, and there have been claims of sightings and items having moved in the bar area overnight, but don't let this put you off. The pub is family friendly, with high chairs provided and a children's menu. Dogs are welcome too, except in the dining room.

Recommended in the area

Hever Castle; Royal Tunbridge Wells; Penshurst Place and Gardens

The Spotted Dog

Address: Smarts Hill, PENSHURST
Tonbridge, TN11 8EE
Tel: 01892 870253
Fax: 01892 870107
Email: info@spotteddogpub.co.uk
Website: www.spotteddogpub.co.uk
Map ref: 4, TQ54
Directions: Off B2188 Penshurst–Fordcombe road
Open: 11–3 6–11 (times vary seasonally, ring for details)
L 12–2.30 D 6–9.30 L 12–2.30 D 6–9.30
Facilities: Garden **Parking:** 60 **Notes:** Free House 9

Built in 1520, the weather-boarded Spotted Dog was erroneously named by a myopic painter who took the leopard on a local coat of arms to be a dog. Beams, open fires, tiled and oak floors, and nooks and crannies characterise the interior. A single, but varied and constantly changing menu has dishes such as honey-baked ham, eggs and chips alongside Thai-style dishes; slow-braised belly of pork; and pan-fried salmon fillet. Harvey and Larkins are on tap, plus guest beers.
Recommended in the area
Chartwell (NT); Penshurst Place and Gardens; Bluebell Railway

The Dering Arms

Address: Station Road, PLUCKLEY
Ashford, TN27 0RR
Tel: 01233 840371
Fax: 01233 840498
Email: jim@deringarms.com
Website: www.deringarms.com
Map ref: 4, TQ94
Directions: From Ashford (M20 junct 9), take A20 N to
Charing; turn left on Pluckley Road; in Pluckley turn left
Open: 11–3 6–11 L 12–2 D 7–9.30 L 12–2
D 7–9.30 **Facilities:** Children welcome Garden **Parking:** 20 **Notes:** Free House 7

The impressive Dering Arms, originally a hunting lodge of the Dering Estate, was built in the 1840s as a replica of the manor house, with curved Dutch gables and uniquely arched windows. Chef/patron James Buss has run the inn with passion and flair for over 20 years, serving ales from Goacher's micro-brewery in Maidstone and an impressive list of wines. The extensive menus reflect his love of fresh seafood, and utilise fresh vegetables from the family farm and herbs from the pub garden.
Recommended in the area
Leeds Castle; Sissinghurst Castle Garden (NT); Bodiam Castle

The Pantiles shopping arcade in Tunbridge Wells.

The Beacon

♦♦♦♦

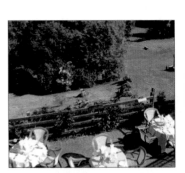

Address:	Tea Garden Lane, Rusthall,
	ROYAL TUNBRIDGE WELLS, TN3 9JH
Tel:	01892 524252
Fax:	01892 534288
Email:	beaconhotel@btopenworld.com
Website:	www.the-beacon.co.uk
Map ref:	4, TQ53

Directions: From Tunbridge Wells take A264 towards East Grinstead. Pub 1m on left

Open: 11–11 (Sun 12–10.30) 🍴 L 12–2.30 D 6.30–9.30 🍴 L 12–2.30 D 6–9.30 Rooms: 3 en suite, S £68.5 D £97 Facilities: Children welcome Garden Parking: 40 Notes: ⊕ Free House ♥ 12

Located 1.5 miles from Tunbridge Wells, with magnificent south-facing views, The Beacon has a fine range of beers and wine to complement the award-winning food, which is produced using local ingredients. Dishes include braised oxtail with root vegetables, parsley mash and buttered cabbage, seafood pie with minted garden peas and natural smoked haddock in Stilton cream.

Recommended in the area

Tunbridge Wells; Penshurst Place & Gardens; Spa Valley Railway

The Farmhouse

Address: 97 High Street, WEST MALLING, ME19 6NA
Tel: 01732 843257
Fax: 01622 851881
Email: info@thefarmhouse.biz
Website: www.thefarmhouse.biz
Map ref: 4, TQ65
Directions: From M20 junct 4, go south on A228, cross
the A20, then look for a right turn for West Malling
Open: 11–11 (Sun 12–10.30) ⌷ L 12–9.30
⌷ L 12–9.30 (Breakfast served 9am–11pm)
Facilities: Children welcome Garden Farm Shop/Deli Market **Parking:** 20 **Notes:** ⌷ ⌷ 13

A handsome Elizabethan building at the heart of the village of West Malling, The Farmhouse markets itself as a pub and eating house. The establishment, which has served travellers and locals alike over the centuries, maintains its relaxed atmosphere, but has been given a contemporary slant, with a stylish bar and two dining areas: one that's warm and airy and the other with its original high ceilings and distinctive decoration. A spacious walled garden overlooks 15th-century stone-built barns and there's an area of decking providing the perfect space to sit outside with a drink on fine summer days. The constantly evolving menu offers a good choice of freshly cooked dishes based on fresh local produce. There is plenty of interest in the deli board, tapas, breads, salads, small dishes, main courses and side orders. Mains range from home-made Harvey's battered cod and chips to wood pigeon breast and confit legs salad with Puy lentils, and bar food is available at lunchtime and in the evening together with daily specials. There are plenty of options for vegetarians, too, including wild mushrooms and aged parmesan risotto with green leaves, and open lasagne, tomato fondue, mushrooms duxelle and baby spinach. In addition to the real ales, 15 brands of malt whisky and a decent selection of wines by the glass, the drinks list extends to a healthy choice of organic fruit juices.

Recommended in the area

Museum of Kent Life; Leeds Castle; Maidstone Carriage Museum

Whalley Abbey.

The Eagle & Child

Address: Maltkiln Lane, BISPHAM GREEN,
             Nr Ormskirk, L40 3SG
Tel: 01257 462297
Fax: 01257 464718
Website: www.ainscoughs.co.uk
Map ref: 6, SD41
Directions: 3m from M6 junct 27, W via A5209; over
Parbold Hill, turn right on B5246 signed Bispham Green
Open: 12–3 5.3–11 (Sun 12-10.30) 🍺 L 12–2
D 6–8.30 🍽 L 12–2 D 6–8.30 Facilities: Children
welcome Garden Parking: 50 Notes: 🐕 🚭 Free House 🍷 6

In 2004 landlady Monica Evans handed over the reins to assistant manager, David Anderson and now it's a more relaxed Monica who does the assisting. No two chairs or tables match in this stone-flagged village pub, where the food, although simply expressed on the menu, is thoughtfully prepared. Thus you are likely to find roast supreme of salmon and celeriac mash; chargrilled lamb cutlet with honey and mint glaze; Thai-style beef stir-fry with noodles; and standards like cod, chips and mushy peas.

Recommended in the area

Wildfowl and Wetlands Trust Martin Mere; Camelot Theme Park; Rufford Old Hall (NT)

The Millstone at Mellor

★★   85% ◉◉   HOTEL

Address: Church Lane, Mellor, BLACKBURN, BB2 7JR
Tel: 01254 813333
Fax: 01254 812628
Email: info@millstonehotel.co.uk
Website: www.millstonehotel.co.uk
Map ref: 6, SD62
Directions: From M6 junct 31 take A59 Clitheroe road,
at rdbt turn right signed Mellor; at next rdbt 2nd exit.
Open: 11–11 (Fri–Sat 11am–12pm, Sun 12–10.30)
🍺 /🍽 L 12–2.15 D 6.30–9.30 Rooms: 23 en suite,
Parking: 45 Notes: 🚭 Shire Hotels Ltd 🍷 12

A charming old inn, in the heart of the Ribble Valley, where good bar food and real ales are served. Main courses in the restaurant might include roast venison with horseradish mash or grilled sea bass. Chef patron Anson Bolton and his team offer daily menus using the finest and freshest produce.

Recommended in the area

Samlesbury Hall; Ribble Valley; Hoghton Tower

The view from the Clitheroe Castle.

The Assheton Arms

Address: Downham, CLITHEROE, BB7 4BJ
Tel: 01200 441227
Fax: 01200 440581
Email: asshetonarms@aol.com
Website: www.assheton-arms.co.uk
Map ref: 6, SD74
Directions: Just N of Clitheroe, turn left off A59 to Chatburn, then follow Downham signs
Open: 12–3 7–11 (all day summer Sun) ⓑ L 12–2 D 7–10 ⓘⓄⓘ L – D – **Facilities:** Children welcome
Parking: 12 **Notes:** ⚑ ⊘ on premises ⊞ Free House ⓟ 18

Better known as the Signalman's Arms from the BBC drama series *Born and Bred*, this country pub is actually named after Lord Clitheroe's family, which owns the whole of Downham. The family has maintained the period integrity of the picturesque village (no aerials, cables or street signs), making it a popular location for filming. The pub has a single bar and comfortable beamed rooms with an open fireplace. Home-cooked food is served, with an emphasis on seafood. Dogs are very welcome.

Recommended in the area

Clitheroe Castle; Pendle Hill; Helmshore Textile Museum

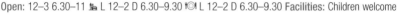

Cartford Country Inn and Hotel

Address: Little Eccleston, PRESTON, PR3 0YP
Tel: 01995 670166
Fax: 01995 671785
Email: cartfordhotel@tiscali.co.uk
Map ref: 6, SD52
Directions: From M55 junct 3, go N on A585, then turn right onto the A586 towards Garstang. Little Eccleston is off to the left, near Great Eccleson, on road to Moss Edge
Open: 12–3 6.30–11 🍴 L 12–2 D 6.30–9.30 🍽 L 12–2 D 6.30–9.30 **Facilities:** Children welcome
Parking: 60 **Notes:** 🐾 🌐 Free House 🍷

This friendly pub is located beside a toll bridge across the River Wyre, with walks along the river in both directions and the beautiful Fylde countryside stretching away to the north. A far cry indeed from the busy motorway to the south, pouring visitors by the thousand into Blackpool. This, together with the good beer, great food and friendly atmosphere, makes the Cartford Country Inn something of a destination pub in the area. Andrew Mellodew has been the owner for nearly 18 years, and his Lancastrian wife Tracy's great grandfather was landlord here in the 1890s. Inside, an open log fire may be blazing if the weather is on the cool side, and there are always games to be played while enjoying a pint of Dishy Debbie, one of several real ales brewed by the Hart Brewery, located right behind the pub. A good range of food on the bar menu includes sandwiches, jacket potatoes, salads, chicken and bacon pasta, lamb Henry and seafood platter. Specials might include spicy curries; lemon sole with crabmeat; and vegetarian options, and in the evenings pizzas are available too. This might sound like pretty standard pub fare, but the quality of the ingredients and skilfull preparation make it stand out.

Recommended in the area

Blackpool; Wyre Estuary Country Park; Marsh Mill

Freemasons Arms

Address: 8 Vicarage Fold, Wiswell, WHALLEY,
Clitheroe, BB7 9DF
Tel: 01254 822218
Email: freemasons@wiswell.co.uk
Website: www.wiswell.co.uk
Map ref: 6, SD73
Directions: From Clitheroe go S on A59, then turn left
onto A671, Wiswell is 1st left
Open: 12–3 6–11 ▧ L 12–2 D 6–9.30 ▧ L 12–2
D 6–9.30 **Notes:** ▦ Free House ♟ 15

Tucked away down a tiny ginnel in the village of Wiswell, the Freemason's Arms has a lovely rural setting at the foot of Pendle Hill. This hidden gem is worth seeking out, particularly for those exploring the Ribble Valley, where the superb scenery can be fully appreciated from numerous walks in the area. The pub dates back at least 200 years and was originally used to house the monks from Whalley Abbey. Secret freemason's meetings are also believed to have been held here, hence the name. Inside there is a spacious bar area with a dining room upstairs. Seats are also available outside, though there is no garden as such. The pub is owned and run with great enthusiasm by Ian Martin, and has a great reputation for its food. Fresh local produce is served in a contemporary style alongside an award-winning 600-bin wine list, many at very reasonable prices. Typical dishes include chargrilled Bowland pork chop; Goosenargh duck confit with sautéed artichokes; and sea bass with anchovy and sage fritters. There's usually a good choice of fish and seafood dishes on the menu too, perhaps brochette of monkfish, scallops and king prawns; sea bass with anchovy and sage fritters; or seared peppered salmon with rösti potatoes. Well-kept local cask ales include Bowland Brewery's Hen Harrier, Black Sheep Bitter and Moorhouse Pride of Pendle, and there is a sizeable selection of vintage Armagnac, cognac and whisky.

Recommended in the area

Pendle Hill; Clitheroe Castle; Trough of Bowland

The Three Fishes

Address: Mitton Road, Mitton, WHALLEY, BB7 9PQ
Tel: 01254 826888
Fax: 01254 826026
Email: enquiries@thethreefishes.com
Website: www.thethreefishes.com
Map ref: 6, SD73
Directions: Go S from Clitheroe on A59 and turn off into Whalley, then take the B6246 for 3m, signed Stonyhurst
Open: 12–11 L 12–2 D 6–9 **Facilities:** Children welcome Garden **Parking:** 55 **Notes:** on premises
 8

Recently completely restored, this 400-year-old pub is proud of its 21st-century revamp, but still upholds traditional values, with real beers, proper home-cooked food and a wonderfully relaxing environment; sprawling sun terraces in summer and crackling log fires in winter. The Three Fishes name is said to come from the arms of Abbott Paslew, last Abbott of Whalley Abbey. The Paslew arms – three fishes pendant – appears as a carved stonework, which is thought to have come from the ruins of the abbey, over the pub entrance. Only cask conditioned beers are served here: Thwaites Traditional, Thwaites Bomber and a monthly guest beer from Bowland Brewery. These are accompanied by draft German lagers and wheat beers, ciders and a selection of wines. The menu is a delicious tribute to Lancashire specialities, British classics and the produce of acknowledged local food heroes. Elm wood platters are a house speciality, with seafood, home-cured meats or pickled vegetables. The inn was founded on the old road between the 16th-century bridge at Lower Hodden and the old ferry at Mitton, and the surrounding area is very scenic, with fabulous views of the Ribble Valley from the garden. The Ribble Way actually goes right past the pub, making this a popular stop for walkers. Dogs are allowed.

Recommended in the area

Stonyhurst College, Stonyhurst; All Hallows medieval church, Mitton; Whalley Abbey, Whalley

The Botanical Gardens in Southport.

The Mulberry Tree

@ @

Address:	Wrightington Bar, WRIGHTINGTON Nr Wigan WN6 9SE
Tel/Fax:	01257 451400
Map ref:	6, SK50
Directions:	M6 junct 27 into Mossy Lea Rd, 2m on right

Open: 12–2 6–9.30 (Fri–Sat 6–10) ⊯ L 12–2 6–9.30 (all day Sun and Fri–Sat 6–10) ⓘ L 12–2 D 6–10 (Sun 12–3) **Parking:** 100 **Notes:**⊞ Free House ♇ 8

The Mulberry Tree dates from 1832, and the award-winning chef proprietor Mark Prescott – ranked among Britain's top ten contemporary chefs – attracts discerning diners from near and far. On the dinner menu are accomplished dishes such as whole roast sea bream with saffron and prawn risotto; crab salad with Bloody Mary dressing; and slow braised lamb shank. Or keep it simple but pricey with Iranian Sevruga caviar followed by fresh lobster with champagne and herb sauce.

Recommended in the area

Astley Hall Museum and Art Gallery; Camelot Theme Park; National Football Museum

A steam train at Loughborough.

Hallaton's village green and butter cross.

The Bewicke Arms

◆◆◆◆

Address:	1 Eastgate, HALLATON, Market Harborough, LE16 8UB
Tel:	01858 555217
Fax:	01858 555598
Website:	www.bewickearms.co.uk
Map ref:	3, SP79
Directions:	W of Leicester off A47

Open: 12–3 6–11 (all day Sun; winter months 7–11)
🍴/🎴 L 12–2 D 7–9.30 **Rooms:** 3 en suite, S £40 D £55 **Facilities:** Children welcome Garden **Parking:** 20 **Notes:** 🖼 Free House 🍷 18

On Easter Monday 1770, a local chatelaine was saved from being gored by a raging bull when a hare ran across the bull's path. In gratitude, she – rather perversely – arranged for two hare pies and a generous supply of ale to be made available to the parish poor every Easter Monday. The Bewicke Arms, a refurbished 400-year-old thatched inn, plays host to this strange annual event. Flowers IPA and Grainstore beers match the seasonal blackboard menu featuring local produce.

Recommended in the area

Rockingham Speedway; Eyebrook Reservoir; Rutland Water

LONDON

The Houses of Parliament and Westminster Bridge.

North Pole Bar & Restaurant

Address: 131 Greenwich High Road, Greenwich, LONDON SE10 8JA
Tel: 020 8853 3020
Fax: 020 8853 3501
Email: north-pole@btconnect.com
Website: www.northpolegreenwich.com
Map ref: 3, TQ38
Directions: From A205 South Circular, join A2 and go west through Blackheath. Turn right into Greenwich
Open: 12–12 🍴 L 12–10.30 🍽 L 12–4 D 6–11
Facilities: Children welcome **Notes:** ⊞ Free House ♟ 20

There really is something for everyone at the North Pole, a wide ranging establishment set over three floors, comprising a ground floor bar, first floor restaurant and a basement DJ Bar, which couldn't be called anything other than The South Pole. Stylish and comfortable, the bar offers an all day menu from noon with delicious roast dinners on Sundays, when top jazz acts perform in the evening. The VIP Room, with its cowhide sofas, plasma TV and bubble tank windows, can be booked free of charge, and can accommodate up to 25 people for a special event. The North Pole is a free house, serving a selection of draught lagers, Caffreys, Guinness and bottled beers, and a larger selection of cocktails – check out Rat Pack Manhattan, the Foxy Brown, and Sex at the Pole. Bar lunches feature such favourites as fish and chips with mushy peas; cheeseburger; fresh pasta; and steak ciabatta, plus a Sunday breakfast menu, while upstairs, the award-winning Piano Restaurant takes pride in its modern European cooking with a French twist. Dishes are elevated by luxurious ingredients such as foie gras, truffles and quails eggs.There is also a new wine list, compiled by the new manager who has come from The Ivy. The restaurant can be hired out privately for weddings and other functions. Facilities for children are provided.

Recommended in the area

Maritime Greenwich World Heritage Site; Greenwich Park; Greenwich Indoor and Outdoor Market

The Grapes

Address: 76 Narrow Street, Limehouse,
LONDON E14 8BP
Tel: 020 7987 4396
Fax: 020 7987 3137
Map ref: 3, TQ38
Directions: At N end of Tower Bridge turn rt on The
Highway; Narrow St is on right, before Limehouse Link
Open: 12–3 5.30–11 (Sat 12–11, Sun 12–10.30)
🛏 L 12–2 D 7–9 🍽 L 12–2.15 D 7.30–9.15
Notes: 🚭 ⊕ 🍷 6

In *Our Mutual Friend*, Dickens describes a pub based at least partly on this venerable establishment as outlasting 'many a sprucer public house'. So it has continued, right into the 21st century, despite the dramatic changes wrought on the river and docks around it. Today, its other claim to fame comes from being an excellent seafood restaurant: lobster bisque and fishcakes jostle with a range of freshly cooked specials; perhaps salmon mornay or halibut with parsley sauce. There's a tiny riverside deck outside, and, as Dickens himself would have appreciated, the landlady was once a Playboy Bunny.
Recommended in the area
Docklands Museum; Limehouse Basin Marina; Canary Wharf

Nags Head

Address: 53 Kinnerton Street,
LONDON SW1X 8ED
Tel: 020 7235 1135
Map ref: 3, TQ38
Directions: Take A4 (or underground) to Knightsbridge;
Kinnerton St is between Lowndes Square and Wilton Place
Open: 11–11 (Sun 12–10.30) 🛏 L 11–9.30
Facilities: Children welcome Notes: 🐾 ⊕ Free House

A true London gem, the Nags Head is an unspoilt drinking house in the heart of Belgravia. It is a small establishment, with wooden floors, panelled walls and low ceilings, built in the early 19th century to cater for the footmen and stable hands who looked after the horses in these Belgravia mews. The proprietors pride themselves on serving a selection of definitive Adnams ales and good pub grub in a relaxed old world manner. The convivial atmosphere is apparent from the moment you step through the door.
Recommended in the area
Hyde Park; Harrods; Buckingham Palace

The Belle Vue

Address:	1 Clapham Common Southside, LONDON SW4 7AA
Tel:	020 7498 9473
Fax:	020 7627 0716
Email:	sean@sabretoothgroup.com
Map ref:	3, TQ38

Directions: At junction of A3 (Long Road) and Clapham Park Road; underground: Clapham Common
Open: 11–11 (Sun and Thu 11–12, Fri–Sat 11am–1am)
L 12.30–3.30 D 6.30–10.00 ◯ L – D –
Notes: ⊞ Free House ♟ 35

In an great location, overlooking the wide green spaces of Clapham Common, this independently-owned free house has made a name for itself under the direction of its discerning team. The Belle Vue was purchased in 2003 by Old Etonians Sean Hall-Smith, former catering director at Glyndebourne, and Alexander Corbett, who is married to Sean's god-daughter, Nicola. It was Nicola who created the welcoming villagey feel here, with wood panelling, traditional old chairs and tables, and artwork and blackboard menus on the walls. Beers on offer include Harveys Sussex Bitter and Courage Directors Bitter, but you could also have a coffee, a hot snack or tapas-style nibbles while surfing the net for free. The daily bistro-style menu specialises in fish and shellfish, such as pan-fried giant tiger prawns in Thai spices; grilled marlin steak with pepper sauce; and dressed Cornish crab salad. Meat dishes on a recent menu included braised leg of rabbit; steak and kidney pie; and Thai green chicken curry, while vegetarian diners are well looked after with such dishes as Mediterranean vegetarian lasagne. Sunday lunchtimes are particularly busy, with roasts, and fish and vegetarian dishes on offer. There are over 30 wines and champagnes available by the glass.

Recommended in the area

London Eye; Battersea Park; Tate Britain

NORFOLK

Burnham Overy Staithe.

Sunset at Cromer.

White Horse Hotel

Address:	4 High Street, BLAKENEY, NR25 7AL
Tel:	01263 740574
Fax:	01263 741303
Email:	enquiries@blakeneywhitehorse.co.uk
Website:	www.blakeneywhitehorse.co.uk
Map ref:	4, TG04

Directions: About 10m W of Cromer on the A149 towards Hunstanton
Open: 11–3 6–11 ఊ L 12–2.15 D 6–9 ⑩ L – D 7–9
Facilities: Children welcome Garden Parking: 14
Notes: ⊕ Free House ♟ 12

The 17th-century White Horse is set in a pretty fishing village with narrow streets of flint-built cottages running down to a small tidal harbour. The locale also provides some excellent provisions for the kitchen. Expect plenty of mussels, crab and other seasonal treats among specials, plus dishes such as Moroccan spiced chicken with pickled lemon and cous cous.

Recommended in the area

North Norfolk Railway; Seal-watching boat trips; Holkham Hall and Bygones Museum

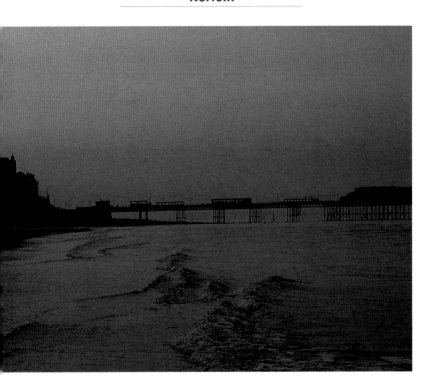

The Lord Nelson

Address:	Walsingham Road, BURNHAM THORPE, King's Lynn, PE31 8HL
Tel/Fax:	01328 738241
Email:	simon@nelsonslocal.co.uk
Website:	www.nelsonslocal.co.uk
Map ref:	4, TF84

Directions: From A149, take B1355 to Burnham Market, then follow signs for Burnham Thorpe off the Fakenham Road

Open: 11–3 6–11 (Sun 6.30–10.30) 🚻 L 12–2 D 7–9

🍽 L 12–2 D 7–9 **Facilities:** Children welcome Garden **Parking:** 30 **Notes:** 🐕 ⊕ Greene King 🍷 13

Dating back 400 years, this pub is in the village where Lord Nelson was born, and the great Admiral used to eat and drink here, hosting a farewell meal for the whole village here in 1793. There is no bar – all drinks are served from the tap room, and the pub is famous for its real beers, direct from the cask. It also has a popular daily-changing menu of freshly prepared food. Outside the massive garden has seating, a barbecue, and wooden play equipment. Dogs are allowed, except in the restaurant.

Recommended in the area

Holkham Hall; Titchwell Nature Reserve; Sandringham House

The George Hotel

Address: High Street, CLEY-NEXT-THE-SEA,
Holt, NR25 7RN
Tel: 01263 740652
Fax: 01263 741275
Email: thegeorge@cleynextthesea.com
Website: www.thegeorgehotelcley.com
Map ref: 4, TG04
Directions: On A149 through Cley-Next-The-Sea,
or approx 4m N of Holt off A148
Open: 11–11 (Sun & BHs 11–10.30) ⓑ L 12–2
D 6.30–9 ⓘⓞⓘ L 12–2 D 6.30–9 Facilities: Children welcome Garden Parking: 15 Notes: 🐾 ⏶ Free
House ⚑ 8

Set within the pretty and historic village of Cley-Next-The-Sea, not far from Cley's famous old windmill, the George Hotel is a classic Edwardian Norfolk inn. This is walking and birdwatching country par excellence, and the wonderful sunsets are also renowned. The first naturalist trust was formed here, and the area's wildlife reserves boast abundant birdlife and local seal colonies. Across the road are the atmospheric marshes, with the sea beyond. The inn has been modernised to create tasteful seating and decor where visitors can mingle comfortably with locals. It has an excellent reputation for its wide selection of real ales and for freshly prepared food made from finest ingredients, supplied from the local area. Locally caught fish and shellfish are a highlight, including smoked salmon and prawns from the Cley Smoke House. The dinner menu includes starters such as pastrami-style smoked salmon with citrus oil; and oysters served with lemon and tarragon olive oil. Main dishes include grilled fillet of red snapper with roasted fennel; Dijon peppered chicken with tagliatelle; and pan-fried strips of lambs' liver served with crispy bacon and Madeira. Puddings might be sticky toffee pudding; lemon and lime posset; or honey and lavender crème brûlée. There are vegetarian options and a kids' menu.

Recommended in the area

Henry Blogg Museum; Felbrigg Hall (NT); North Norfolk Railway

The Saracen's Head

Address: ERPINGHAM, Norwich, NR11 7LX
Tel: 01263 768909
Fax: 01263 768993
Email: saracenshead@wolterton.freeserve.co.uk
Website: www.saracenshead-norfolk.co.uk
Map ref: 4, TG13
Directions: From A140, 2.5m N of Aylsham, turn off to go through Erpingham, pass Spread Eagle on left, follow signs to Calthorpe. Through Calthorpe, the pub is 1m on right in field – do not bear right to Aldborou gh
Open: 12–3 6–11.30 (Sun 12–3, 7–10.30) ⮞ L 12.30–2 D 7.30–9 ⮞ L 12.30–2 D 7.30–9
Facilities: Garden Parking: 50 Notes: ⊕ Free House

Self-acknowledged as a 'funny place in the middle of nowhere', The Saracen's Head is acknowledged by its loyal devotees as a funny place that is definitely worth seeking out. People come from far and wide to enjoy the food, drink and overnight accommodation here. A free house, the inn serves Adnams Best Bitter and Woodforde's Wherry, and the menu reflects the proprietor's love for county and country, while incorporating a number of continental twists, depending to a large extent what is in season. The blackboard changes daily as Robert Dawson-Smith and his team cook up many a wild and tame treat. As an indication of the style of cooking, a recent menu included starters of Morston mussels with cider and cream; grilled halloumi on a lavender croûte with sun blush tomatoes and cream; and game and cranberry terrine. This was followed by such main courses as baked Cromer crab with apple and sherry; Gunton venison with a red fruit jus; and roast lamb with red and white beans. Desserts ranged from old fashioned treacle tart and bread-and-butter pudding to poached pears in spicy red wine.

Robert's daughter Rachel has devoted a lot of time and artistic talent to drawing out the beauty of the inn, which was built in 1806 as the coach house to Wolterton Hall. She has built on the great character of the downstairs areas created by her father over the years, and added elements of the Tuscan farmhouse theme, based on influences from her time spent in that region of Italy. Two new bedrooms have been added and the existing four refurbished to provide six en suite rooms (two suitable for families) with a colourful, comfortable, arty feel. The Shed in the pub's courtyard garden, run by Rachel as a workshop for furniture, paintings and other retro or rustic items, is a great place to rummage for a vintage find.

Recommended in the area

Wolterton Hall; Bure Valley Railway; Norfolk Broads; Norwich

Victoria at Holkham

★ ★   79% ◉◉ HOTEL

Address: Park Road, HOLKHAM, NR23 1RG
Tel: 01328 711008
Fax: 01328 711009
Email: victoria@holkham.co.uk
Website: www.victoriaatholkham.co.uk
Map ref: 4, TF84
Directions: On A149, 3m W of Wells-next-the-Sea
Open: 12–11 ⭐❙ L 12–2.30 D 7–9 Rooms: 10 en suite,
S £95 D £115 Facilities: Children welcome Garden
Parking: 30 Notes: 🐕 allowed in lounge and bar areas ⊞ ♟ 12

Thomas William Coke opened his new hotel in 1838, the year after the young Queen Victoria had elevated him to the peerage, and he named it in her honour. The Victoria's immediate neighbour is the Coke family's ancestral home, the 18th-century Holkham Hall, just a few minutes' walk from the beach. The interior of the colonial-style Victoria is opulent and colourful, with furniture and accessories from Rajasthan. Outside there is a courtyard where barbecues are popular in summer. Food here is fresh, seasonal and local, which means crabs from Cromer, oysters from Thornham, mussels from Brancaster and venison, beef, game and eels from the estate. Favourite among its two-rosette awarded dishes are the more prosaic fish and chips and 10oz Holkham rib-eye steak, while more complex treats from the restaurant menu might include steamed beef and Guinness pudding with young carrots, shallot purée and oysters; or pan-fried sea bass with puy lentils, baby gem lettuce and artichoke cream. Real ales on tap come from Adnams and Woodfordes (a Norfolk brewery), plus a guest IPA from a local microbrewery. There is also an extensive wine list, with 12 wines served by the glass. The ten bedrooms in the main building have been augmented with three cleverly converted ancient follies dotted around Holkham Park. The hotel also has children's facilities.

Recommended in the area

Holkham Hall; Wells and Walsingham Light Railway; Peddars Way and Norfolk Coast Path

Walpole Arms

Address: ITTERINGHAM, Aylsham, NR11 7AR
Tel: 01263 587258
Fax: 01263 587074
Email: goodfood@thewalpolearms.co.uk
Website: www.thewalpolearms.co.uk
Map ref: 4, TG13
Directions: Turn off A140 into Aylsham and head out in Blickling direction. After passing Blickling Hall (NT), take 1st right to Itteringham
Open: 12–3 6–11 (Sun 7–10.30) ⓑ L 12–2 D 7–9
🍴 L 12–2 D 7–9 Facilities: Children welcome Garden Parking: 100
Notes: 🐾 ⌖ Noble Rot Associates Ltd 🍷 12

After ten years producing BBC TV's *Masterchef* programme, Richard Bryan decided to put his food knowledge into practice. He and an old friend, wine merchant Keith Reeves, took over this small pub, originally owned by Robert Horace Walpole, a direct descendant of Britain's first prime minister. The oak beams, logs fires and polished wood were everything they hoped for in a bar, and required little more than spring cleaning. Everything else, though, needed major construction work, and rebuilding finished just hours before Richard's buddy, *Masterchef* presenter Loyd Grossman, arrived for the opening ceremony. The pub's status, as a place for customers who simply want to enjoy a good pint of locally brewed ale, has not been compromised, and they are made just as welcome as diners in the 40-seat restaurant, which has its own private bar. A daily-changing menu, available in the bar as well as the restaurant, might feature rib-eye steak with mushroom polenta, green beans, port jus and salsa verde; Glamorgan sausages with potato, walnut and celeriac mash, green beans and apple compôte; and crispy parcels of goat's cheese and spinach with Israeli cous cous and a Jewish sweet potato-based dish called tzimmes. A lunctime snack menu is equally interesting.

Recommended in the area

Norfolk Wildlife Park; Bure Valley Railway; Pensthorpe Waterfowl Park

The Wildebeest Arms

Address: 82–86 Norwich Road,
STOKE HOLY CROSS,
Norwich, NR14 8QJ
Tel: 01508 492497
Fax: 01508 494946
Email: wildebeest@animalinns.co.uk
Map ref: 4, TG20
Directions: S of Norwich off A140 Ipswich road
Open: 12–3 6–11 (Sun 12–3 7–10.30) L 12–2 D 7–10 **Facilities:** Children welcome Garden
Parking: 40 Free House 12

The extensive open-plan, oak-beamed bar and dining area with dark wooden furniture, sunny yellow rag-washed walls, allied to soft lighting and a slight African theme, lend a homely feel to the comfortable atmosphere of The Wildebeest Arms. The invariably friendly and efficient service is a notable plus; meals are served at substantially proportioned tree-trunk tables or, if preferred on brighter days, in the garden. If reputation is everything, then these days The Wildebeest has it in spades: cooking from the open kitchen is of a modern style and has both the quality and price to bring in customers from miles around East Anglia. The menus are exceptional for a pub and particularly well compiled, blending a classic base with French and British elements. Typical examples are North Norfolk crab tian, rosemary marinated chump of spring lamb or glazed vanilla rice pudding with roast banana. The wines too, are eye-catchingly well priced. Because of its high regard locally, this is a pub where booking is essential, especially for dinner. The Wildebeest is a free house serving Adnams Ales and 12 wines by the glass.

Recommended in the area

Caistor St Edmund Roman Town; Sainsbury Centre for Visual Arts; Norwich Castle Museum

Chequers Inn

Address: Griston Road, THOMPSON,
Thetford, IP24 1PX
Tel: 01953 483360
Fax: 01953 488092
Email: richard@chequers_inn.wanadoo.co.uk
Website: www.thompsonchequers.co.uk
Map ref: 4, TL99
Directions: N of Thetford off A1075 Watton road
Open: 11.30–2.30 6.30–11 (Sun 12–3, 6.30–10.30)
L 12–2 D 6.30–9.30 L 12–2 D 6.30–9.30
Rooms: 3 en suite, S £40 D £60 Facilities: Children welcome Garden Parking: 35
Notes: Free House 7

This historic 16th-century pub has over the years done time as a manor court, doctor's surgery and meeting room. Many original features remain, including exposed beams and a timber and thatched roof swooping almost to the ground. A regularly-changing menu encompasses both traditional pub favourites and dishes such as baked sea bream with thyme and sunblushed tomato.

Recommended in the area

Pingo trail; Thompson Water; Peddars Way

Lifeboat Inn

★★ 74% ◉ HOTEL
Address: Ship Lane, THORNHAM, PE36 6LT
Tel: 01485 512236
Fax: 01485 512323
Email: reception@lifeboatinn.co.uk
Website: www.lifeboatinn.co.uk
Map ref: 4, TF74
Directions: E of Hunstanton on A149; pub 1st left
Open: 11–11 L 12–2.30 D 6.30–9.30 D 7–9.30
Rooms: 22 en suite, S £68 D £96 Facilities: Children welcome Garden Parking: 100 Notes: Free House 10

Retaining many original features, this 16th-century inn overlooks the salt marshes and Thornham Harbour. Inside, the warm glow of paraffin lamps enhances the welcoming atmosphere, while the adjoining conservatory has an ancient vine. The best available fish and game feature on the frequently changing menus of traditional country fare. Bowls of steaming mussels are legendary, harvested daily by local fishermen. Popular bar meals include roast loin of pork and Lifeboat fish pie.

Recommended in the area

Peddars Way and Norfolk Coast Path; Sandringham; Norfolk Lavender

The Crown Hotel

Address:	The Buttlands, WELLS-NEXT-THE-SEA, NR23 1EX
Tel:	01328 710209
Fax:	01328 711432
Email:	reception@thecrownhotelwells.co.uk
Website:	www.thecrownhotelwells.co.uk
Map ref:	4, TF94
Directions:	On A149, 21m west of Cromer

Open: 11–11 ⓑ L 12–2.30 D 6.30–9.30 ⓘⓞⓘ D 7–9
Facilities: Children welcome Garden Notes: 🐾 ⊕ Free House 🍷 12

The Crown is a handsome former coaching inn overlooking the tree-lined green known as the Buttlands in Wells-Next-The-Sea. This superb location is just a few minutes from the beach on the North Norfolk coast. Striking contemporary furnishings work well with the old-world charm of the 17th-century building, and the bar, with its open fire and ancient beams, is an appealing place for a drink – Adnams Ales, Woodforde's Wherry, 12 wines by the glass – or light meal from the interesting bar menu. This might include marinated pork belly with stir-fried noodles and hot-and-sour sauce; smoked haddock chowder; or beef burger with Gruyere cheese, sweet onions and pepper relish. The Crown Restaurant, awarded an AA Rosette for the quality of its food, offers dishes freshly prepared from the finest ingredients, in modern and traditional styles with a hint of Pacific Rim. A recent menu included such starters as flash-fried squid, bacon and black pudding; cream of curried parsnip soup; and grilled goat's cheese. Main courses featured Thai marinated duck breast with seared scallops and chilli jam; steamed North Sea cod with ginger, lemongrass and lime; and roast partridge breasts and confit legs. A private dining room seating 20 is also available. Twelve recently refurbished en suite bedrooms are offered, including two family suites. Dogs on leads are permitted.

Recommended in the area

Holkham Hall; Wells and Walsingham Light Railway; Blakeney Point (NT)

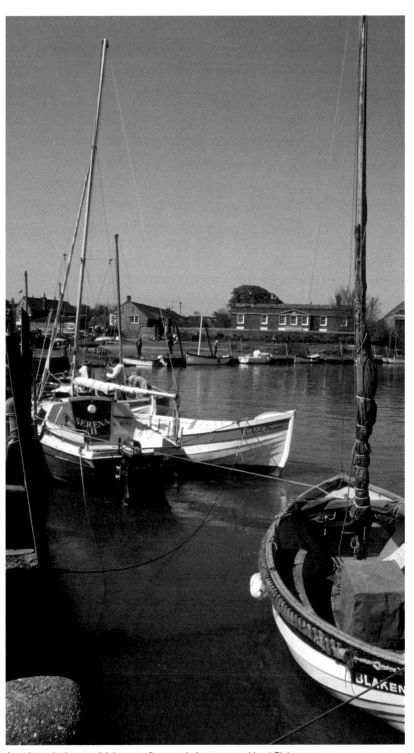

A yacht and other small leisure craft moored along a quayside at Blakeney

Church of St Mary and All Saints near the River Nene.

The Queen's Head

Address: Main Street,
BULWICK, NN17 3DY
Tel: 01780 450272
Map ref: 3, SP99
Directions: About 5m N of Corby, just off the A43 Stamford road
Open: 12–3 6–11 L 12–2.30 D 6–9.30
L 12–2.30 D 6–9.30 **Facilities:** Children welcome
Garden **Parking:** 40 **Notes:** Free House 9

The Queen's Head is believed to have been a pub since 1647, but it's history goes back even further, with parts of the building dating back to 1400. It was named after Charles II's wife, Catherine of Braganza (known, apparently, for her very elaborate hair styles), and is the only pub in this charming village. Its cosy interior is a warren of small rooms, with low beamed ceilings, flagstone floors and four open fireplaces, and the lively local social life adds greatly to the atmosphere. The pub has a resident darts and dominos team, and a group of bellringers who each Wednesday show off their skills at the 12th-century church opposite the pub. Special events and themed nights are also organised, including the popular Hog Roast for Spring Bank Holiday. The landlord is very keen on real ale, and always keeps Shepherd Neame's Spitfire, Rockingham Ales and Newby Wyke on tap, plus guest ales. Hearty pub food includes some interesting and unusual dishes, such as chicken and goat's cheese wontons with lemon and mixed herb cous cous; vanilla roasted monkfish tail with spinach, fondant potato and spiced port jus; and noisettes of roasted lamb with red pepper and Savoy cabbage. All ingredients are fresh and locally sourced where possible, with an emphasis on fish and game when in season. Outside there is a very pretty patio, candle-lit at night, which is a great place to enjoy lunch or dinner in the summer, when it echoes with the sounds of peacocks from Bulwick Hall.

Recommended in the area

Kirby Hall; Deene Park; Rockingham Raceway

George and Dragon

Address: Silver St, CHACOMBE,
nr Banbury, OX17 2JR
Tel: 01295 711500
Fax: 01295 710516
Email: thegeorgeanddragon@msn.com
Map ref: 3, SP44
Directions: NE of Banbury; from M40 junct 11 take
A361 Daventry road. Chacombe is 1st turn on right
Open: 12–11 (Sun 12–10.30) ⓑ L 12–2.30
D 6.30–9.30 ⓞ L 12–2.30 D 6–9.30
Facilities: Children welcome Garden **Parking:** 40 **Notes:** ⌗ ⓦ Free House

Set in a pretty conservation village surrounded by lovely countryside, it's hard to believe that the
George and Dragon could be so well placed for travellers on the busy M40 and for the business
community of nearby Banbury. There's a welcoming feel to its three bars, with their low beams, simple
wooden chairs and settles, log fires and warm terracotta decor. Owned now by the Everard Brewery
of Leicester, the pub serves Everard Tiger and Beacon, along with weekly guest ales. Blackboard
menus list an interesting selection of British food, and every endeavour is made to source ingredients
locally. A standard lunchtime menu features sandwiches, baked potatoes and omelettes alongside
a great range of dishes such as lobster soup; fish pie; warm sausage with potato salad; and lamb
burger. A different menu is available in the evenings, designed to meet all tastes but still staunchly
British. Look for starters such as goat's cheese and caramelised pears; rabbit and prune pâté;
or potted prawns, which could be followed by main courses that might include steak and Everard Tiger
beer pie; lambs' liver and bacon; baked trout in butter sauce; and venison kebabs. Desserts offer such
tempting treats as a chocolate fondue or marmalade bread-and-butter pudding. A traditional Sunday
roast is also available. Menus change weekly, but the most popular dishes remain.

Recommended in the area

Heritage Motor Centre; Sulgrave Manor; Stratford-upon-Avon

Peterborough Cathedral.

The Falcon Inn

Address: FOTHERINGHAY, Nr Oundle, PE8 5HZ
Tel: 01832 226254
Fax: 01832 226046
Website: www.huntsbridge.com
Map ref: 3, TL09
Directions: N of Oundle off A605 Peterborough road
Open: 11.30–3 6–11 (Sun 12–3, 7–10.30) (Sat 6–12
last orders 10pm) ⛺ L 12–2.15 D 7–9.30 ⊙ L
12–2.15 D 6.15–9.30 **Facilities:** Children welcome
Garden **Parking:** 30 **Notes:** ⊞ Free House ⚲ 20

This attractive 18th-century, stone-built inn is set in a garden redesigned by in-demand landscape
architect Bunny Guinness. Inside, it's chef/patron Ray Smikle who works the magic, well known for
endowing his cooking with vibrancy, flavour and colour. You can settle in the locals' tap bar, the smart
rear dining room or the conservatory and choose from the blackboard snack selection or the seasonal
carte. Typical dishes are penne pasta with cannellini beans and roast garlic; slow-braised daube
of beef with horseradish mash; and salmon fillet with tomato, onion and pak choi compote.

Recommended in the area

Nene Valley Railway; Sacrewell Farm & Country Centre; Rutland Water

The Crown

Address: Helmdon Road, WESTON, nr Towcester, NN12 8PX
Tel: 01295 760310
Fax: 01295 760310
Email: info@thecrownweston.co.uk
Website: www.thecrownweston.co.uk
Map ref: 3, SP54
Directions: From Brackley, go north on the A43 Towcester road, then turn left onto B4525; look for right turn to go through Melmdon to Weston
Open: 12–3 6–12 (Sun 6–11.30) L 12–2.30 D 6–9.30 L – D – **Facilities:** Garden **Parking:** 10
Notes: Free House 6

This is a place that's oozing with history: a hostelry since the reign of Elizabeth I, the first documented evidence of The Crown pins the year down to 1593 and the first recorded owner was All Souls College, Oxford. Current owner Robert Grover has more recently completed a refurbishment of the building and brought renown to the pub for its excellent food, all prepared from fresh ingredients. A typical menu might start with goat's cheese and sun-dried tomato tart; or moules marinière and French bread. Mains range from the simple Charolais minute steak and caramelised onion baguette, or shepherd's pie with steamed vegetables, to lamb casserole with mint and apricots, vegetables and herb mash; wild mushroom risotto; or breast of duck with potato, Savoy cabbage, bacon rösti and kumquat sauce. Desserts take in a selection of ice creams and sorbets, as well as raspberry crème brûlée; lemon curd and ginger sponge pudding; and spiced apple pie with custard. A 25-bin wine list has been carefully selected to complement the food, and beer drinkers are rewarded with Greene King IPA, Hook Norton Best, Black Sheep, Landlord and other fine ales.

Recommended in the area

Sulgrave Manor; Silverstone; Canons Ashby House (NT)

NORTHUMBERLAND

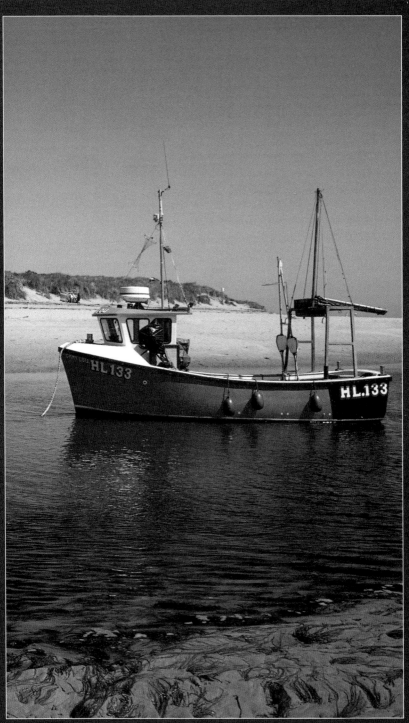

The River Aln at Alnmouth.

Victoria Hotel

★★ 80% HOTEL

Address: Front Street, BAMBURGH, NE69 7BP
Tel: 01668 214431
Fax: 01668 214404
Email: enquiries@victoriahotel.net
Website: www.victoriahotel.net
Map ref: 10, NU13
Directions: From A1, approx half-way between Alnwick and Berwick-upon-Tweed, turn onto B1341 or B1342 for 4m to Bamburgh. Pub is in centre by village green
Open: 11–11 (Fri–Sat 11–12) ⮕ L 12–9 D 7–9 🍴 L 12–2 D 7–9 **Rooms:** 29 en suite, S £44 D £78
Facilities: Children welcome **Parking:** 6 **Notes:** 🐾 ⊞ Free House 🍷 6

The sturdy exterior of the Victoria Hotel is a prominent feature on the village green, the whole scene overshadowed by the magnificent Bamburgh Castle. After substantial refurbishment, this establishment presents a cool, contemporary appearance – particularly in the brasserie, with its stylish domed glass ceiling – but the welcome remains as warm as ever, and the location is very appealing. The general managers, Sue and Alan Baldwin, offer Wallsend and Mordue beers in the bar, and the brasserie menu offers modern cooking that is inspired by the availability of superb local ingredients. Starters here might include Seahouses smoked haddock fishcakes served with a salsa vierge; Seahouses crab wrapped ins smoked salmon, with a tapenade dressing; or tian of Farne Island crab with tiger prawns and black olive tapenade. To follow, there might be Cajun-spiced Gressingham duck breast on a creamed leek and orange sauce; Coldingham wild boar loin with caramelised baby apples in a scrumpy sauce; or darne of wild salmon on baby spinach with a red wine and thyme sauce. Glazed lemon tart with raspberries; dark chocolate mousse with crème Anglaise and blackcurrant sorbet; or a selection of Northumbrian cheeses with oat cakes, grapes and chutney could round off the meal.

Recommended in the area

Bamburgh Castle; Holy Island and Farne Islands; Grace Darling Museum

The Pheasant Inn

◆◆◆◆

Address: Stannersburn, FALSTONE, NE48 1DD
Tel/Fax: 01434 240382
Email: enquiries@thepheasantinn.com
Website: www.thepheasantinn.com
Map ref: 6, NY78
Directions: From A68 N of Hexham, turn onto B6320;
or from A69 take B6079, B6320; signs 'Kielder Water'
Open: 11–3 6–11 (times vary, ring for details)
L 12–2.30 D 7–9 L 12–2.30 D 7–9 Rooms: 8 en
suite, S £45 D £80 Facilities: Children welcome Garden Parking: 30 Notes: Free House

Since 1985 the Kershaw family has offered warm hospitality and good food at this pub amid glorious scenery in the heart of the national park. Among the wholesome dishes are home-made soups; steak and kidney pie; roasted Northumbrian lamb with rosemary and redcurrant jus; fresh fish of the day; home-made game and mushroom pie, pan-fried breast of marinated chicken; and vegetarian and salad choices. Bedrooms are grouped around a small courtyard, which has a stream running through.

Recommended in the area

Kielder Water; Hadrian's Wall; Alnwick Castle and Gardens

Queens Head Inn

Address: GREAT WHITTINGTON, NE19 2HP
Tel: 01434 672267
Map ref: 7, NZ07
Directions: W of Newcastle upon Tyne, off the
A68 and the B6318
Open: 12–3 6–11 L 12–2 D 6.30–9 L 12–2
D 6.30–9 Facilities: Children welcome Garden
Parking: 20 Notes: Free House

Just to the north of Hadrian's Wall country, surrounded by beautiful wooded countryside, stands this stone-built village pub. It holds plenty of character with its exposed stone walls, open fireplaces and old English fixtures, and the atmosphere is inviting and unpretentious in the bar and lounge. Here, displays of bric-a-brac and a mixture of banquette, pew and old spoke-back chair seating make a fine setting for enjoying a pint of locally-produced ale from Matfen Brewery. Cooking with Northumberland flair is offered in the dining room, where recent menus have included such dishes as pork tenderloin on an orange and onion marmalade, with black pudding fritters and cider and sage jus. Desserts major on old favourites like sticky toffee pudding.

Recommended in the area

Hadrian's Wall and Roman Forts; Northumberland National Park; Belsay Hall, Castle and Gardens

The Anglers Arms

Address:	Weldon Bridge, LONGFRAMLINGTON, Morpeth, NE65 8AX
Tel:	01665 570271
Fax:	01665 570041
Email:	johnyoung@anglersarms.fsnet.co.uk
Website:	www.anglersarms.com
Map ref:	10, NU10

Directions: Approx 10m N of Morpeth via A1, then A697 Wooler road, turning left onto B6344; or 8m S of Alnwick via A1; turn right at signs for Weldon Bridge

Open: 11–11 (Sun 12–11) 🍴 L 12–9.30 D 12–9.30 🍽 L 12–2 D 7–9 **Facilities:** Children welcome Garden **Parking:** 30 **Notes:** 🐕 ⊕ Free House

As its name suggests, this former coaching inn has a riverside location on the Coquet, by picturesque Weldon Bridge in the heart of rural Northumberland. Fishing rights for a stretch of the bank are free to residents, with day permits available. Visitors will also relish the landscape of the Cheviot Hills and the sandy beaches at Warkworth or Bamburgh. The inn is a family-run establishment, dating from the 1760s, housing charming collections of antiques, bric-a-brac, fishing memorabilia and hand-painted tiles. Outside is a half-acre of garden with play equipment for children and space for adults to sit and relax. For accommodation, guests can choose between en suite bedrooms with tea/coffee facilities, televisions and direct dial phones, or flats sleeping two or four people. An old Pullman railway carriage provides a unique restaurant setting, complete with silver service. A good range of dishes is on offer, such as rack of Border lamb, or cod and crab fishcakes, and includes tempting vegetarian options and local nettle cheese. Bar meals, in the country inn-style, and sandwiches are also served. Exceptional value is offered by the Early Bird and Fish Friday menus. The inn is a popular venue for private functions and is licensed for civil partnerships.

Recommended in the area

Alnwick Castle; Brinkburn Priory; Cragside House (NT)

The ancient woodland of Sherwood Forest.

The Martins Arms Inn

Address: School Lane, COLSTON BASSETT, NG12 3FD
Tel: 01949 81361
Fax: 01949 81039
Map ref: 8, SK73
Directions: E of Nottingham. Take A52 Grantham road; turning off via Bingham and Langar; or off A46 Leicester–Newark road
Open: 12–3 6–11 (Sun 7–10.30) ⓫ L 12–2 D 6–10 ⓲ L 12–2 D 6–9 **Facilities:** Garden **Parking:** 35
Notes: ⓫ Free House ♀ 7

So popular is this award-winning inn that it has made appearances on both regional and national television. It is a listed 18th-century building, set close to the old market cross in this stunning village in the Vale of Belvoir, an area that is renowned for its Stilton cheese. The interior has a real country house feel to it, with period furnishings, traditional hunting prints and seasonal fires in the Jacobean fireplace. Outside there is an acre of landscaped grounds, which includes a herb garden and well established lawns, backing on to National Trust land. The inn is a free house, serving a good range of real ales – Marston's Pedigree, Interbrew Bass, Greene King Abbot Ale, Timothy Taylor Landlord – from hand pumps. The wine list also offers seven wines by the glass. Good regional ingredients are a feature of the menu. Take, for example, the classic ploughman's lunch comprising Melton Mowbray pork pie, Colston Bassett stilton or cheddar, home-cured ham, pickles and bread. Alternatives in the bar include game pie, or fresh gnocchi with oven roasted tomatoes, peppers, spinach and parmesan cream. Typical restaurant dishes are cod fillet with lobster ravioli, potato rösti and creamed leek sauce; and bacon-wrapped rump of lamb with potato fondant and Puy lentils. Dogs are allowed in the garden only, with water provided.

Recommended in the area

Belvoir Castle; Grantham Canal; National Watersports Centre

OXFORDSHIRE

Magdalen College, Oxford University.

St Mary's Anglican Convent, Wantage.

The Boars Head

♦♦♦♦ ⊛ ⊛

Address:	Church Street, ARDINGTON, Wantage, OX12 8QA
Tel/Fax:	01235 833254
Email:	info@boarsheadardington.co.uk
Website:	www.boarsheadardington.co.uk
Map ref:	3, SU48

Directions: Off A417 E of Wantage
Open: 12–3 6.30–11 🍽 L 12–2.30 D 7–10
🍴 L 12–2.30 D 7–10 **Rooms:** 3 en suite, S £75 D £85
Facilities: Children welcome Garden **Parking:** 20 **Notes:** ⊞ Free House ♇ 8

Revenue from this pub used to fund the village's gas lamps. Times have changed, but the pub remains an unspoilt delight, and an eclectic, elegant menu has been impressing locals and visitors in the smart dining room. The speciality here is fish – delivered daily from Cornwall – and there's a tinge of luxury to dishes like seared scallop with pork belly and Pinot Noir, or Angus beef fillet in pastry with seared foie gras. For dessert try prune and almond tart with Armagnac ice cream.

Recommended in the area

White Horse at Uffington; Newbury Races; Didcot Steam Railway Centre

The Abingdon Arms

Address: High Street, BECKLEY, Oxford, OX3 9UU
Tel: 01865 351311
Email: chequers89@hotmail.com
Map ref: 3, SP51
Directions: From M40 junct 8 take A40 towards Oxford; at Headington rdbt, follow signs for Beckley
Open: 12–3 6–11 (all day Sat–Sun) 🍴 L 12–2.30 D 7–9.30 🍽 L 12–2.30 D 7–9.30
Facilities: Garden **Parking:** 20 **Notes:** 🌐 Brakspear 🍷 8

This pub is a real find, either for travellers on the M40 needing refreshment or for anyone visiting the nearby city of Oxford. It's a pretty country hostelry that is the hub of the local community, a situation that is relished by owners Michelle and Neil Wass, and this makes for an inviting ambience for casual visitors too. The interior has been brought up to date with very smart decor, but there's still a nice traditional atmosphere, particularly in winter when log fires add a warm glow. The food here is another reason why The Abingdon Arms is so popular, with a specials menu supporting the regularly-changing main menu. This, too, is augmented at lunchtime with bar snacks such as locally reared organic pork sausages; hot chicken and bacon salad; and sandwiches and filled ciabattas. On the main menu, you'll find starters such as marinated crab with chilli, coriander and rocket; crispy duck and orange salad; and prawns in a filo basket with aioli, while main courses to look out for include sea bass with crab and spinach mash and beurre blanc sauce; slow-roasted shoulder of lamb; sizzling fajitas with guacamole, salsa and cheese; or chicken stuffed with brie and bacon, served with wild mushrooms. There are vegetarian options on the menu too, including starters such as goat's cheese bruschetta with toasted walnuts, followed, perhaps, by a shitake mushroom risotto. If you don't want to eat, a pint of Brakspear's ale is equally enjoyable, and in summer there's no better place to enjoy it than on the pub's patio, with spectacular views of Otmoor.

Recommended in the area

Waterperry Gardens; Blenheim Palace; Oxford Colleges

The Vines

Address: Burford Road, BLACK BOURTON,
Black Bourton, OX18 2PF
Tel: 01993 843559
Fax: 01993 840080
Email: info@vineshotel.com
Website: www.vinesblackbourton.co.uk
Map ref: 3, SP20
Directions: From A40 Witney, take A4095 to Faringdon,
then 1st right after Bampton to Black Bourton
Open: 12–3 6–11 (Mon 6–11) ♿ L 12–2 D 6.30–9.30
🍴 L 12–2 D 6.30–9.30 Facilities: Children welcome Garden Parking: 70 Notes: ⊞ Free House ♟ 7

A handsome building of mellow local stone in a picturesque village setting, The Vines is a great place from which to explore the Cotswolds. The restaurant and bar were designed by John Clegg from the BBC *Real Rooms* team, and the effect is unexpected and very striking. Food is offered from the carte or special daily menu, with dishes prepared from fresh local produce. Fish, which is a highlight, arrives each day from a local supplier. A meal might begin with a Thai chicken salad with cashew nuts and baby leaves, then continue with pan-fried sea bass with spicy tomato sauce, with a dessert such as orange and passion fruit tart or crème brûlée with home made shortbread bringing the meal to a satisfactory conclusion. An alternative venue for a drink or a snack is the comfortable lounge with its leather sofas. Spacious bedrooms are equipped with leisure and business guests in mind, with desks and internet access as well as televisions, shaver sockets, hairdryers, toiletries, a hospitality tray and access to an iron and ironing board on request. Additional accommodation is available in a new detached wing overlooking the lovely village church. These rooms also have direct dial telephones. The hotel, which has a children's license, provides a large, secure car park, spacious gardens and a patio for use in fair weather. Don't miss the great Aunt Sally game.

Recommended in the area

Cogges Manor Farm Museum; Cotswold Wildlife Park; Blenheim Palace

The Lord Nelson Inn

Address: BRIGHTWELL BALDWIN,
nr Watlington, OX49 5NP
Tel: 01491 612497
Fax: 01491 612118
Website: www.lordnelson-inn.co.uk
Map ref: 3, SU69
Directions: From M40 junct 6 take B4009 towards
Benson and Wallingford, then right onto B480
Open: 11–3 6–11 ⓑ L 12–2.30 D 6–10.30
⑩ L 12–2.30 D 6–10.30 Facilities: Garden Parking:
20 Notes: ⊕ Free House ⦿ 20

This traditional 300-year-old inn, furnished with beautiful antiques, is set in an unspoilt village,
opposite the church, and its exterior will be familiar to *Midsomer Murders* fans. In 1905 it was forced
to close by the local lord who was trying to stop his workers from drinking, and did not reopen until
1971. There is a comprehensive wine list, and all the dishes are freshly cooked to order by the inn's
experienced chefs. There are also some good hearty bar snacks and a varied Sunday lunch menu.
Recommended in the area
Stonor Park; The Rideway; Wallingford Museum

The Lamb Inn

★★★ 78% ◉◉ HOTEL
Address: Sheep Street, BURFORD, OX18 4LR
Tel: 01993 823155
Fax: 01993 822228
Email: info@lambinn-burford.co.uk
Website: www.cotswold-inns-hotels.co.uk/index.aspx
Map ref: 3, SP21
Directions: On A40 Oxford–Cheltenham road. Follow
signs for Burford. Off High Street
Open: 11–11 ⓑ L 12–2.30 D 6.30–9.30
⑩ L 12.30–2.30 D 7–9.30 Rooms: 15 en suite, S £115 D £145 Facilities: Children welcome

Garden Notes: ⤳ ⊘ on premises ⊕ Free House ⦿ 9

If your idea of a traditional English inn includes stone flagged floors, real ale and log fires, the 500-
year-old Lamb will not disappoint. The chef uses locally produced and organic meat, cheese and
vegetables whenever possible. Menus change regularly, and might include smoked haddock and trout
risotto; vine tomato, halloumi and basil tart; and middle eastern lamb shank with pepper cous cous.
Recommended in the area
Minster Lovell Hall and Dovecote; Bourton-on-the-Water; Cotswold Wildlife Park

Sir Charles Napier

Address: Spriggs Alley, CHINNOR, OX39 4BX
Tel: 01494 483011
Fax: 01494 485311
Website: www.sircharlesnapier.co.uk
Map ref: 3, SP70
Directions: From M40 junct 6, take B4009 to Chinnor
Open: 12–3.30 6.30–12 ⓑ L 12–2.30 D 7–9.30
🍽 L 12–2.30 D 7–10 **Facilities:** Children welcome
Garden **Parking:** 50 **Notes:** ⊕ Free House 🍷 15

Once voted among the 50 most romantic spots in the world, the Sir Charles Napier is in the scenic Chiltern Hills surrounded by beech woods and fields. The furnishings are eclectic, and wonderful sculptures exhibited throughout the year encourage you to linger. In summer, lunch is served on the terrace beneath vines and wisteria, overlooking the herb gardens and lawns. An exhaustive wine list complements the blackboard dishes and imaginative seasonal menus that have earned this pub two AA Rosettes. Typical dishes are halibut with pea purée, and sea bream with saffron and crayfish tails.

Recommended in the area

The Chiltern Hills; West Wycombe Park; Garsington Opera

The George

Address: 25 High Street, DORCHESTER, OX10 7HH
Tel: 01865 340404
Fax: 01865 341620
Email: thegeorgehotel@fsmail.net
Website: ww.thegeorgedorchester.com
Map ref: 3, SU59
Directions: Off A4074 Oxford–Wallingford road
Open: 11.30–11 (Sun 12–10.30) ⓑ L 12–2.15
D 7–9.45 🍽 L 12–2.15 D 7–9.45 **Rooms:** 17 en suite,
S £75 D £95 **Facilities:** Garden **Parking:** 60
Notes: ⊕ Neville & Griffin Ltd 🍷 6

This historic 15th-century inn, in the heart of the pretty village, has bags of charm, and DH Lawrence was a frequent visitor. There are inglenook fireplaces in the bar and a fine vaulted ceiling in the restaurant. The bar menu has dishes like smoked haddock and spinach fishcake, or beef olives in red wine sauce and various toasties. In the restaurant pome tian of crab and avocado with parmesan crisp might be followed by bacon and praline duck breast with savoy cabbage and herb mash.

Recommended in the area

Didcot Railway Centre; Thames Path; Harcourt Arboretum

The Five Horseshoes

Address:	Maidensgrove, HENLEY-ON-THAMES, RG9 6EX
Tel:	01491 641282
Fax:	01491 641086
Email:	admin@thefivehorseshoes.co.uk
Website:	www.thefivehorseshoes.co.uk
Map ref:	3, SU78

Directions: From Henley-on-Thames take A4130, after 1m take B480 to the right, signed Stonor. At Stonor, turn left and go through woods and over common; pub on left.
Open: 12–3.30 6–11 (Sat 12–11, Sun 12–6) 🍴 L 12–2.30 D 6.30–9.30 🍽 L 12–2.30 D 6.30–9.30 **Facilities:** Children welcome Garden **Parking:** 85 **Notes:** 🚭 ⊞ Brakspear 🍷 9

The Five Horseshoes is a 17th-century pub located in an area of outstanding natural beauty. The pub's interior is oozing with old world character, with brass, wrought iron, wooden beams, open fires and pub games. Traditional home-cooked food is ably prepared from fresh local produce and the same menu is available throughout the bar and restaurant, augmented by seasonal specials. Dishes change regularly and range from a platter of rustic breads with Spanish olives and roasted garlic, or home made pork pie with piccalilli and cheese, to tasty seafood casserole; pumpkin risotto; and slow roasted belly of pork. Brakspear's Ordinary, Special and seasonal ales are served alongside a list of fine wines, including a good choice by the glass. Outside, the two large beer gardens offer truly amazing views of the surrounding valley and the Chiltern Hills. Barbeques are held during summer weekends, with a spit roast on the first weekend of every month. The larger of the two gardens is available for exclusive hire and is ideal for parties and weddings, with a marquee for special occasions. The pub is an obvious watering hole for hikers and mountain bikers, who are made very welcome, but are asked to leave their muddy boots at the door. Dogs are permitted in the gardens and bar.

Recommended in the area

Henley-on-Thames; Stonor House & Gardens; Maidensgrove Common

The Crown Inn

Address: PISHILL, Henley-on-Thames, RG9 6HH
Tel: 01491 638364
Fax: 01491 638364
Email: jcapon@surfree.co.uk
Website: www.crownpishill.co.uk
Map ref: 3, SU78
Directions: NW of Henley-on-Thames. Take A4130
Wallingford road, then fork right onto B480,
Open: 11.30–2.30 6–11 (Sun 12–3, 7–10.30)
L 12–2.30 D 7–9.30 L 12–2.30 D 7–9.30
Facilities: Children welcome Garden **Parking:** 60 **Notes:** Free House 8

A pretty brick and flint former coaching inn, The Crown has enjoyed a chequered and colourful history. It began life in medieval times, serving ale to members of the thriving local monastic community, and in later years served as a refuge for Catholic priests escaping Henry VIII's draconian rule. It contains the largest priest hole in the country, complete with a sad story about one Father Dominique, who met his end here. Later still, in the 'swinging 60s', the barn housed a nightclub hosting the likes of George Harrison (who for many years had a home in nearby Henley-on-Thames) and Dusty Springfield. Today, this appealing inn is renowned for its food, offered from a seasonally changing menu. It features such starters as dolcelatte, wild mushroom and tarragon filo parcel with plum compote; ham and potato terrine with apple and sage chutney; and roast chicken and basil risotto with parsnip chips. The main courses include king scallops and tiger prawns in a Thai dressing; pan-fried calves' liver with smoked bacon and fried onions in a red wine sauce; and half a roasted duck served with black cherry sauce and straw potatoes. Regularly appearing desserts include sticky toffee pudding with toffee sauce; banoffee pie; bread-and-butter pudding; or a selection of five mini-desserts. On a fine summer day, it is pleasant to sit in the extensive gardens overlooking the valley.

Recommended in the area

Stonor Park; Greys Court, (NT); River and Rowing Museum

The Bliss Tweed Mill, Chipping Norton.

The Shaven Crown Hotel

Address:	High Street, SHIPTON-UNDER-WYCHWOOD, OX7 6BA
Tel:	01993 830330
Fax:	01993 832136
Email:	relax@theshavencrown.co.uk
Website:	www.theshavencrown.co.uk
Map ref:	3, SP21

Directions: On A361 Burford–Chipping Norton road
Open: 12–2.30 5–11 (all day Sat–Sun) 🐾 L 12–2
D 6–9.30 ⏐◎⏐ L 12–2 D 7–9 **Facilities:** Children
welcome Garden **Parking:** 15 **Notes:** 🐕 🌐 Free House 🍷 10

It was built around 700 years ago as a monastery hospice, then Elizabeth I used it as a hunting lodge. When she gave it to the village in 1580 it became the Crown Inn, and a brewery renamed it in 1930. During his two years here, Philip Mehrtens has successfully focused on the food, which includes bar food such as steak and kidney pie, and sausage and mash, and a main menu featuring dishes like chicken breast with plum and orange sauce; and pasta with pesto, wild mushrooms and mozzarella.
Recommended in the area
Minster Lovell Hall and Dovecote; Cotswold Wildlife Park; Birdland

Crooked Billet

Address: STOKE ROW, Henley on Thames, RG9 5PU
Tel: 01491 681048
Fax: 01491 682231
Website: www.thecrookedbillet.co.uk
Map ref: 3, SU68
Directions: From Henley take A4130 Oxford road, turn left at Nettlebed on B481, then right for Stoke Row.
Open: 12–11 (Sun 12-10.30) ⓣ L 12–2.30 D 7–10 ⓣⓞⓣ L 12–2.30 D 7–10 **Facilities:** Children welcome Garden **Parking:** 50 **Notes:** ⊘ on premises ⓦ Brakspear ⓣ 12

The remote location of this charmingly rustic pub was a boon to highwayman Dick Turpin, who avoided the law and courted the landlord's daughter here. Later, it became a favourite watering hole of George Harrison, who lived nearby, and was frequented by several of his famous friends. So popular is it still with local celebrities that Kate Winslet held her first wedding reception here. It's easy to see why it is so popular, and you certainly don't have to be a celebrity to appreciate its pretty farmland setting and its fascinating history, dating back to 1642. This low-beamed old inn is simply achingly romantic. Extensive and carefully thought-out menus are created by award-winning chef/proprietor Paul Clerehugh, who is so keen to use local produce that he's even been known to swap a meal here for locals' excess harvests. The menu is both lengthy and luxurious: seafood is a speciality, with Sevruga caviar served with oysters, sour cream and smoked salmon blinis as a starter, and fillets of Dover sole with grilled king prawns and Puy lentils as a main course. Game is also a strength, including, unusually, hare braised with lardons, mushrooms, baby onions and thyme, served with herb dumplings. Dishes are tantalising, complex and well-balanced, with starters such as a selection

of Italian salami, served with artichoke, mozzarella, olives and sun-blushed tomato; or crispy-fried salt and pepper squid with warm chick pea and roast vegetable salad; or main courses such as breast of chicken stuffed with goats' cheese and baked in pancetta, served with warm chorizo salad, Puy lentils, crispy potato, rocket and tarragon dressing. Vegetarians are not neglected: they might find sage and pecorino polenta with asparagus and artichoke heart salad, or leek and Oxford blue pancakes with roast winter roots and buttered spinach on the menu. Desserts are quite irresistable: try the gooseberry fool and honey comb. On a hot day, enjoy the heavenly combination of classic cocktails in the garden.

Recommended in the area

Mapledurham House; Greys Court (NT); Beale Park

The Mason's Arms

Address: Banbury Road, SWERFORD,
Chipping Norton, OX7 4AP
Tel: 01608 683212
Fax: 01608 683105
Email: themasonschef@hotmail.com
Website: www.masons-arms.com
Map ref: 3, SP33
Directions: NE of Chipping Norton, off A361 Banbury
road. Take 2nd exit at rdbt; pub is 4m further on left
Open: 10–3 6–11 ♿ L 12–2.15 D 7–9.15 ⊕ L

12–2.15 D 7–9.15 **Facilities:** Children welcome Garden **Parking:** 50 **Notes:** ⊞ Free House ⬥ 6

A former Masonic lodge built of local honey-coloured stone, this free house is situated in beautiful
surroundings just a stone's throw from the Hook Norton Brewery. Traditional charm is balanced
by plenty of modern comforts under the enthusiastic ownership of Bill and Charmaine Leadbeater.
The chef/proprietor trained with Gordon Ramsay and Marco Pierre White, so it's not surprising that the
food has a stand out quality. So do the ingredients – all the meat is from rare breeds and traceable;
poultry is free range; fish is delivered daily. The menu, boldly entitled Bill's Food, has a distinctly
continental outlook, featuring unusual and frequently changing dishes. Starters might include smoked
halibut with avocado parfait and cider and apple dressing, while main course options of chargrilled
marlin loin; steamed vegetable pancake wrap; and Gloucester Old Spot pork done three ways have
featured on recent menus. A treat for four to share, given 48 hours' notice, is whole roast leg of
Oxford Down lamb with rosemary and garlic, dauphinoise potatoes, haricot verts and rosemary jus. Bar
snacks take in a wide range of pub favourites, while the beers on offer include Hook Norton Best and
Brakspear Special. There's also a good choice of malt whiskies. In summer the garden, with its large
lawned area, is the perfect place to sit with a drink and admire the view.

Recommended in the area

Burford Wildlife Park; Hook Norton Brewery and Pottery; Wiggington Waterfowl Sanctuary

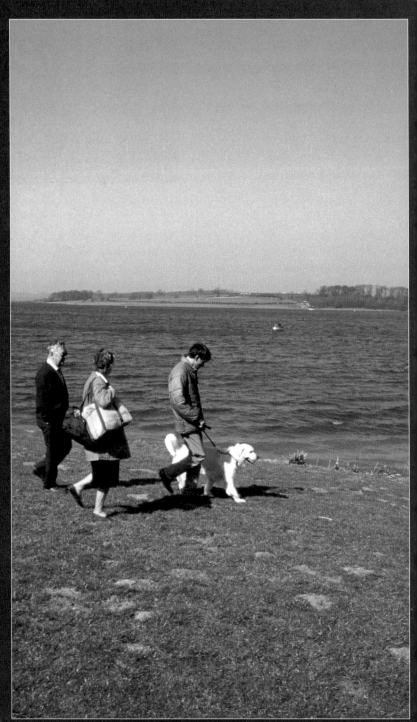

Rutland Water.

Fox & Hounds

Address: 19, The Green, EXTON,
nr Oakham, LE15 8AP
Tel: 01572 812403
Fax: 01572 812403
Email: sandra@foxandhoundsrutland.co.uk
Website: www.foxandhoundsrutland.co.uk
Map ref: 3, SK91
Directions: Take A606 from Oakham towards Stamford; at Barnsdale turn left; after 1.5m turn right towards Exton village. Pub located in centre next to village green.
Open: 11–3 6–11 (closed Mondays) L 12–2 D 6.30–9 L 12–2 D 6.30–9 **Facilities:** Children welcome Garden **Parking:** 20 **Notes:** Free House 8

At the centre of the pretty village of Exton, with its many thatched houses, stands the Fox & Hounds, an imposing 17th-century building overlooking the village green. The large walled garden at the back is big enough to accommodate medium sized functions and a play area is provided for children. There is plenty of good walking in the vicinity and, with its reputation for good food and hospitality, the inn makes an ideal stop for refreshment. The pub is a free house serving Greene King IPA, Grainstore Real Ales and John Smiths Smooth. It offers a full menu of Italian and English dishes, with a lunchtime choice of filled ciabattas, paninis, salads and sandwiches. For the evenings, the menu has dishes such as rack of lamb with apricots and rosemary; and linguini with jumbo prawns, and the Italian chef/proprietor has created an impressive list of more than 25 authentic, thin-crust pizzas, which are certainly not on the small side. The popularity of the inn is further enhanced during special events in the village, such as the Spring Bank Holiday street market. Four en suite double bedrooms are available, with views over the garden or the village green. The rooms are equipped with televisions and tea and coffee-making facilities. Dogs are permitted with water provided.

Recommended in the area

Barnsdale Gardens; Rutland Water; Burghley House

Part of Oakham school and grounds.

The Old Plough

Address:	2 Church Street, Braunston, OAKHAM, LE15 8QT
Tel:	01572 722714
Fax:	01572 770382
Email:	the oldplow@aol.com
Website:	www.oldploughrutland.com
Map ref:	3, SK80

Directions: At railway crossing in Oakham, bear left and take 2nd left signed Braunston.

Open: 11–11 (Fri–Sat 11–12) ⓑ/ⓣⓞⓘ L 12–2.30 D

6–9.30 Facilities: Children welcome Garden Parking: 30 Notes: ⌁ ⊕ Free House ⓨ 9

This genteel old coaching inn, which dates back to 1783, has been tastefully modernised to retain its traditional identity. Owned by the Grainstore Brewery, expect lots of speciality evenings and various weekend entertainments, and their enthusiasm for good food extends to candlelit dinners in the picturesque conservatory, as well as light lunches on the terrace. Expect favourites like liver, bacon and onions; Cajun chicken; and steak and kidney pudding.

Recommended in the area

Rutland Water; Oakham Castle; Eyebrook Reservoir

SHROPSHIRE

The Iron Bridge.

Ludlow Castle.

Unicorn Inn

Address: Corve Street, LUDLOW, SY8 1DU
Tel: 01584 873555
Fax: 01584 876268
Website: www.unicorninn.com
Map ref: 2, SO57
Directions: From A49, take B4361 into Ludlow; Corve St is off this road
Open: 12–3 6–11 (Sun 12–3.30, 6.30–10.30)
🍴 L 12–2.15 D 6–9.15 🍽 L 12–2.15 D 6–9.15
Facilities: Children welcome Garden **Parking:** 3
Notes: 🐾 ⊞ Free House 🍷 8

Mike and Rita Knox gave up city careers in finance and human resources to run the Unicorn, getting occasional kicks now from long-distance endurance driving (London to Cape Town; Rio de Janeiro to Tierra del Fuego and back). Bar food here might include Greek-style orange and herb lamb, and farmhouse sausages with bubble and squeak, while the restaurant offers smoked turkey steak with pink peppercorn sauce; fillets of red mullet with tagliatelle nero; and lamb saddle for two to share.

Recommended in the area

Shropshire Hills Discovery Centre; Acton Scott Working Farm; Stokesay Castle

The Hundred House Hotel

★★ 76% ◎◎ HOTEL

Address: Bridgnorth Road, NORTON, nr Shifnal, TF11 9EE
Tel: 01952 730353
Fax: 01952 730355
Email: reservations@hundredhouse.co.uk
Website: www.hundredhouse.co.uk
Map ref: 2, SJ70
Directions: On A442, 6m N of Bridgnorth, 5m S of Telford centre
Open: 11–2.30 6–11 (Sun 11–10.30) L 12–2.15 D 6–9 L 12–2.15 D 6–9 **Rooms:** 10 en suite, S £69 D £99 **Facilities:** Children welcome Garden **Parking:** 40
Notes: Free House 16

The Phillips family – Henry, Sylvia and sons David and Stuart – have been running this engagingly off-beat pub with love and great tenderness for nearly a quarter of a century. The guest book gives a clue: instead of the usual platitudes, guests tend to write pertinent and believable comments like: 'Halfway to heaven'; and 'Can't say a thing, we're off to the swing, thanks for the best part of our European fling'. The swing, in one of the bedrooms, is just one of the quirks that set the Hundred House apart. Downstairs is a warren of lavishly decorated bars and dining rooms, hung with bunches of drying herbs and flowers. This main part of the house is Georgian, but in the courtyard there's a timbered, thatched barn that dates back to the 14th century and was used as a courthouse in medieval times. There's a good range of ales on offer, including Heritage Bitter, Highgate Saddlers Bitter, Everards Tiger and Bombardier. Food here is in the modern English/Continental style, all according to season where possible. In the bar/brasserie there are speciality sausages, rib-eye steaks, and grilled aubergine and halloumi rolls, while the carte offers such dishes as lamb, fennel and apricot casserole; breast of stuffed chicken; roulade of spinach and sweet potato; and such fish dishes as steamed fillet of monkfish with a casserole of mussels and prawns; or seared tuna with tomato salsa. There's a long and lovely dessert menu, with such offerings as double chocolate mousse with orange crème Anglaise; hot treacle tart; and warm pears poached in red wine and served with crème fraîche ice cream and spiced apricot compote.

Recommended in the area

Ironbridge Gorge; Bodenham Arboretum and Earth Centre; Severn Valley Railway

The Countess's Arms

Address: WESTON HEATH, nr Shifnal, TF11 8RY
Tel: 01952 691123
Fax: 01952 691660
Email: thecountessarms@hotmail.com
Website: www.countessarms.co.uk
Map ref: 2, SJ71
Directions: From M54 junct 3, take A41 Newport Road, cross A5 at rdbt and continue for about 1.5m to Weston Heath
Open: 12–11 (Sun 12–10.30) ⓑ L 12–6 D 6–9.30
ⓘ L 12–6 D 6–9.30 **Facilities:** Children welcome Garden **Parking:** 100 **Notes:** ⊞ Free House ⓣ 10

In the owners' own words, this is 'a large contemporary eatery in a refurbished traditional pub'. The owner in question is the Earl of Bradford, a well-known restaurateur and food critic, whose splendid family seat is Weston Park, just down the road. Formerly known as The Plough, The Countess's Arms (named for the earl's wife) has had a transformation, involving the removal of all the internal floors and walls and the addition of an extension. Customers in the spacious gallery bar able to look down on the blue glass mosaic-tiled bar below. Head chef Patrick Champion has brought the earl's concept of fun eating to fruition with his interesting menus. Bar snacks feature oriental dim sum, and chicken liver parfait with onion marmalade and French stick, alongside sausage with bubble and squeak. A stylish, modern approach to cooking results in main course dishes such as lamb chump, Dauphinoise potatoes, roasted cherry tomatoes and redcurrant jus; roast duck breast with rosti potato, braised red cabbage and kirsch sauce; and Cajun-spiced chicken salad. Fishy choices could include poached sea bass with shitake mushrooms, spring onions and jasmine rice; salmon fillet on crushed potatoes; and sautéed prawns, mussels and clams with gnocchi and basil dressing. There's an excellent wine list, and beer drinkers can savour Robsinsons, St Austell Tribute and Woods Hopping Mad.

Recommended in the area

Weston Park; Lilleshall Abbey; Royal Air Force Museum

Wells Cathedral.

The Hunters Rest

◆◆◆◆

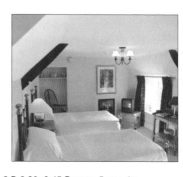

Address: King Lane, Clutton Hill,
CLUTTON, BS39 5QL
Tel: 01761 452303
Fax: 01761 453308
Email: info@huntersrest.co.uk
Website: www.huntersrest.co.uk
Map ref: 2, ST65
Directions: From A37 Bristol–Wells road turn onto
A368 towards Bath, in 100 mtrs turn right; continue 1m
Open: 11.30–3 6–11 (all day Fri, Sat, Sun) ⓑ/🍽 L 12–2 D 6.30–9.45 **Rooms:** 5 en suite,
S £62.50 D £87.50 **Facilities:** Children welcome Garden **Parking:** 80 **Notes:** 🐾 ⊕ Free House 🍷 14

Originally a hunting lodge that was built for the Earl of Warwick in about 1750, the inn is situated amid beautiful countryside high on Clutton Hill overlooking the Cam Valley to the Mendip Hills and the Chew Valley to the port of Bristol. Historic character, including beams, exposed stonework and log fires, has been complemented by modern amenities, creating a cosy atmosphere inside. There's a landscaped garden outside, complete with a miniature railway to carry passengers around the grounds. The beers served here include Otter Ale, Sharps Own, Hidden Quest and Butcombe, and there is a reasonably priced wine list with a good choice by the glass. Home-made dishes from the menu range through bakehouse rolls and giant oggies (pasties) with a variety of fillings, to grills and other popular pub fare, while the list of daily specials might include rack of lamb with rosemary and garlic gravy, or salmon fishcakes with dill mayonnaise. The inn is conveniently located for access to Bath, Bristol and Wells and offers accommodation in individually designed bedrooms. These include four-poster suites, antique furniture, direct dial telephones with data links, televisions and VCRs, and all have wonderful views across the surrounding countryside.

Recommended in the area

Bath; Cheddar Caves; Wells Cathedral

The Wheatsheaf

Address:	COMBE HAY, Bath, BA2 7EG
Tel:	01225 833504
Tel:	01225 836123
Email:	info@wheatsheafcombehay.co.uk
Website:	www.wheatsheafcombehay.co.uk
Map ref:	2, ST75

Directions: From Bath take A367 Exeter road to Odd Down, then at park go left towards Combe Hay. Follow for 2m to thatched cottage and turn left
Open: 10.30–3 6–11 (Fri–Sat 11–11, Sun 12–4)
🛏/🍽 L 12–2.30 D 6.30–9.30 Facilities: Garden Parking: 100 Notes: 🐕 Children 🍺 Free House 🍷 6

You'll find The Wheatsheaf, a stylish inn and superior dining destination, nestling within the village of Combe Hay, an area of outstanding natural beauty close to Bath. The real ales, local ciders and a Eurocentric wine list are as much a draw as the highly acclaimed seasonal menus, which feature such offerings as terrine of home-smoked partridge with green tea jelly and Combe Hay apple chutney, or crisp pork belly with south coast scallops and pork juices.

Recommended in the area

Bath; Wells; Longleat House and Safari Park

Carew Arms

Address:	CROWCOMBE, Taunton, TA4 4AD
Tel:	01984 618631
Fax:	01984 618428
Email:	info@thecarewarms.co.uk
Website:	www.thecarewarms.co.uk
Map ref:	2, ST13

Directions: Midway Taunton–Minehead, off A358.
Open: 11–3 6–11 (Apr–Sep phone for details) 🛏 L 12–2 D 7–9.30 🍽 L 12–2.30 D 7–10 Facilities: Children welcome Garden Parking: 40 Notes: 🍺 Free House 🍷 8

The Carew Arms, set in the Quantock Hills, has been welcoming travellers since the 16th century, and its front bar, with original flagstone floor and deep inglenook fireplace, remains unaltered, while the kitchen and dining facilities have been sympathetically refurbished. In fine weather, the south-facing garden is ideal for a quiet drink or light lunch. Chef proprietor Reg Ambrose, backed up by a strong team, devises creative menus with all round appeal. Good use is made of local seafood, and the local beers include Exmoor, Cotleigh and Otter Ales. Dogs are welcome.

Recommended in the area

Exmoor National Park; Coleridge Cottage (NT); West Somerset Railway

The Crown Hotel

★★★ 74% ⑨⑥ HOTEL

Address: EXFORD, Exmoor National Park, TA24 7PP
Tel: 01643 831554
Fax: 01643 831665
Email: info@crownhotelexmoor.co.uk
Website: www.crownhotelexmoor.co.uk
Map ref: 2, SS83
Directions: From M5 junct 24 take A39 to Dunster, then A396 to Wheddon Cross and B3224 to Exford
Open: 12–3 6–11 (Apr–Sep 11–11) ⓑ L 12–2 D 6.30–9.30 ⑩ L – D 7–9 **Rooms:** 17 en suite, S £65 D £99 **Facilities:** Children welcome Garden **Parking:** 20 **Notes:** ⋈ ⊕ Free House ♉ 8

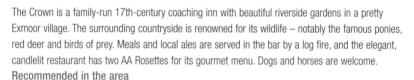

The Crown is a family-run 17th-century coaching inn with beautiful riverside gardens in a pretty Exmoor village. The surrounding countryside is renowned for its wildlife – notably the famous ponies, red deer and birds of prey. Meals and local ales are served in the bar by a log fire, and the elegant, candlelit restaurant has two AA Rosettes for its gourmet menu. Dogs and horses are welcome.

Recommended in the area

Tarr Steps; Dunkery Beacon; Dunster Castle

The Horse & Groom

Address: East Woodlands, FROME, BA11 5LY
Tel: 01373 462802
Fax: 01373 462802
Email: horse.and.groom@care4free.net
Website: www.horseandgroom.care4free.net
Map ref: 2, ST74
Directions: On A361 S of Frome, just E of junct with B3092, turn S towards East Woodlands; pub 1m on left
Open: 11.30–2.30 6.30–11 (Sun 12–3, 7–10) ⓑ L 12–2 D 6.30–9 ⑩ L 12–2 D 6.30–9
Facilities: Children welcome Garden **Parking:** 20 **Notes:** ⋈ ⊕ Longleat Estate ♉ 7

Thoroughly rural, with views of fields, an award winning garden, and even a stableyard where you can leave your horse while you quaff a quick half, this pub has a flagstoned bar, where you can peruse the lengthy menus. Co-owner Kathy Barrett managed a Devon teashop until chef Rick Squire chanced by; their subsequent joint endeavor has resulted in bar food such as steaks, chops and baguettes, and more elaborate dinners: perhaps roast haunch of venison; or smoked artichoke and potato filo tart.

Recommended in the area

Longleat House and Safari Park; East Somerset Railway; Brokerswood Country Park

The Lord Poulett Arms

◆◆◆◆

Address: High Street, HINTON ST GEORGE, TA17 8SE
Tel: 01460 73149
Email: steveandmichelle@lordpoulettarms.com
Website: www.lordpoulettarms.com
Map ref: 2, ST41
Directions: 2m N of Crewkerne, 1.5m S of A303
Open: 12–3 6.30–11 ⏚/◉ L 12–2 D 7–9 **Rooms:** 4
en suite, S £59 D £88 **Facilities:** Children welcome
Garden **Parking:** 10 **Notes:** ⌁ ⊕ Free House ⏄ 7

In one of Somerset's loveliest villages, this 17th-century
thatched inn has been lovingly restored, exposing its
flagstone floors and several fireplaces, and it is furnished
throughout with country antiques. The monthly changing
menu majors on fresh, local seasonal and often organic produce, including a great seafood selection
from Dorset and game from Exmoor.
Recommended in the area
Montacute House (NT); Fleet Air Arm Museum; Worldwide Butterflies

The Notley Arms

Address: MONKSILVER,
Taunton, TA4 4JB
Tel: 01984 656217
Website: www.thenotleyarms.co.uk
Map ref: 2, ST03
Directions: From A39 near Washford, go S on B3190,
then fork left on B3188
Open: 12–2.30 6.30–11 (Closed Monday lunctime)
⏚ L 12–2 D 7–9 **Facilities:** Garden **Parking:** 26
Notes: ⌁ ⊕ Enterprise Inns ⏄ 10

Built in the 1860s and named after a prominent local family, the Notley Arms is all you could ask
for in an English country drinking and dining pub. The owners, who come from Zimbabwe, cook all
the dishes themselves with a distinct bias towards traditional but imaginative British cuisine, using
fresh regional produce. However, you can also expect a sprinkling of ostrich steaks, biltong, droewors
and bobotie. Real beers include Exmoor Ale, Bath Ales and Wadworth 6X. The pretty garden bordered
by an Exmoor stream has well tended flower borders and toys to keep the children happy.
Recommended in the area
Exmoor National Park; Combe Sydenham Country Park; Cleeve Abbey

George Inn

Address: High St, NORTON ST PHILIP,
            nr Bath, BA2 7LH
Tel: 01373 834224
Fax: 01373 834861
Email: georgeinnnsp@aol.com
Website: www.thegeorgeinn-nsp.co.uk
Map ref: 2, ST75
Directions: From Bath take A36 for Warminster, after
6m take A366 on right to Radstock, village 1m
Open: 11–2.30 5.30–11(all day weekends during
summer) ﹩ L 12–2 D 7–9.30 ⏀ L 12–2 D 7–9.30 Facilities: Garden Parking: 26
Notes: ﹩ ⊕ Wadworth ⏀ 6

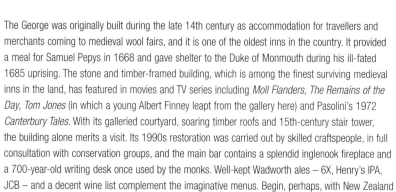

The George was originally built during the late 14th century as accommodation for travellers and
merchants coming to medieval wool fairs, and it is one of the oldest inns in the country. It provided
a meal for Samuel Pepys in 1668 and gave shelter to the Duke of Monmouth during his ill-fated
1685 uprising. The stone and timber-framed building, which is among the finest surviving medieval
inns in the land, has featured in movies and TV series including *Moll Flanders*, *The Remains of the
Day*, *Tom Jones* (in which a young Albert Finney leapt from the gallery here) and Pasolini's 1972
Canterbury Tales. With its galleried courtyard, soaring timber roofs and 15th-century stair tower,
the building alone merits a visit. Its 1990s restoration was carried out by skilled craftspeople, in full
consultation with conservation groups, and the main bar contains a splendid inglenook fireplace and
a 700-year-old writing desk once used by the monks. Well-kept Wadworth ales – 6X, Henry's IPA,
JCB – and a decent wine list complement the imaginative menus. Begin, perhaps, with New Zealand
green lipped mussels in a garlic sauce; goat's cheese and caramelised red onion tart; deep-fried

Somerset brie, with cranberry dip; or one of the
home made soups, served with locally baked
granary bread. Follow this with an individual
beef Wellington, with red wine gravy; chicken
breast stuffed with sun dried tomato, olive, garlic
and mozzarella; fillet of local trout with butter
glaze and toasted almonds; or fillet of sea bass
on roast vegetables with balsamic dressing.
The mouthwatering desserts on offer might
include chocolate and orange bavarois; bread-
and-butter pudding; or a brandy snap basket
filled with toffee fudge ice cream. Meals can be
enjoyed in the main dining room or smaller
Charterhouse room, both extending right up
into the beamed roof.

Recommended in the area

Westwood Manor; Brokerswood Country Park;
Farleigh Hungerford Castle

The Three Horseshoes Inn

★★★★ ◉ INN

Address: Batcombe, SHEPTON MALLET, BA4 6HE
Tel: 01749 850359
Fax: 01749 850615
Map ref: 2, ST64
Directions: Take A359 from Frome to Bruton.
Batcombe is signed on right
Open: 12–3 6.30–11 ⦿ L 12–2 D 7–9 **Parking:** 25
Notes: ⌂ ⊕ Free House ⦿ 10

Formerly an inn with its own smithy, the 17th-century building of honey-coloured stone has been transformed into a dining pub that attracts local regulars and gastro diners alike in both the bar area and restaurant. The lovely rear garden overlooks the 15th-century tower of the parish church. Original features of the building include a fine Grade II listed brick chimney that rises out of the kitchen. The atmosphere is cosy and relaxed, with attentive service from the owners and their small team of staff. Exposed beams, terracotta walls and an inglenook fireplace are features of the long, low main bar, where real ales are served from hand pumps, including Bats in the Belfry (brewed for them), Butcombe Bitter and Adnams. Also on offer are draft ciders and a well balanced wine list that includes 10 wines available by the glass. Cooking is traditionally based, including home-cured hams, home-made sausages and home-made dishes prepared from local organic and Soil Association certified growers or farmers' markets. Daily specials might include Fowey mussels marinières with crusty bread and a large pot of fries, and the carte includes starters such as pan-fried organic chicken livers en croûte, with a bacon, brandy and parsley cream sauce and main courses such as home-made bangers and mash with onion gravy. Gourmand quiz dinners are a regular feature. There are three stylishly decorated letting bedrooms, two with en suite facilities and one with a private bathroom. Breakfast for gastronauts is cooked by the owner/chef. Dogs are allowed (water and biscuits provided).

Recommended in the area

Longleat House and Safari Park; Stourhead (NT); Wincanton Racecourse

The Greyhound Inn

◆◆◆◆

Address: STAPLE FITZPAINE, Taunton, TA3 5SP
Tel: 01823 480227
Fax: 01823 481117
Email: info@thegreyhoundinn.fsbusiness.co.uk
Website: www.thegreyhoundinn.fsbusiness.co.uk
Map ref: 2, ST21
Directions: From M5 junct 25, take A358 Yeovil road, in 1m turn right, signed Staple Fitzpaine, at t-junct go left, pub is on right at crossroads.
Open: 12–2.30 6–11 (Fri 5.30–11; all day Sun) ⓑ L 12–2 D 7–9 ⓞ D 7–9 **Rooms:** 4 en suite, S £55 D £80 **Facilities:** Children welcome Garden **Parking:** 60 **Notes:** ⌘ ⊞ Free House ⓨ 7

This attractive and award-winning 16th-century free house, with its flagstone bars and open fires, serves a good choice of real ales and traditional Somerset cider. The menu features a variety of dishes using the finest local ingredients, including cheeses, pork, beef and lamb. Fish is delivered daily from Brixham. Typical seafood dishes include smoked haddock and mussel chowder, and crab farcie.

Recommended in the area

Taunton Racecourse; Willow and Wetlands Visitor Centre; Hestercombe Garden

The Fountain Inn & Boxer's Restaurant

Address: 1 Saint Thomas Street, WELLS, BA5 2UU
Tel: 01749 672317
Fax: 01749 670825
Email: eat@fountaininn.co.uk
Website: www.fountaininn.co.uk
Map ref: 2, ST54
Directions: In city centre, junct Tor St and St Thomas St
Open: 10.30–2.30 6–11 (Sun 12–3, 7–10.30) ⓑ L 12–2 D 6–10 ⓞ L 12–2.30 D 6–10
Facilities: Children welcome **Parking:** 24
Notes: ⊞ Innspired ⓨ 23

Built in the 16th century to house cathedral builders, this popular pub has a charmingly unpretentious bar. All food is freshly cooked using local produce, with a varied bar menu plus a restaurant upstairs for starters like seafood mornay with parmesan, mains like pan-fried rib-eye with blue cheese sauce.

Recommended in the area

Wells Cathedral; Bishop's Palace; Wells Museum

Minehead's Victorian town centre.

Crossways Inn

Address:	Withy Rd, WEST HUNTSPILL,
	Highbridge, TA9 3RA
Tel:	01278 783756
Fax:	01278 781899
Email:	crossways.inn@virgin.net
Website:	www.crossways-inn.com
Map ref:	2, ST34

Directions: 3.5m from M5 junct 22 or 23, on A38
Open: 12–3 5.30–11 (Sun 12–4.30, 7–10.30)
 L 12–2 D 6.30–9 L 12–2 D 6.30–9

Facilities: Children welcome Garden **Parking:** 60 **Notes:** Free House 8

The seasoned enthusiasm of Anna and Mike Ronca, who bought this 17th-century coachinG inn more than 30 years ago, is nicely balanced by the youthful exuberance of their kitchen team. The result is an ever-changing menu of good home-cooked food, served with several real ales, and a small but interesting wine list. Look out for favourites like fiery chicken wings with chilli, sour cream and chive dip; venison sausage with chasseur sauce and cheesy spring onion mash; and cod and prawn mornay.
Recommended in the area
Burnham-on-Sea; Helicopter Museum; Quantock Hills

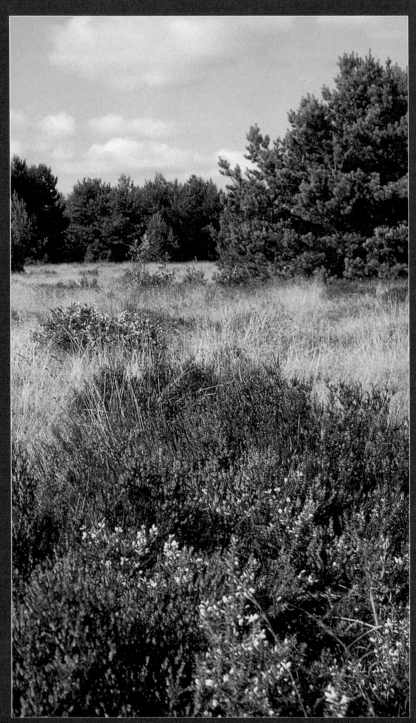

Heath and woodland at Cannock Chase.

The Holly Bush Inn

Address:	Salt, STAFFORD, ST18 0BX
Tel:	01889 508234
Fax:	01889 508058
Email:	geoff@hollybushinn.co.uk
Website:	www.hollybushinn.co.uk
Map ref:	7, SJ92
Directions:	4m NE of Stafford. From A51 go 1m N of

junct with A518 turn left for Salt; cross railway, canal and river then turn right. From M6 junct 14, follow signs Uttoxeter, turn left on B5066. 1m turn left at brown signs

Open: 12–11 L 12–9.30 D 12–9.30 **Facilities:** Children welcome Garden **Parking:** 25 **Notes:** Free House 12

In an area cut through by several major trunk roads, it's good to find such a peaceful spot, and then take time to discover the glorious Staffordshire countryside that lies hidden away from the highways. The Holly Bush Inn was licensed during the reign of Charles II (1660–85), although the building itself dates from around 1190, and heavy carved beams, open fires and cosy alcoves still characterise the comfortably old-fashioned interior. Like most other landlords, owner Geoff Holland aims to serve good quality real ales and wines. What helps to differentiate Geoff, though, is his insistence on providing non-processed, mostly organic, fully traceable food, and on minimising his hostelry's impact on the environment by setting up a worm farm. Traditional British dishes on the main menu include grilled pork chops with a honey and whole-grain mustard glaze; braised lamb and apples flavoured with nutmeg and allspice; and breaded wholetail scampi. Daily specials might be butternut squash and goat's cheese lasagne; fillet of beef Wellington; chargrilled red snapper with Jamaican spiced chutney; and baked perch with watercress sauce. Holly Bush mixed grill is a favourite plateful. At lunchtime triple-decker sandwiches, jacket potatoes and toasties are available. Beers include Adnams, Pedigree and guest ales.

Recommended in the area

Shugborough Hall (NT); Weston Park; Cannock Chase

The Crown Inn

Address: Den Lane, WRINEHILL, Crewe, CW3 9BT
Tel: 01270 820472
Fax: 01270 820547
Email: mark_condliffe@hotmail.com
Map ref: 6, SJ74
Directions: From Newcastle-under-Lyme; take A525 W, then turn N on A531. From M6 junct 16, go W on A500, then south on A531
Open: 12–3 6–11 (Sun 6–10.30, closed Monday lunchtimes) 📖 L 12–2 D 6.30–9.30 **Facilities:** Garden **Parking:** 36 **Notes:** ⊕ Free House 6

A former coaching inn with a village setting, The Crown stands six miles equidistant from Crewe and Newcastle-Under-Lyme. The interior is largely open plan but retains its oak beams and large inglenook fireplace, and the recently renovated garden has an attractive patio area for dining. A family-run free house for some 30 years, the pub has a great reputation for its real ales. There is always a choice of five traditional cask ales, including Marstons Pedigree, Adnams Bitter and Banks's Original, and there will be a regularly changing guest beer. Wine is an integral part of the inn's drinks portfolio, including six wines offered by the glass. Food also plays a significant part in this establishment's success, and it is renowned in the area for its generous portions and consistent good quality. The menu changes on a monthly basis with dishes reflecting the time of year and the fresh produce available locally. The team here is well established. Charles and Sue Davenhill bought the pub in 1977, and were joined in the business by their daughter and son-in-law, Anna and Mark Condliffe, in 2001. Mother and daughter are both vegetarians, so the food on offer always includes meat-free choices and a vegan dish. Meat-eaters are spoilt for choice, with such dishes as piri-piri chicken; Cumberland grill; and tuna cooked Chinese style, and desserts include sticky toffee pudding and ice cream sundae.

Recommended in the area

The Potteries; Bridgemere Garden World; Trentham Gardens and Monkey Forest

SUFFOLK

Dunwich beach.

The Swan Inn

Address: Swan Lane, BARNBY, NR34 7QF
Tel: 01502 476646
Fax: 01502 562513
Map ref: 4, TM49
Directions: Just off the A146 Lowestoft–Beccles road
Open: 11–3 6–12 🍺 L 12–2 D 7–9.30 🍽 L 12–2
D 7–9.30 **Facilities:** Children welcome Garden
Parking: 40 **Notes:** 🍺 Free House

If you like fish, you will love The Swan, where the menu
lists up to 80 different seafood dishes – hardly surprising, since it's owned by a family of Lowestoft
fish wholesalers. The distinctive pink-painted building, set in a picturesque village, dates from 1690,
and comprises a lively bar that is at the centre of local social life, and the rustic Fisherman's Cove
restaurant. The menu includes smoked sprats; Italian seafood salad; lobster thermidor; skate wing
in black butter; baby scallops and crevettes in garlic butter; grilled Dover sole; crab gratin; and
poached salmon in tarragon. For anyone who doesn't like fish, there are various steaks on the menu
plus home-cooked gammon salad.
Recommended in the area
Africa Alive; New Pleasurewood Hills; East Anglia Transport Museum

Cornwallis Country Hotel

Address: BROME, Eye, IP23 8AJ
Tel: 01379 870326
Fax: 01379 870051
Email: info@thecornwallis.com
Website: www.thecornwallis.com
Map ref: 4, TM17
Directions: Just S of Diss, turn off A140 onto B1077
Eye road. Pub is 30 metres on the left
Open: 11–11 🍺 L 12–2.30 D 6–9.30 🍽 L 12–2.30
D 6–9.30 **Facilities:** Children welcome Garden
Parking: 400 **Notes:** 🍺 Free House 🍷 16

New owners have arrived at this handsome looking building, which dates from 1561 and was formerly
the Dower House to Brome Hall. Within its 20 peaceful acres are an avenue of limes, some impressive
yew topiary and a pretty water garden, while inside many of the original beams, panels and oak and
mahogany settles remain. Virtually everything emanating from the kitchen is fresh and locally supplied,
from roasted cod and chorizo mash with wilted spinach and cockles, to cannelloni of butternut squash
Recommended in the area
Euston Hall; Banham Zoo; Bressingham Steam Museum and Gardens

The Trowel & Hammer Inn

Address: Mill Road, COTTON, Stowmarket, IP14 4QL
Tel: 01449 781234
Fax: 01449 781765
Website: www.trowelandhammer.co.uk
Map ref: 4, TM06
Directions: From A14 junct 47, NW of Stowmarket,
follow signs to Haughley, then Bacton, then turn left for
Cotton. From Stowmarket, head N on B1113
Open: 12–11 (Fri–Sat 12pm–1am) ⓑ L 12–3 D 6–9.30
(Sun 12–9) **Facilities:** Children welcome Garden
Parking: 50 **Notes:** ⊞ Free House

Hidden away down Mill Road, in the heart of the Suffolk countryside, this cosy pub was once a haunt of the poet Milton. Well maintained and draped in wisteria, this pub really doesn't look its age from the outside, but the interior gives a much clearer picture, and the addition of a new bar has augmented the amenities without detracting from the traditional style. Old oak timbers, red carpets and imaginative lighting make for a pleasant and relaxed atmosphere. Watch out for the herd of elephants – a family of nine carved out of solid teak, making their way from the entrance to the swimming pool in the garden where the thatched table umbrellas add to the safari theme. A license for civil weddings is held for both The Breeze House and the Cotton Club. The internationally themed menu has starters listed by country of origin – samosas (India); spring rolls and chicken dumplings (China); antipasti (Italy). Main courses include pizzas and pasta dishes such as tomato, mozzarella and basil gnocchi, plus curries; chicken cooked in various ways (New Yorker, Tuscan and Dijonnaise); beer-battered cod or haddock; and traditional Sunday roasts. Exotic dishes include kangaroo and crocodile. Lighter dishes include sandwiches and jacket potatoes. Real ales come from Suffolk's own Adnams brewery, Mauldens and Nethergate breweries, and Greene King's IPA and Abbot ales, plus Guinness and lagers.

Recommended in the area

Museum of East Anglian Life; Euston Hall; Framlingham Castle

Racehorses are put through their paces in fields near Newmarket.

The Star Inn

Address: The Street, LIDGATE, Newmarket CB8 9PP
Tel: 01638 500275
Fax: 01638 500275
Email: tereaxon@aol.com
Map ref: 4, TL75
Directions: 7m SE Newmarket on B1063 Clare road
Open: 11–3 6–11 🍴 L 12–2 D 7–10 ⦿ L 12–2 D
7–10 Facilities: Children welcome Garden Parking: 12
Notes: ⊕ Greene King

From the outside, this inn, formed from two lovely colour-washed Elizabethan cottages, seems entirely traditional. It is only once you pass through the beamed bars, furnished with oak and pine, and enter the simple dining room that you discover The Star's secret – a Catalan landlady who has put together an innovative menu of Spanish and British dishes. It has become popular with trainers on Newmarket race days, and with dealers and agents from all over the world during bloodstock sales, all tucking into such dishes as paella Valenciana; and lamb kidneys in sherry. Well trained staff are happy to translate where needed.

Recommended in the area

Newmarket Races; National Horseracing Museum and Tours; Ickworth House, Park and Gardens (NT)

The Crown and Castle

★ ★   85% ◉ ◉   HOTEL

Address: ORFORD, IP12 2LJ
Tel: 01394 450205
Email: info@crownandcastle.co.uk
Website: www.crownandcastle.co.uk
Map ref: 4, TM45
Directions: From A12 take B1078 to Orford. Pub is 50
metres from the Castle
Open: 12–3 7–11 (Sun 7–10.30) ⓑ L 12.15–2.15
D – ⓘ L 12.15–2.15 D 7–9.30 **Rooms:** 18 en suite,
Facilities: Garden **Parking:** 18 **Notes:** ⌁ ⊘ on premises
⊞ Free House ⓦ 18

Proprietors Ruth and David Watson have quite a track
record in the hospitality business, having previously owned
Hintlesham Hall and the Fox and Goose Inn at Fressingfield. Ruth is well known as a food writer and
the couple have put The Crown and Castle firmly on the culinary map. Orford is an unspoilt village, and
the red-brick inn stands in Orford's old market square, next to the remains of the 12th-century castle,
overlooking the estuary on Suffolk's heritage coast. The terrace, where you can sit outside with a drink,
overlooks the castle's Norman keep. The inn actually dates from the 16th century but underwent
a drastic Victorian re-modelling. Contemporary touches in the interior design make a stylish statement,
but the atmosphere is delightfully relaxed, with stripped floors and simply set tables. Cooking has a
modern approach with high-end skill, creativity and quality. Menus showcase fresh, locally sourced
produce and many of the dishes are featured in Ruth's cookbooks. An impressive list of wine, including
18 by the glass, is offered alongside Greene King IPA and Aspalls Cider. Some of the bedrooms have
been designated for families and well-behaved pets.

Recommended in the area

Orford Castle; Orford Ness (NT), Snape Maltings

The Church of St Edmund, Stowmarket.

Crown Hotel

★★　85% ◉◉　HOTEL

Address:	The High Street, SOUTHWOLD, IP18 6DP
Tel:	01502 722275
Fax:	01502 727263
Email:	crown.hotel@adnams.co.uk
Website:	www.adnamshotels.co.uk
Map ref:	4, TM57

Directions: from A12, 19m S of Lowestoft, take A1095
Open: 8–3 6–11 (all day peak times) ⓑ L 12–2.30
D 7–9.30 ⓘ L 12–2.30 D 7–9.30 **Rooms:** 14 (13 en
suite) **Parking:** 18 **Notes:** ⊘ on premises ⊞ Adnams ☙ 20

Combining the appeal of a pub, wine bar and restaurant, this small hotel is always buzzing with lively informality. The Crown is one of two Adnams' owned hotels in the home of their renowned brewery, and has an excellent reputation for it food, wine and, of course, beer. Originally a posting inn, the building dates from 1750 and its central location is just two minutes from the beach. Visit the cellar and kitchen store in the hotel's yard for a full selection of wines and bottled beers.

Recommended in the area

Minsmere RSPB Reserve; Suffolk Wildlife Park; Suffolk Heritage Coast

SURREY

The River Thames at Hampton Court.

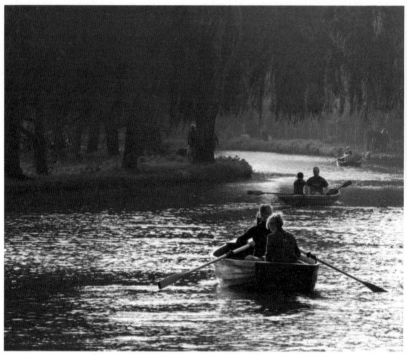

The River Thames at Guildford.

The Woolpack

Address: The Green, ELSTEAD,
nr Godalming, GU8 6HD
Tel: 01252 703106
Fax: 01252 705914
Map ref: 3, SU94
Directions: From A3 SW of Guildford, take Milford
exit and follow signs for Elstead on the B3001
Open: 11–3 5.30–11 (Sat 11–11, Sun 12–10.30)
L 12–2 D 7–9.30 L 12–2 D 7–9.30
Facilities: Children welcome Garden **Parking:** 15
Notes: Punch Taverns 11

The Woolpack is a traditional village inn, on the village green, and is surrounded by some of Surrey's most beautiful countryside. As the name suggests, it was once a centre for the local wool trade and there is plenty of intriguing memorabilia in the cosy, low-beamed setting. You can enjoy one of several real ales or test out the reputation of the renowned, generously-portioned 'Old English' style dishes: perhaps macaroni cheese; haddock, egg and prawn pie; or Cumberland sausages on mustard mash.

Recommended in the area

Loseley Park; Winkworth Arboretum (NT); Witley Common (NT)

Hare and Hounds

Address: Common Road, LINGFIELD, RH7 6BZ
Tel: 01342 832351
Fax: 01342 832351
Email: hare.hounds@tiscali.co.uk
Map ref: 3, TQ34
Directions: From M25 junct 6, go S on A22 East Grinstead road, then follow signs for Lingfield Racecourse into Common Road
Open: 11.30–11 ▸ L 12–2.30 D 7–9.30 ⦿ L 12–2.30 D 7–9.30 **Facilities:** Garden **Parking:** 40 **Notes:** ⌗ ⊕ Punch Taverns ♇ 8

The promise of this friendly establishment is that, despite a commitment to providing food of unusual excellence, it remains at heart a proper pub. This means there are plenty of real ales, including Greene King IPA, Flowers Original and Old Speckled Hen, and a friendly bunch of locals who enjoy nothing more than a convivial conversation at the bar. There's a peaceful atmosphere throughout because the pub is entirely free of the electronic interference that has ruined many good places, and the walls are decked with a changing display of original art works, all of which are for sale. There's also a lovely split level garden to enjoy when the weather is sunny. The food, however, really is a highlight. The menu is eclectic, and everything – bread, pasta, ice cream – is made on the premises. You might begin the culinary experience with a dish of linguini, spinach, parmesan, poached egg and truffle oil, before choosing between enticing main courses that might include slow-roasted belly of pork with chorizo mash and Granny Smith, tomato and basil salsa; or baked stuffed aubergine, with crostini and basil dressing, rocket, pink grapefruit and parmesan salad. The equally unusual desserts take some classic ideas and give them a startling twist, resulting in such mouthwatering delights as rhubarb, apple and rice brûlée, or chocolate brioche Belle Hélène.

Recommended in the area

Standen (NT); Godstone Farm; Hever Castle

The Inn @ West End

Address: 42 Guildford Road, WEST END, GU24 9PW
Tel: 01276 858652
Fax: 01276 485842
Email: greatfood@the-inn.co.uk
Website: www.the-inn.co.uk
Map ref: 3, SU96
Directions: From the M3 junct 3, go S for 3m on the A322 towards Guildford; pub is just beyond the Gordon Boys rdbt.
Open: 12–3 5–11 🍴 L 12–2.30 D 6–9.30
🍴 L 12–2.30 D 6–9.30 **Facilities:** Garden
Parking: 35 **Notes:** ⌖ ⊕ Free House ♟ 12

The name gives a hint that The Inn @ West End is a modern place. It is a restaurant pub run by owners (Gerry and Ann Price) who pride themselves on the great food, wine and atmosphere here. Indeed, its role as a focus for local social life has seen it being described as more of a community centre than a pub or restaurant, with special events such as quiz nights and wine tastings, and involvement in a variety of clubs and societies. In addition to the dining room, the bar and the garden room, there is a private gastronomic cellar, available for private hire, and the garden offers further facilities in the shape of a lovely dining patio and a boules terrain. An interesting wine list takes in wines from all over the world, but with a leaning towards Portugal and Spain. There is also an impressive Champagne section. Real beers include Scottish Courage, Courage Best and Fuller's London Pride. Food is fresh and local, with fish and game dishes as a speciality on the modern British menu. Fish is acquired on weekly buying trips to Portsmouth Harbour and game comes directly from the farm for processing – they even have their own plucking machine here. Dogs are allowed.

Recommended in the area

Windsor Great Park; Airborne Forces Museum; Thorpe Park

EAST SUSSEX

Fulking Escarpment.

The Causeway in Horsham leads to the spired Norman church.

The Coach and Horses

Address: DANEHILL, RH17 7JF
Tel: 01825 740369
Fax: 740369
Map ref: 3, TQ42
Directions: From E Grinstead, take A22 S then go right on A275 for 2m to Danehill, left onto School Lane for 0.5m
Open: 11.30–3 6–11 ⅃ L 12–2 D 7–9 ⏀ L 12–2 D 7–9 **Facilities:** Garden **Parking:** 30 **Notes:** ⊮ ⏀ Free House ⏀ 10

Built in 1847 of local sandstone, virtually in Ashdown Forest, The Coach and Horses is ideal for walkers and lovers of stunning scenery. Homely winter fires and neatly tended gardens add plenty of character and colour, and half-panelled walls, highly polished wooden floorboards and vaulted beamed ceilings give the place a charming, timeless feel. Food plays a key role in the pub's success, with a good selection of lunchtime sandwiches and a constantly changing evening menu. Fish features regularly, with dishes like tuna loin with lemon buttered spring onions; pan-fried turbot with sesame noodles; pan-fried sea bass with buttered spinach; and poached witch sole with confit of white cabbage.

Recommended in the area

Sheffield Park (NT); Bluebell Railway; Wakehurst Place (NT)

The Hatch Inn

Address: Coleman's Hatch, HARTFIELD, TN7 4EJ
Tel: 01342 822363
Fax: 01342 822363
Email: Nickad@bigfoot.com
Map ref: 3, TQ43
Directions: From E Grinstead, take A22 S; turn left at
Forest Row rdbt, and go 3m to Colemans Hatch; turn right
Open: 11.30–3 5.30–11 (all day Sun, Sat in summer
and BHs) ⓑ L 12–2.30 D 7–9.15 ⓘ L 12–2.30
D 7–9.15 Facilities: Garden Notes: ⌀ ⊘ on premises
⌂ Free House ♟ 10

Classically picturesque and reputed to date back to 1430, The Hatch Inn was converted from three
cottages thought to have housed workers for the local water-driven hammer mill and it may also have
been a smugglers' haunt at one time; it is named after the coalmen's gate at the nearby entrance
to Ashdown Forest. The pub is superbly placed for combining a visit with a country walk (dogs are
welcome), and features in a number of 'top ten pubs' lists, as well as serving as a filming location for
television dramas and advertisments. There are two large beer gardens for al fresco summer dining,
one of which enjoys views out over the forest, and is only minutes away from the restored Poohsticks
Bridge, immortalised in A.A. Milne's 'Winnie the Pooh' stories. Cooking by the owner Nicholas Drillsma,
who trained as a chef in both the UK and the US, combined with the customer service background for
his partner Sandra, have created a recipe for success. Quality ingredients and imaginative techniques
make for an exciting menu, which includes a good selection of light bites and home-cooked traditional
dishes. These might include starters such as hot duck salad with fresh mango and field mushrooms
and main courses like pork tenderloin on crushed celeriac, with a sweet mustard seed cream sauce.
No reservations are available at lunchtime and evening booking is essential.

Recommended in the area

Ashdown Forest; Standen (NT); Royal Tunbridge Wells

The Middle House

Address: High Street, MAYFIELD, TN20 6AB
Tel: 01435 872146
Fax: 01435 873423
Map ref: 4, TQ52
Directions: From Tunbridge Wells go S on A267 for approx 8m, then turn left for Mayfield
Open: 11–11 (Sun 12–10.30) ⓑ L 12–2 D 7–9.30
⓽ L 12–2 D 7–9 **Facilities:** Children welcome Garden
Parking: 25 **Notes:** ⊕ Free House ⓨ 9

Dominating the heart of this 1,000-year-old village, the Middle House is truly a family-run business: Monica and Bryan Blundell are the owners, son Darren is general manager, daughter Kirsty manages the restaurant, her husband, Mark, is the head chef, and second daughter Nicky helps out. This is said to be one of the finest timber-framed buildings in Sussex, with ornate patterns in wood on its facade, and was built in 1575 for Sir Thomas Gresham, Elizabeth I's Keeper of the Privy Purse and founder of the London Stock Exchange. It remained a private residence until the 1920s, and retains a fireplace by the renowned master carver Grinling Gibbons and wattle-and-daub infill. The splendid oak-panelled formal restaurant, seating 70, still incorporates the private chapel. Here, an extensive carte is offered, featuring starters such as caramelised roasted fig and goat's cheese gateau, served with a balsamic glaze; or asparagus and brie in a filo parcel, served with a cheron sauce. Main course dishes might include local marinated venison loin, with infused red cabbage and apple; chicken breast filled with brie and mango wrapped in filo pastry with chablis, cream and chive sauce; half a shoulder of lamb slowly roasted with redcurrant and rosemary sauce; and two whole boneless quail filled with duck liver pâté, wrapped in bacon, with a red wine jus. More than 40 dishes, including various vegetarian and fish dishes, are served in the bar, where beers on offer include Harvey Best, Greene King Abbot Ale, Black Sheep Best, Theakston Best and Adnams Bitter.

Recommended in the area

Bateman's (NT); Spa Valley Railway; Royal Tunbridge Wells

Star Inn

Address: Church Street, OLD HEATHFIELD, TN21 9AH
Tel: 01435 863570
Fax: 01435 862020
Email: heathfieldstar@aol.com
Website: www.thebestpubsinsussex.co.uk
Map ref: 4, TQ52
Directions: From Tunbridge Wells, take the A267 S for approx 14m, then turn left on A265 for Heathfield
Open: 11.30–3 5.30–11 ⓔ L 12–2.15 D 7–9.30
⓪ L 12–2.15 D 7–9.30 **Facilities:** Children welcome Garden **Parking:** 20 **Notes:** ⛵ ⊕ Free House

A lovely creeper-clad building of honey-coloured stone, the Star was originally built as an inn for the stonemasons who constructed the village church, All Saints, during the 14th century. The enchanting surroundings include an award-winning summer garden, with colourful shrubs, oak tables shaded by umbrellas, a fountain and, of course, flowers. From the garden there are views across High Weald, a designated Area of Outstanding Natural Beauty. It certainly inspired J M W Turner, who captured the scene in a painting. This is wonderful walking country, and there are also plenty of historic towns and villages to be explored. Equally appealing is the atmospheric low-beamed bar with its huge inglenook fireplace. Traditional ales include Harvey Best, Shepherds Neame, Master Brew and Bishops Finger. Bar food focuses on fresh fish from Billingsgate or direct from the boats at Hastings. The range of dishes includes such favourites as seafood chowder; snails with garlic and herb butter; fish and chips; stuffed supreme of chicken; and Arborio risotto with sun blushed tomatoes, leeks, garlic and crayfish tails, finished with cream, white wine and aged parmesan. The restaurant upstairs, which has a fine barrel ceiling, has seven tables, seating around 45 people in all, and is ideal for family and corporate functions. Dogs are allowed, with a dog watering hole provided.

Recommended in the area

Bateman's (NT); Bentley Wildfowl and Motor Museum; Michelham Priory

River Rother, Rye.

The Ypres Castle Inn

Address: Gun Garden, RYE, TN31 7HH
Tel: 01797 223248
Email: info@yprescastleinn.co.uk
Website: www.yprescastleinn.co.uk
Map ref: 4, TQ92
Directions: In town centre, off Fishmarket (A259)
Open: 11.30–3.30 6–11 (Fri–Sat 11.30–12, Sun 12–4)
🏊 L 12–2.30 🍴 L 12–2.30 D 7–9 Facilities: Children
welcome Garden Notes: 🐾 ⊕ Free House 🍷 11

Known locally as 'The Wipers', the building was two weather-boarded cottages in 1640, and nearly 200
years elapsed before it became a pub. Buildings in the citadel area of this ancient Cinque Port are tightly
packed, and the pub is unique for having a garden. Colourful art and furnishings help make the interior
warm and friendly. From its seasonal, mainly locally sourced menu might come grilled fillet of sea bass;
seared Rye Bay scallops; Gloucester Old Spot pork steak with cider and apple sauce; caramelised onion
and goats cheese tartlet; and daily specials. The bar lunch menu includes tomato and roast red pepper
soup and hearty ploughman's lunches with organic crusty bread. On Friday night there's live music.
Recommended in the area
Rye Castle Museum; Lamb House; Rye Nature Reserve

The Dorset Arms

Address: WITHYHAM, Nr Hartfield, TN7 4BD
Tel: 01892 770278
Fax: 01892 770195
Email: pete@dorset-arms.co.uk
Website: www.dorsetarms.com
Map ref: 3, TQ43
Directions: 4M W of Tunbridge Wells; Take A264 E Grinstead road, then turn left onto B2110 Edenbridge Road. Withyham is between Groombridge and Hartfield
Open: 11–3 6–11 (Sun 12–3, 7–10.30) ⓑ L 12–2 D 7–9 ⓘ L 12–2 D 7–9 Facilities: Garden Parking: 20 Notes: 🐕 ⊕ Harveys of Lewes

Local records suggest that this tile-hung, family-run pub and restaurant at the edge of the Ashdown Forest has been an inn since the 18th century. Its origins go much further back – to the 15th century when it was an open-halled farmhouse. Today it retains its original flagstone floors, and among the many interesting Tudor and later period features that remain are the ice-house buried in the hillside behind the building, the oak-floored bar, a magnificent open log fireplace, and the massive wall and ceiling beams in the restaurant. There's seating on the lawn outside for fine summer days. As a focus of village life, the Dorset Arms hosts periodic quiz nights and occasional live music. When it comes to the food on offer, wherever possible owner Peter Randell sources ingredients locally, including what some customers claim to be the best fillet steaks in the area. Starters might include oak-smoked salmon with brown bread; deep-fried tempura battered king prawns with chilli dip; or crispy whitebait. Continue with a fillet steak, wrapped in bacon and in a port and redcurrant sauce; a halibut steak, poached in white wine; medallions of pork fillet with mushrooms in a stilton, white wine and cream sauce; or perhaps seared scallops with bacon and onions. For dessert, one of the favourites is warm chocolate fudge brownies with ice cream. Prize-winning real ales come from Harveys of Lewes.

Recommended in the area

Tunbridge Wells; Groombridge Place; Spa Valley Railway

The Weald and Downland Open Air Museum.

George & Dragon

Address: BURPHAM, Arundel, BN18 9RR
Tel: 01903 883131
Map ref: 3, TQ00
Directions: Off A27 1m E of Arundel, signed Burpham
Open: 11–2.30 6–12 (Oct–Apr, closed Sun eve)
L 12–2 D 7–9.30 D 7–9 **Parking:** 40
Notes: Free House

Down a 2.5m cul-de-sac in a tranquil village, this lovely old pub is opposite the church and next to the cricket pitch. The historic town of Arundel is very close, as are some beautiful country walks over the downs and by the River Arun. The interior is full of old world character with beams and worn flagstone floors providing a backdrop for the modern prints hung on the walls. Smaller rooms have been opened out for more space, but there are still some nooks and crannies for an intimate meal or drink. A selection of real ales includes Harvey Best, Brewery-on-Sea Spinnaker Bitter, Fuller's London Pride and King Brewery Red River, but this is very much a dining pub with a good choice of dishes from the carte and specials board.

Recommended in the area

Arundel Castle; Wildfowl and Wetlands Trust; Amberley Working Museum

Royal Oak Inn

★★★★★ ⬡ ⬭ INN

Address: Pook Lane, East Lavant,
CHICHESTER, PO18 0AX
Tel: 01243 527434
Fax: 01243 775062
Email: enquiries@royaloaklavant.co.uk
Website: www.thesussexpub.co.uk
Map ref: 3, SU80
Directions: Off A286 just N of Chichester
Open: L 12–2 D 6–9.30 L 12–2 D 6–9.30
Rooms: 5 en suite and 3 cottages **Facilities:** Children welcome Garden **Parking:** 24 **Notes:** 12

This 200-year-old coaching inn (with resident ghost) set in a pretty Downland village, has been given a new lease of life with a stylish conversion comprising the inn, a barn and a cottage round an attractive courtyard. The interior design of the bar and restaurant achieves effortless rustic chic, and a simple contemporary menu is served. The bedrooms are in the barn, cottage and main house, and all rooms have flat-screen TV and CD player, a library of DVDs and broadband internet access.

Recommended in the area

Chichester; Goodwood; Weald & Downland Open Air Museum; seaside

The King's Arms

Address: Midhurst Road, FERNHURST,
nr Haslemere, GU27 3HA
Tel: 01428 652005
Fax: 01428 658970
Website: www.kingsarmsfernhurst.com
Map ref: 3, SU82
Directions: On A286 between Haslemere and Midhurst,
1m S of Fernhurst
Open: 11.30–3 5.30–11 ⓑ L 12–2.30 D 7–9.30
⦿ L 12–2.30 D 7–9.30 **Facilities:** Children welcome
Garden **Parking:** 45 **Notes:** 🚂 ⊞ Free House ♟ 10

A Grade II listed property of Sussex stone, the pub and its outbuildings date from the 17th century and are prettily decorated with hanging baskets, flowering tubs, vines and creepers. These days The Kings Arms comprises a free house and restaurant – a genuine gastro pub – surrounded by rolling Sussex farmland, close to Goodwood Racecourse and Cowdray Park. Outside, the large garden has splendid views of the Sussex Downs. The L-shaped interior is cosy, with low oak-beamed ceilings and a large inglenook fireplace in the restaurant area. Real ales, including Horsham Best Bitter, Ringwood 49er, Hogsback TEA and Caledonian IPA, are well kept and there is an extensive wine list. The food, a fusion of modern British and traditional, is all home made from fresh, locally sourced produce. A lighter lunch menu runs alongside the main menu, both of which change slightly on a daily basis. Game dishes, such as a pot roast of rabbit, play a major part in the winter fare and fish is always has a presence, bought direct from south coast boats. Typical dishes might include monkfish loin in Parma ham with courgette ribbons and a prawn and saffron sauce; poached finnan haddock topped with poached egg; or smoked salmon and hollandaise sauce. Alternatives could be Barbary duck breast; rack of English lamb; or roasted butternut squash filled with fresh herb risotto. Dogs are welcome in the bar.

Recommended in the area

Hollycombe Steam; Uppark (NT); South Downs Way

Heyshott Church.

Unicorn Inn

Address: HEYSHOTT, Midhurst, GU29 0DL
Tel: 01730 813486
Fax: 01730 815672
Map ref: 3, SU81
Directions: From Midhurst, on the A272, go S on the A286 Chichester Road, then turn left for Heyshott
Open: 11.30–3 6.30–11 Sun 12–4, closed Mon eve in winter 🍺 L 12–2.30 D 7–9.30 🍽 L 12–2.15 D 6.30–9.15 **Facilities:** Garden **Parking:** 24
Notes: 🌐 🍷 10

A cosy village inn, dating from 1750, the Unicorn is located in the South Downs Area of Outstanding Natural Beauty, and is equally popular with walkers and cyclists as it is with locals. There are stunning views from the beautiful south-facing gardens. The atmospheric bar, with its beams and a large log fire, is part of the original building. Also in perfect historical tune is the subtly lit, cream-painted restaurant, with oil paintings of individual flowers. Locally sourced food includes fish from Selsey and Portsmouth, and Unicorn Inn ale is brewed specially for the pub by the Hampshire Brewery in Romsey.
Recommended in the area
South Downs Way; Weald and Downland Open Air Museum; Chichester

The Half Moon Inn

Address: KIRDFORD, Nr Billingshurst, RH14 0LT
Tel: 01403 820223
Fax: 01403 820224
Email: halfmooninn.kirdford@virgin.net
Website: www.the-halfmoon-inn.co.uk
Map ref: 3, TQ02
Directions: Off the A272 between Billingshurst and Petworth. At Wisborough Green follow Kirdford signs
Open: 11–3 6–11 (closed Sun eve) ⊾ L 12–2.30 D 6–9.30 ⦿ L 12–2.30 D 6–9.30 **Facilities:** Garden
Parking: 12 **Notes:** ⊕ Laurel Pub Partnerships

Officially one of the prettiest pubs in the south of England, this appealing red-tiled 16th-century village inn is covered in climbing rose bushes, and sits directly opposite the church in this unspoilt Sussex village near the River Arun. Although people who call in just to have a drink are very welcome, The Half Moon is mainly a dining pub. The interior, with its low beams and log fires, is where the well-presented cask ales and lagers are on offer, along with a varied wine list that includes four available by the glass. The talented young team in the kitchen specialise in British cooking 'with a twist'. Lunch choices from the bistro menu might include such starters as twice-cooked blue cheese soufflé; chicken liver pâté; and medallions of lobster. Main courses that follow could feature pan-fried venison with black pudding mash; fillet of salmon on a bed of buttered pasta; and pork and leek sausages with apple mash. The list of home made desserts has recently included ginger crème brûlée; rhubarb crumble with custard; and lemon tart with clotted cream. Expect lunchtime snacks like battered haddock with chips; Caesar salad; and lamb curry with coriander rice. At dinner, the menu is broadly similar, but the atmosphere changes with candlelight, tablecloths and polished glassware. The well-tended gardens are an added draw on summer days, and the pub offers a pamphlet detailing local country walks.

Recommended in the area

Arundel Castle; Goodwood; Petworth House (NT)

Black Horse Inn

Address:	Nuthurst Street, NUTHURST, Horsham, RH13 6LH
Tel/fax:	01403 891272
Email:	clive.henwood@btinternet.com
Website:	www.theblackhorseinn.info
Map ref:	3, TQ12
Directions:	4m S of Horsham, off A281, A24, A272
Open:	12–3 6–11 (all day Sat–Sun and BH's)

L 12–2.30 D 6–9.30 L 12–2.30 D 6–9.30
Facilities: Children welcome Garden Front and rear patio
Parking: 28 Notes: Free House 6

Once on the main route from Brighton to Horsham, this used to be a smugglers' hideout, with a secret passage from the pub to the church which can still be seen. Quietly hidden away, it retains plenty of original features: stone-flagged floors, an inglenook fireplace and an exposed wattle and daub wall. The pub has a reputation for good ales and homemade, freshly prepared food, with universal appeal and menus that specify gluten-free and vegetarian options. There are some very tempting desserts.
Recommended in the area
Four local pub walks; Wakehurst Place; Pulborough Brooks Nature Reserve; Leonardslee Gardens

The Green Man Inn and Restaurant

Address:	Church Road, PARTRIDGE GREEN, RH13 8JT
Tel:	01403 710250
Fax:	01403 713212
Email:	info@thegreenman.org
Website:	www.thegreenman.org
Map ref:	3, TQ11
Directions:	On B2135, just S of junct A24 and A272

Open: 11.30–3.30 6.30–12 L 12–2.15 L 12–2.15 D 7–9.30 Facilities: Children welcome Garden Parking: 30 Notes: 6

This stylish gastro pub offers a seasonal menu with daily specials, and the chefs use only fresh and locally sourced ingredients. Tapas, bar snacks and sandwiches are available at lunchtime, while the restaurant offers starters such as deep-fried halloumi with chilli and tomato jam and mains like pan-ried calves' liver with streaky bacon, or lamb shank with root vegetable jus.
Recommended in the area
Amberley Working Museum; Parham House & Gardens; Holly Gate Cactus Garden

Royal Oak Inn

Address: The Street, POYNINGS, BN45 7AQ
Tel: 01273 857389
Fax: 01273 857202
Email: ropoynings@aol.com
Website: www.royaloakpoynings.biz
Map ref: 3, TQ21
Directions: From Brighton go N on the A23, then take the A281 left (signed Henfield and Poynings); follow signs into Poynings village
Open: 11–11 (Sun 12–10.30) ⓑ L 12–9.30 D 12–9.30
Facilities: Garden **Parking:** 35 **Notes:** 🐾 ⊕ Free House 🍷 10

Beautifully located in the folds of the South Downs, the Royal Oak is just a short walk from the Devil's Dyke yet only a few minutes' drive from the city of Brighton and several other south coast resorts. Built as a small hotel and tea gardens during the 1880s, the inn has recently undergone a comprehensive refurbishment. It has a smart cream-painted exterior, and inside you'll find solid oak floors, old beams hung with hop bines and crackling log fires along with more contemporary decor and comfy sofas. For summer enjoyment, there is a large garden with splendid views of the Downs, providing the backdrop for award-winning barbecues. The popular free house, under the ownership of Paul Day and Lewis Robinson has, for more than a decade, maintained a commitment to good quality pub food featuring locally sourced produce. These include Sussex cheeses and grass-fed beef from the neighbouring farm's pedigree Sussex beef herd. The season's main menu is supported by daily specials from the chalkboard and occasional themed menus. Favourite regular dishes include roast Gressingham duck breast; deep-fried cod fillet in beer batter; pan-fried local sea bass fillet; local sausages with mash and caramelised onions; or hand-made lamb burger with feta and tzatziki. A good choice of ales includes Harveys Sussex, Abbot Ale, Greene King Morland and Old Speckled Hen. Dogs on leads are welcome.

Recommended in the area

Brighton; South Downs Way; Bramber Castle (NT)

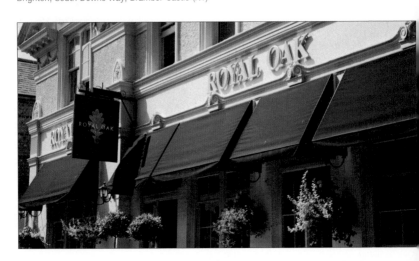

The Countryman Inn

Address: Countryman Lane, SHIPLEY, RH13 8PZ
Tel: 01403 741383
Fax: 01403 741115
Email: countrymaninn@btopenworld.com
Website: www.countrymanshipley.co.uk
Map ref: 3, TQ12
Directions: From Billingshurst, take the A272 E, through Coolham, then r onto Smithers Hill Lane. Not into Shipley village, but over river and left on Countryman Lane
Open: 11–3.30 6.30–11 (Sat 11–11, Sun 12–4 7–10.30)
⚜ L 11.30–2.30 (Sun 12–3) D 6.30–9.45 (Sun 12–3 7–9.30) **Parking:** 40

As you might guess from its name, The Countryman is a rural hostelry, and it offers superb country views. Along with the nearby village of Shipley, it is set within the 3,500-acre Knepp Castle Estate, where the land is being returned to its natural state, with wild grasses and flora encouraging native birds to nest. Fallow deer, free-ranging Tamworth pigs, Exmoor ponies and English longhorn cattle have been introduced. The inn maintains a traditional style, serving a minimum of three cask-conditioned ales, such as Harvey's Sussex and Horsham Best, in the cosy bar, which is warmed by a roaring log fire in winter. Bar snacks include ploughman's lunches and appetising salads, perhaps with Selsey crab or smoked salmon and feta cheese. In the restaurant, hearty home-cooked meals are offered from a seasonal menu using free-range meat and locally produced vegetables. Favourites include roast pheasant; minted lamb; braised oxtail; venison and beef pie; and fresh fish straight from boats working out of Shoreham and Newhaven. There are more exotic options, such as Mexican burritos and lamb tagine, and choices for vegetarians, too. Such meals are complemented by an international list of over 30 wines. In summer there are plenty of tables outside for those who prefer to enjoy their meal in the garden, which is planted with flowers and shrubs and overlooks open farmland.

Recommended in the area

Leonardslee Gardens; Shipley Windmill; Holly Gate Cactus Garden

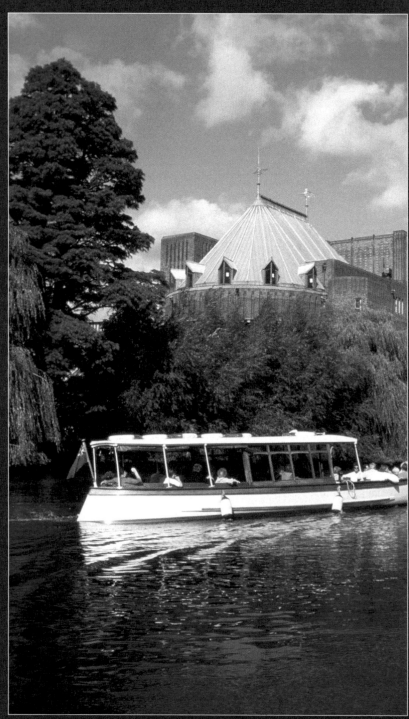

The Royal Shakespeare Theatre, Stratford-upon-Avon.

The Golden Cross

Address: ARDENS GRAFTON, B50 4LG
Tel: 01789 772420
Fax: 01789 773697
Website: www.thegoldencross.net
Map ref: 3, SP15
Directions: From the Stratford-upon-Avon ring road, take the B439 W to Cranhill and turn right. From Evesham, go N on A46, then right on B439, left at Cranhill
Open: 12–3 5–11 (all day Sat–Sun) 🍴 L 12–2.30 D 6–9
🍴 L 12–2.30 D 7–9.30 Facilities: Children welcome Garden Parking: 80 Notes: 🛢 Free House 🍷 8

The Golden Cross is a lovely country inn with plenty of rustic charm, recently refurbished by the new proprietors, Pat and Steve Wainwright. The mellow bar is characterised by massive beams, a log fire and flagstone floors softened by rugs. In contrast, the spacious dining room has a more contemporary mood, with its restful decor and beautifully laid tables. In summer there is seating on the beautiful new dining patio under giant umbrellas overlooking the extensive lawns. Sensibly priced, freshly prepared food is offered from a frequently changing menu. The bar menu features such dishes as traditional toad in the hole; beer battered fish and chips; and warm chicken and roast pumpkin salad, while the restaurant offers more adventurous options like pork tenderloin with Thatcher's cider sauce; confit leg of lamb with roast vegetables and lavender gravy; or breast of guinea fowl with shallot and red wine jus. A daily specials board lists the chef's interesting fish dishes, such as grilled sea bream with samphire; grilled red mullet and king prawn with saffron mussel sauce and leek mash; or River Exe mussels marinière style. Beautifully kept cask ales include Tetley Cask, Hook Norton, UBU Purity Brewing and a monthly-changing guest beer. Live music is a regular feature on a Thursday night, with a variety of musical styles being represented. Dogs are allowed in the garden only.

Recommended in the area

Stratford-upon-Avon; Anne Hathaway's Cottage; Ragley Hall

King's Head

Address: 21 Bearley Road, ASTON CANTLOW,
Solihull, B95 6HY
Tel: 01789 488242
Fax: 01789 488137
Website: www.thekh.co.uk
Map ref: 3, SP16
Directions: From Stratford-upon-Avon, take A3400
Henley-in-Arden road then turn left through Wilmcote for
Aston Cantlow; alternatively, take A46 W towards Alcester
and turn right through Billesley

Open: 11–3 5.30–11 🍴 L 12–2.30 D 6.30–9.30 🍽 L 12–2.30 D 6.30–9.30 **Facilities:** Children welcome Garden **Parking:** 60 **Notes:** 🐕 🍺 Independent 🍷 8

A wisteria-hung black and white timbered pub in a pretty village setting, the King's Head dates from the 15th century and is full of historic character. It is said that William Shakespeare's parents held their reception here after their wedding in Aston Cantlow church in 1557. Inside you will find the comfy village bar furnished with wooden settles, a massive inglenook fireplace and an old-fashioned snug. The main room has a flagged stone floor, inviting window seats and oak tables. Outside there is a large hedged beer garden where food is served in summer. A single modern British menu serves all areas and features such main courses as salmon, lemongrass and chive fishcake with tomato salsa; slow-cooked lamb shank on spiced aubergine and saffron cous cous; and the famous King's Head Duck Supper, with braised white cabbage in brown sugar. Other options range from a bowl of chilli marinated olives and rustic breads to roast venison pavé with parsnip and pear purée and Calvados sauce. Private dining, weddings and private events are all catered for. Well-kept real ales on hand pumps include Greene King Abbot Ale, Purity Gold, and Mitchell and Butler Brew XI, and the wine list offers eight wines by the glass. The pub has facilities for children, and dogs are also permitted with water provided.

Recommended in the area

Stratford-upon-Avon; Mary Arden's House; Coughton Court (NT)

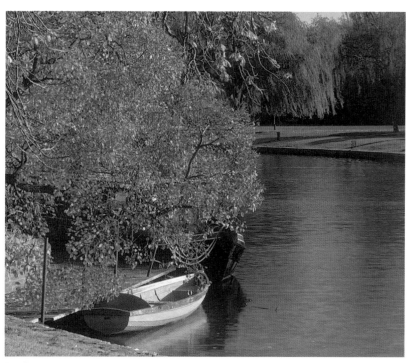

The River Avon.

Golden Lion Inn

★★★ 74% HOTEL

Address: Easenhall, RUGBY, CV23 0JA
Tel: 01788 832265
Fax: 01788 832878
Email: reception@goldenlionhotel.org
Website: www.goldenlionhotel.org
Map ref: 3, SP57
Directions: From A426 between M6 junct 1 and Rugby, take B4112 through Newbold on Avon, then 2nd left
Open: 11–11 ⓜ L 12–2 D 6–9.30 ⓞ L 12–2 D 6–9.30
Rooms: 21 en suite, S £50 D £60 **Facilities:** Children welcome Garden **Parking:** 80 **Notes:** ⊗ on premises ⓦ Free House ⓥ 7

The atmosphere here is informal: the beamed bar, for example, has a rug-strewn stone floor, mellow décor and scrubbed pine tables, while the dining-room is light and airy. A quarterly menu blends more traditional dishes (perhaps given a modern twist) with more inventive ones, such as pan-fried red snapper over coriander crushed potatoes with Thai butter; or marinated tuna loin over cous cous.

Recommended in the area

Webb Ellis Rugby Football Museum; Garden Organic Ryton; Stanford Hall

The Durham Ox Restaurant and Country Pub

Address: Shrewley Common, SHREWLEY,
Warwick, CV35 7AY
Tel: 01926 842283
Fax: 0121 705 9315
Email: reservations@durham-ox.com
Website: www.durham-ox.com
Map ref: 3, SP26
Directions: From M40 junct 15, take A46 to Warwick, then left on A4177. Fork left on B4439 for Shrewley
Open: 12–11 ㋹ L 12–3 D 6–10 ㋡ L 12–3 D 6–10
Facilities: Children welcome Garden **Parking:** 100
Notes: ㋙ Greene King ㋰ 12

The Durham Ox is an award-winning country pub and restaurant with warm and inviting open fires and old beams, but a shot of city smart attitude gives it a competitive edge. Food is key to its success, and a range of classic and contemporary dishes is offered, changing regularly with the seasons. Children are made welcome with their own special menu. The restaurant brings a contemporary look to the decor and furnishings in a traditional setting with a splendid oak floor. The bar has been extended to accommodate further seating in curved booths and leather chairs. Food options in the bar take in generously cut sandwiches and hot main dishes served alongside real ales and a selection of wines and spirits. Large gardens include a safe children's play area and a decked terrace, the perfect place to sit out on a sunny day. There is also an outside bar and barbecue, plus room for a marquee, which lends itself well to weddings, private functions and corporate events. Special celebrations throughout the year include Valentine's Day, Mothering Sunday, Easter, Father's Day, Bonfire Night, Christmas and New Year.

Recommended in the area

Warwick Castle; Hatton Country World; Baddesley Clinton (NT)

St John's Church, Devizes.

The Crown

Address: ALVEDISTON, Nr Salisbury, SP5 5JY
Tel: 01722 780335
Fax: 01722 780836
Map ref: 2, ST92
Directions: 2.5m S of the A30 Salisbury–Shaftesbury rd
Open: 12–3 6.30–11 (Sun 12-3, 7-10.30) ➤ L 12–2.30
D 6.30–9 ⊙ L 12–2 D 6.30–9.30 **Facilities:** Children
welcome Garden **Parking:** 40 **Notes:** ⊕ Free House 10

In the heart of the chalk valley, on the edge of Cranborne
Cahse, The Crown is a 15th-century thatched inn with extensive gardens, a vine-covered terrace, open
Inglenook fireplaces and low beams. Since they took over the pub in July 2004, Karen and Phil are
gaining an increasing number of loyal customers, and it is little wonder that people travel to this old
world inn, especially when you consider the choice of real ales, fine wines and a substantial menu that
uses fresh local produce whenever possible. The cosy bar and restaurant set the scene for food that
can range from a simple sandwich to fresh fish and rib-eye steaks. Listed daily on chalk boards expect
to find plenty of starters and an average of 17 main course dishes.

Recommended in the area

Old Wardour Castle; Farmer Giles Farmstead; Wilton House

The Boot Inn

Address: High Street, BERWICK ST JAMES,
        Salisbury, SP3 4TN
Tel: 01722 790243
Fax: 01722 790243
Email: kathieduval@aol.com
Map ref: 3, SU03
Directions: On B3083, between A303 at Winterbourne
Stoke and A36 at Stapleford, NW of Salisbury
Open: 12–3 6–11 (Sun 7–10.30; closed Mon lunch)
➤ L 12–2.30 D 6.30–9.30 **Facilities:** Children welcome
Garden **Parking:** 18 **Notes:** 🐾 ⊕ Wadworth

The attractive ivy-covered stone and flint inn dates from the 16th century and part was formerly used
as a cobblers' – hence the name. It is surrounded by picturesque countryside and has award-winning
gardens. The interior provides a traditional setting for real ales such as Wadworths 6X and Henrys IPA.
Quality home-cooked food is prepared from fresh local produce, including herbs and vegetables from
the garden. Game is available in season and fresh fish according to availability. Dogs are welcome.

Recommended in the area

Stonehenge; Salisbury Cathedral; Wilton House, Wilton

The Kings Arms

Address: Monkton Farleigh,
BRADFORD-ON-AVON, BA15 2QH
Tel: 01225 858705
Fax: 01225 858999
Email: enquiries@kingsarms-bath.co.uk
Website: www.kingsarms-bath.co.uk
Map ref: 2, ST86
Directions: Off the A363 Bath to Bradford-on-Avon
road, follow brown tourist signs to Kings Arms
Open: 12–11 (Sun 12–10.30) ☕ L 12–10.30
Facilities: Children welcome Garden **Parking:** 45 **Notes:** ⚑ ⊕ Innspired ♥ 8

This warm and friendly pub dates from the 11th century, and conversion into an alehouse took place in the 17th century. Original features remain, including the mullioned windows, flagged floors and a vast inglenook fireplace – said to be Wiltshire's largest. Traditional English dishes include salmon fillet with roasted tomato sauce; game casserole (usually venison, pheasant, guinea fowl and rabbit) with herb dumplings; crispy Old Spot pork belly; Wiltshire pork sausage; and oven-baked lemon sole.
Recommended in the area
Bath; Lacock Abbey; Fox Talbot Museum & Village; Avon Valley Railway

The Dove Inn

◆◆◆◆

Address: CORTON, Warminster, BA12 0SZ
Tel: 01985 850109
Fax: 01985 851041
Email: info@thedove.co.uk
Website: www.thedove.co.uk
Map ref: 2, ST94
Directions: Off A36 (W of junct with A303) signs Corton
and Boyton. Cross railway, turn rt at T-junct; in 1m turn rt
Open: 12–2.30 6–11 (Sun 7–10.30) ☕ L 12–2 D 7–9
🍽 L 12–2 D 7–9 **Rooms:** 5 en suite, S £55 D £75 **Facilities:** Children welcome Garden **Parking:** 24
Notes: ⚑ ⊕ Free House ♥ 10

This is a thriving traditional pub in a beautiful village close to the River Wylye. The bar has a central fireplace, and the large garden is the site of summer barbecues. The food is based on West Country produce, much of it sourced within a few miles, and the menu includes a good selection of fish dishes such as salmon with creamed leeks and ginger. Real ales include Oakhill, Wadworth and Hopback.
Recommended in the area
Stonehenge; Bath; Longleat

The Beckford Arms

Address: FONTHILL GIFFORD, nr Tisbury,
             Salisbury, SP3 6PX
Tel/fax: 01747 870385
Email: beck.ford@ukonline.co.uk
Map ref: 2, ST93
Directions: 2m from A303 (Fonthill Bishop turning, next
to Beckford Estate) midway between Hindon and Tisbury
Open: 12–11 (Sun 12–10.30) ⓑ L 12–2.15 D 7–9
🍴 L 12–2.15 D 7–9 Facilities: Children welcome
Garden Parking: 40 Notes: 🐕 ⏀ Free House 🍷 6 6

The Costellos have transformed this rural retreat over the past few years. It's now tastefully rustic, complete with scrubbed plank tables topped with huge candles, and warm terracotta-painted walls. Well-presented dishes range from starters such as sweet chilli and coriander fish cakes, or a selection of Continental meats with caper berries and gherkins, to main courses of pan-fried pavé of salmon; or roasted breast of Barbary duck. Desserts are seriously rich, and a Baileys and Horlicks crème brûlée may require a brisk walk. The sun-trap patio and delightful garden are perfect for summer sipping.

Recommended in the area

Salisbury; Wilton House; Stonehenge

The White Hart

Address: FORD, Nr Chippenham, SN14 8RP
Tel: 01249 782213
Fax: 01249 783075
Email: whitehart.ford@eldridge-pope.co.uk
Website: www.roomattheinn.info
Map ref: 2, ST87
Directions: From M4 junct 17 take A350 S, then A420 W
Open: 11–11 (Sun 12–10.30) ⓑ L 12–3 D 6–9
🍴 L 12–2.30 D 7–9.30 Facilities: Children welcome
Garden Parking: 80 Notes: 🐕 ⏀ Eldridge Pope 🍷 8

In a peaceful village, deep in the Wyvern Valley, this 15th-century coaching inn is in a location used for the original *Dr Doolittle* film (with Rex Harrison) in the late 1960s, and in more recent years has appeared in a Carlsberg advertisement. It's a mellow stone building with old beams and log fires, including a traditional bar and candlelit dining rooms. Typical dishes include stuffed squid; venison medallions; and rib-eye steak with pepper sauce. In summer, drinks can be taken out onto the grass area to the rear of the pub, and meals can be enjoyed alfresco on the patio or pub front.

Recommended in the area

Dyrham Park (NT); Bath; Lacock Abbey, Fox Talbot Museum & Village;

The Angel Coaching Inn

Address: High Street, HEYTESBURY, BA12 0ED
Tel: 01985 840330
Fax: 01985 840931
Email: admin@theangelheytesbury.co.uk
Website: www.theangelheytesbury.co.uk
Map ref: 2, ST94
Directions: From A303 take A36 toward Warminster; after approx 8m turn left then 2nd right into Heytesbury High Street
Open: 12–12 🍽 L 12–2.30 D 7–9.30 🍴 L 12–2.30 D 7–9.30 Facilities: Children welcome Garden
Parking: 20 Notes: 🚭 🍺 Greene King 🍷 10

Co-owned by TV chef Antony Worrall Thompson and event management supremo Tim Etchells, this 16th-century inn, surrounded by stunning countryside on the edge of Salisbury Plain, is a striking blend of original features and contemporary comfort. Worrall Thompson is the executive chef, but day-to-day it's Paul Kinsey, the resident chef, who produces the wealth of sumptuous dishes made from only the freshest seasonal ingredients. Diners can eat in the restaurant, the bar, or, during the summer months, alfresco in the secluded courtyard garden. Steaks are a speciality, coming from the nearby Pensworth Farm and from Castle Brae in Scotland, and matured for 35 days in the inn's own ageing rooms. Other main courses include seared fillet of local venison with celeriac purée, roasted artichoke and pepper sauce; grilled portobello mushroom on brioche with garlic-parsley butter and truffle oil; assorted cured meats and pâté with pickles and olives; salad of pork belly, bacon, soft-boiled egg, croutons and baby gem lettuce; and fresh tagliatelle with pan-fried scallops, mussels, clams and tiger prawns. Desserts include chocolate and raspberry terrine with white chocolate cream; sticky toffee pudding with vanilla ice cream; and peach and vanilla cheesecake.

Recommended in the area

Stonehenge; Longleat; Farmer Giles Farmstead

Gold Hill, Shaftesbury.

Angel Inn

Address: High Street, HINDON, Salisbury, SP3 6DJ
Tel: 01747 820696
Fax: 01747 820054
Email: info@theangelathindon.com
Website: www.theangelathindon.com
Map ref: 2, ST93
Directions: 1.5m S of A303 nr Chicklade, signs Hindon
Open: 11–3 5–11 ⓑ L 12–2.30 D 7–9.30 ⓞ L
12–2.30 D 7–9.30 **Facilities:** Children welcome Garden
Parking: 20 **Notes:** 🐾 ⊕ Free House ♟ 14

Rustic charm meets urbane sophistication in this elegant Georgian coaching inn, with wooden floors, beams, large stone fireplaces and comfortable leather seating. Here you can enjoy hand-pulled real ales in a traditional atmosphere. The brasserie, however, has contemporary appeal in both its menu and stylish interior design. A comprehensive selection takes in seared king scallop and crispy pancetta salad; medallions of pan-fried steak with tiger prawns and a whisky cream sauce; and confit of duck leg on honeyed kumquats. Outside is an attractive paved courtyard, ideal for dining alfresco.

Recommended in the area

Stonehenge; Shaftesbury Abbey; Old Wardour Castle

The Lamb at Hindon

◆◆◆◆

Address: High Street, HINDON, Salisbury, SP3 6DP
Tel: 01747 820573
Fax: 01747 820605
Email: info@lambathindon.co.uk
Website: www.lambathindon.co.uk
Map ref: 2, ST93
Directions: Follow signs Hindon from A303, at Fonthill Bishop turn right onto B3089. In Hindon, Lamb is on left.
Open: all day (incl breakfast from 7.30am) ⓑ L 12–2.30 D 6.30–9.30 ⓘ L 12–2.30 D 6.30–9.30 **Rooms:** 14 en suite, S £65 D £90 **Facilities:** Garden **Parking:** 24 **Notes:** ⌖ ⊕ Youngs ⓣ

The Lamb is set in the centre of a charming Wiltshire village just 20 minutes from Salisbury. It began trading as a public house as long ago as the 12th century and by 1870 it supplied 300 horses to pull coaches on the London–West Country route. The inn is part of the Boisdale group, with two other establishments in London (Belgravia and Bishopsgate), and this is reflected in the distinctive interior design and in the quality of the food and wine. The building still has plenty of historic character, with beams, inglenook fireplaces, and wood and flagstone floors, all set off by fine antique furniture, old paintings and open fires. Food is served from breakfast to dinner in the dining room or the intimate Whisky and Cigar Bar. Dishes are prepared from carefully sourced ingredients, including fresh fish and game in season. A recent dinner menu featured main courses such as Macsween haggis; Gloucester Old Spot sausages with Beaune mustard mash and gravy; and the 'famous Boisdale' burger, plus a fish of the day and pie of the day. The Meeting Room, in a sunken area just off the main dining room, is available for private dining or meetings. The bedrooms are richly decorated, some with tartan carpets. Each room has entertainment in the form of LCD screens and Sky television.

Recommended in the area

Longleat; Stonehenge; Stourhead House & Gardens

The Compasses Inn

★★★ ◉ INN

Address: LOWER CHICKSGROVE,
Nr Tisbury, SP3 6NB
Tel: 01722 714318
Fax: 01722 714318
Email: thecompasses@aol.com
Website: www.thecompassesinn.com
Map ref: 2, ST92
Directions: From A30, 1.5m W of Fovant, take 3rd right
to Chicksgrove, 1.5m, then left on Lagpond Ln for 1m
Open: 12–3 6–11 (Winter Sun eve 6-8.30) 🍽 L 12–2 D 7–9 🍴 L 12–2 D 7–9 **Rooms:** 4 en suite,
S £65 D £85 **Facilities:** Children welcome Garden **Parking:** 30 **Notes:** 🐾 ⊕ Free House 🍷 7

You'll find this thatched inn tucked away down a single track lane in a tiny hamlet amid beautiful
rolling countryside, which in turn forms part of a designated Area of Outstanding Natural Beauty. The
Compasses is a 14th-century building of great character, and beyond the latched door there's a long,
low beamed bar with high-backed stools, stone walls, worn flagstone floors and a large inglenook
fireplace. Here, a wood-burning stove is lit in the colder months. Adjacent to the bar is a dining room,
ideal for private parties. There is a regularly changing blackboard menu of dishes freshly prepared
from seasonal produce, and a choice of ales including Interbrew Bass, Wadworth 6X, Ringwood Best
and Chicksgrove Churl. Extra seating is set out in the big garden, which has a grassed area and some
wonderful views. If you want to make the most of the lovely location and stay over, there are lovely
double bedrooms and a detached cottage accessed separately from the inn. All the bedrooms have
hospitality trays and remote control televisions, one room is perfect for families, with an additional
single bed, and z-beds for children are available. Children's facilities also extend to a play area in the
garden. Dogs, too, are made welcome.

Recommended in the area

Longleat Safari Park; Stonehenge; Farmer Giles Farmstead

The Vine Tree

Address: Foxley Road, Norton,
MALMESBURY, SN16 0JP
Tel: 01666 837654
Fax: 01666 838003
Email: enquries@thevinetree.co.uk
Map ref: 2, ST98
Directions: From M4 junct 17, take the A429
Cirencester road N, then 3rd turning left onto a minor
road for Hullavington and Norton

Open: 12–3 6–11 (Sun 12–10.30) ⓑ/◎ L 12–2 D
7–9.30 **Facilities:** Children welcome Garden **Parking:** 100 **Notes:** ⌘ ⊕ Free House ♛ 25

In a former life co-owner Tiggi Wood organised the catering at Glyndebourne and Formula One events;
she even trained chefs in Paris. Partner Charlie Walker travelled internationally for Rothmans and now
handles the financial and marketing side of the business. The building had a former life too, as a mill,
but even in those days beverages were passed out through front windows to passing carriages. Today,
of course, customers are welcomed inside, and the inviting central bar has a large open fireplace that
burns wood throughout the winter months. There's an abundance of old beams, flagstone and oak
floors, and resident ghosts – at least two, so they say, one of which is a small boy in polo kit. Cooking
here is modern British in style, and the menu changes daily in response to the availability of fresh local
produce. An interesting selection of dishes includes light snacks, vegetarian meals, fish and seafood
from Cornwall. The menu might include such mouthwatering options as caramelised Barbary duck
breast; local wood pigeon; and pan-fried foie gras. To complement the food on offer, Tiggi and Charlie
specialise in stocking a wide selection of wines. Entertainment is also provided, in the form of jazz and
blues bands, once a month. In addition to the sun-trap terrace, there's a lovely two-acre garden that
children can play in, and two boules terrains.

Recommended in the area

Westonbirt National Arboretum; Malmesbury Abbey and Gardens; Cotswold Water Park

The George and Dragon

Address: High Street, ROWDE, SN10 2PN
Tel: 01380 723053
Fax: 01380 723053
Email: thegandd@tiscali.co.uk
Map ref: 2, ST96
Directions: From Devizes, take the A342 Chippenham rd to Rowde. Pub is on main road, near junct with Marsh Lane (B3101)
Open: 12–3 7–11 (Sat–Sun 12–4; closed Mon morning) ⊫ L 12–3 D 7–10 ⊚ L 12–3 D 7–10
Facilities: Children welcome Garden **Parking:** 14 **Notes:** ⌑ ⊘ on premises ⊞ Free House ♟ 11

Successfully combining the charm of a 16th-century inn with the relaxed atmosphere of a modern gastro-pub, the George and Dragon is located on Rowde High Street, a stone's throw from the Kennet and Avon Canal and the dramatic Caen Hill flight of locks. In summer the garden is a delight, with its lawned area and cottage-style flower borders, and there's seating for an alfresco meal or a quiet drink. During winter there are welcoming log fires in the panelled bars and dining room, and an interesting original feature is a carved Tudor rose on one of the old beams in the restaurant. Seafood delivered directly from Cornwall is the speciality of the house, so diners can take their pick from the latest catch. The choise is huge, and may comprise sea bass, lobster, lemon sole, John Dory, mackerel, scallops, turbot, mussels, halibut, mackerel, squid and oysters. Blackboards above the bar list the fish dishes of the day, while the carte offers a range of local meat and game options. The emphasis is on home-made delicacies, and this extends from the complementary bread served at the start of the meal, to the delicious desserts and ice creams, and the chocolate fudge served with coffee. Draught beers include Butcombe Bitter, Milk Street Brewery ales, and Bath Ales Gem. Children's facilities are available, and dogs are permitted, with water provided.

Recommended in the area

Bowood House and Gardens; Lacock Abbey, Fox Talbot Museum & Village; Avebury

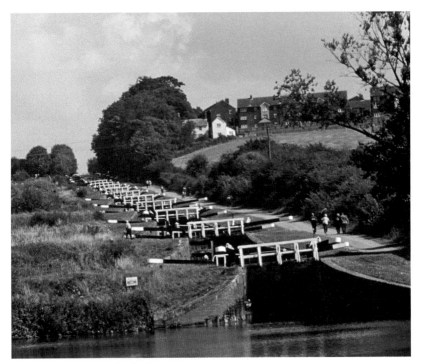

Flight of locks along canal at Devizes.

The Bridge Inn

Address: 26 Church Street, WEST LAVINGTON,
Devizes, SN10 4LD
Tel/Fax: 01380 813213
Email: portier@btopenworld.com
Website: www.the-bridge-inn.co.uk
Map ref: 3, SU05
Directions: On A360, approx 6m S of Devizes.
Open: 12–3 6.30–11 ♿ L 12–2 D 6.30–9 ○ L 12–2
D 6.30–9 **Facilities:** Garden **Parking:** 20 **Notes:** ⊞ ♥ 11

Located on the outskirts of a village on the edge of Salisbury Plain, the Bridge Inn is a small but
perfectly formed pub and restaurant with a beamed bar and log fire. Local paintings, offered for sale,
cover the walls of the bar and restaurant, and outside in the large garden there is a boules pitch. The
food-led establishment caters for all appetites, with light lunches, a regular a la carte and a specials
board, and the kitchen produces English food with a French twist. To sum up the atmosphere and
appeal of this pub, it is a well-known place frequented both by locals and those from further afield.
There is no smoking at The Bridge Inn

Recommended in the area

Longleat; Stonehenge; Lacock Abbey, Fox Talbot Museum & Village

Worcester.

The Bell Tower Church, Evesham.

The Fleece Inn

Address:	The Cross, BRETFORTON, Evesham, WR11 7JE
Tel:	01386 831173
Email:	nigel@thefleeceinn.co.uk
Website:	www.thefleeceinn.co.uk
Map ref:	3, SP04

Directions: From Evesham/A46 follow signs for B4035 Chipping Campden. At Bretforton, turn rt at village hall **Open:** 11–11 (Sun 12–10.30), Winter 11–3 6–11 (Sat 11–11 Sun 12–10.30) ♿ L 12–2.30 (Sun 12–4) D 6.30–9 **Facilities:** Children welcome Garden **Notes:** ⊕ Free House ♟ 12

The Fleece was built as a longhouse 600 years ago and its last private owner, Lola Taplin, who died in the snug in 1977, was a direct descendant of the man who built it, and she bequeathed it to the National Trust. In 2004, it caught fire but a massive restoration ensued and it looks as good as ever. Homemade dishes include local sausage of the day with mash, pork belly marinated in plum cider brewed on the premises and a fresh fish dish of the day. Look out for Morris dancers, folk singing and asparagus.

Recommended in the area

Chipping Camden; Hidcote Manor (NT); Cotswold Way

Crown & Sandys Arms

Address: Main Road, OMBERSLEY, WR9 0EW
Tel: 01905 620252
Fax: 01905 620769
Email: enquiries@crownandsandys.co.uk
Website: www.crownandsandys.co.uk
Map ref: 2, SO86
Directions: From M5 junct 6, take A449 towards Kidderminster. After 6m, fork left into Ombersley. Pub is on this road, just before rdbt in village centre

Open: 11–3 5–11 ⓑ L 12–2.30 D 6–10 ⓘ L 12–2.30 D 6–10 **Facilities:** Children welcome Garden **Parking:** 100 **Notes:** ⊘ on premises ⊞ Free House ⓦ 10

The Crown and Sandys is a classy establishment run by Rachael and Richard Everton, who used to own the village delicatessen and wine shop, so expect excellent wines here as well as a good selection of traditional draught ales. The interior design, modern in concept, looks great against a backdrop of original beams and fireplaces in what was formerly a coaching inn. Catering for civil receptions and weddings is a speciality, and outside there is a large beer garden with a Japanese-style terrace. The food is as contemporary as the decor, and there are three restaurants to choose from according to your mood. Freshly-made sandwiches, paninis, baguettes and hot dishes are offered at lunchtime, and daily specials could include Moroccan lamb tagine; salmon en croute; or local pheasant breast, pan-fried and flamed in whisky. The carte changes seasonally, and offers an interesting dishes such as pot roasted blade of beef with a mini kidney and mushroom pie with fondant potato and red wine jus or corn fed chicken breast coated with parmesan bread crumbs, courgette and tomato risotto and balsamic jus. A good variety of home-made pizzas is also available from Monday to Friday. For anyone wanting to stay overnight, there are five en suite bedrooms, all equipped with tea and coffee facilities, digital and terrestrial television, direct-dial telephones, hairdryers, and ISDN internet connections.

Recommended in the area

Worcester; Hawford Dovecote (NT); Witley Court

The Fountain Hotel

Address: Oldwood, St Michaels,
TENBURY WELLS, WR15 8TB
Tel: 01584 810701
Email: enquiries@fountain-hotel.co.uk
Website: www.fountain-hotel.co.uk
Map ref: 2, SO56
Directions: From A49 just N of Leominster, take A4112 towards Tenbury Wells. From Ludlow, go S on A49, then E on A456 to Tenbury Wells; take A4112 Leominster rd, 1m
Open: 9–11 ⓑ L 9–9 D 9–9 ⓞ L 12–10 D 12–10
Facilities: Garden Children welcome Alfresco dining **Parking:** 60 **Notes:** ⊕ Free House ♟ 20

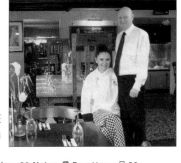

This country pub was first established in 1855, when it began serving beer and cider to the Welsh drovers herding their sheep across the border to English markets. In those days, it was known as The Hippodrome, after the horse racing that took place on the adjacent Oldwood Common. The building is older, though, serving first as a farmhouse, and displays the vernacular black-and-white architecture of the region. Now it has something of a nautical theme – publican Russell Allen is a well-travelled big-game fisherman – and there's a 1,000 gallon aquarium filled with exotic fish, including a leopard shark, which is an object of enormous fascination to children and adults alike. Russell's wife Michaela, is the chef, and, not surprisingly, there's plenty of award-winning fish dishes on the menu, sometimes including Tay Salmon caught in Scotland by Russell's father. All the food here is home made and freshly cooked; look out for Beef and Fountain Ale pie with Yorkshire pudding; Seafood Roulade; poached cod and parsley; and Best Herefordshire steaks and a vast array of vegetarian dishes sauce. Beers include Old Speckled Hen, XX Mild, Greene King IPA, Wye Valley Bitter and the exclusive Fountain Ale. There is also a large, secluded garden with a children's play area and heated patio, and an organic herb and vegetable plot where produce for the kitchen is grown.

Recommended in the area

Burford House Gardens; Berrington Hall; Ludlow Castle; Ludlow, Hereford and Worcester Racecourses

NORTH YORKSHIRE

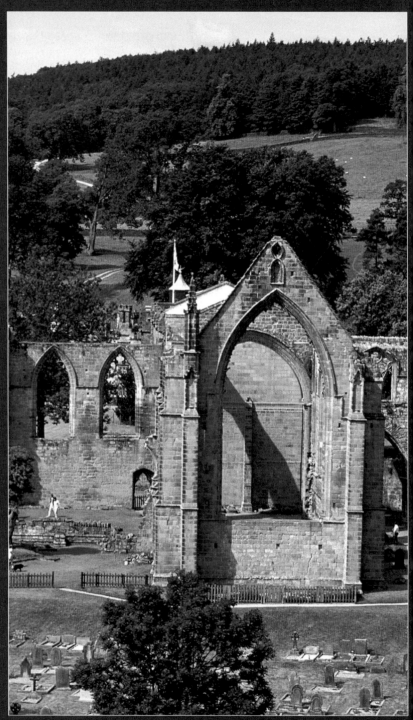

The ruins of Bolton Priory, Wharfedale.

Newby Hall, near Ripon.

Crab & Lobster

◉◉

Address:	Dishforth Road, ASENBY, Thirsk, YO7 3QL
Tel:	01845 577286
Fax:	01845 577109
Email:	reservations@crabandlobster.co.uk
Website:	www.crabandlobster.co.uk
Map ref:	8, SE37

Directions: From A1(M) junct 49 take A168 towards Thirsk, then follow signs for Asenby

Open: 11.30–11 ♨/☺ L 12–2.30 D 7–9.30

Facilities: Children welcome Garden **Parking:** 120 **Notes:** ⚓ ⊘ on premises ⊕ Scottish Courage ♟ 16

A visit to this unique 17th-century hotel is quite an experience. It is an Aladdin's Cave of antiques and artefacts from around the world, often described as a jungle of bric-à-brac, and you are bound to find something to amuse. It is equally famous for its innovative cuisine and special gourmet extravaganzas, and the menus show influences from France and Italy, with some oriental dishes too. Typical main dishes might be brill fillet with crab and wilted spinach; oriental beef pancakes; or braised lamb shank.

Recommended in the area

Norton Conyers; Aldborough Roman Site; Newby Hall and Gardens

257

The Three Hares Country Inn

Address: Main Street, BILBROUGH,
Nr York, YO23 3PH
Tel: 01937 832128
Fax: 01937 834626
Email: info@thethreehares.co.uk
Website: www.thethreehares.co.uk
Map ref: 8, SE54
Directions: Off A64, SW of York; alternatively, from A1(M), leave at junct 45 and take A64 towards York, turning left after approx 8m for Bilbrough
Open: 12–12.30 🍽 L 12–2.30 D 7–9 **Facilities:** Children welcome Garden **Parking:** 35
Notes: 🍺 Free House 🍷 10

Under new ownership, this 18th-century country pub remains a haven for lovers of high quality food, real ales, and good wines at affordable prices. It is set in a quiet village not too far from York, and has been carefully refurbished to create a friendly and welcoming pub. One particularly interesting feature is that the old village forge can still be seen in the restaurant, and the bar areas are equally appealing. Starters such as chicken liver parfait with red onion marmalade; calamari, pak choi and sweet chilli dressing; or fresh soup of the day might precede main courses options like confit duck leg; roast cod with asparagus, poached egg with dressed spinach and hollandaise sauce; or roast loin of lamb, with potato fondant, tomato petals and confit garlic with olive sauce. Specials include baked Whitby fish and seafood pie, glazed with cheese and served with vegetables; or sausage and mash with an onion jus. Several vegetarian options are offered, too. In addition, breakfast is served from 10.30am on York race days and a set-price Sunday lunch offers good value. The list of guest ales on tap changes regularly, and there is also a good list of wines by the glass. As a focus of village life, The Three Hares provides a variety of entertainment and special events during the year.

Recommended in the area

York; Beningborough Hall (NT); Lotherton Hall

The market place, Boroughbridge.

The Black Bull Inn

Address: 6 St James Square, BOROUGHBRIDGE,
Nr York, YO51 9AR
Tel: 01423 322413
Fax: 01423 323915
Map ref: 8, SE36
Directions: From A1(M) junct 48 take B6265 E for 1m
Open: 11–11 (Sun 12–10.30) 🍽 L 12–2 D 6–9
🍽 L 12–2 D 6–9 **Facilities:** Children welcome
Parking: 4 **Notes:** 🐾 🌐 Free House 🍷 10

Anthony and Gillian Burgess always hankered after owning a free house, but after leaving their jobs in the declining textile industry, chose a tenancy in Saltaire; ten years later they bought The Black Bull. The frontage dates from 1262, so perhaps its ghosts are no surprise, including one that is purported to have upended the glasses in the restaurant one night. Bar snacks include hot and cold sandwiches; Thai beef; and battered haddock, chips and mushy peas,, while the restaurant offers chargrills; rump of English lamb; tenderloin of pork; and a range of tasty 'sizzlers'. Tuna steak with prawns and wild mushroom glazed with gruyère is one of the fish specials.

Recommended in the area

Knaresborough Castle and Museum; Newby Hall and Gardens; Fountains Abbey and Studley Royal

The Red Lion

★★ 72% ◉ HOTEL

Address:	By the Bridge, BURNSALL, Skipton, BD23 6BU
Tel:	01756 720204
Fax:	01756 720292
Email:	redlion@daelnet.co.uk
Website:	www.redlion.co.uk
Map ref:	7, SE06

Directions: From Skipton take A59 E. At Bolton Bridge, take the B6160 for Bolton Abbey and Grassington, and continue for 7m to Burnsall

Open: 8–11.30 ᴸ L 12–2.30 D 6–9.30 ℝ L 12–2.30 D 7–9.30 Rooms: 14 en suite, S £62.50 D £125 Facilities: Children welcome Garden Parking: 70 Notes: ➤ ⊕ Free House ♟ 14

Within the southern part of the Yorkshire Dales National Park, the Red Lion is home to Andrew and Elizabeth Grayshon, their family and friendly staff. It's a riverside pub, with large gardens and terraces, adjacent to a five-arch bridge in a picturesque village setting. The place is full of old world charm, with oak floors and panelling in the traditional Dales bar, where there's a choice of cask conditioned real ales. The dining room has mullioned windows overlooking the village green. The Grayshon's two son-in-laws, James and Olivier, offer imaginative menus in the bar and restaurant, complemented by an extensive wine list. Dishes are freshly made and include lunchtime snacks, salads and light meals. Typical examples from the main restaurant menu might include such starters as fresh Whitby crab risotto; or locally shot pheasant, partridge and venison terrine; followed by main courses like medallions of Wharfedale beef fillet with seared foie gras, wild mushrooms and garlic crostini; or goats' cheese parcels on a rocket and watercress salad. Home-made desserts are a treat, including lemon tart with lemon sorbet and tuille biscuit, and sticky toffee pudding with banoffi ice cream.

Recommended in the area

Grassington National Park Centre; Stump Cross Caverns; Skipton Castle

Abbey Inn

Address: BYLAND ABBEY, Coxwold, York, YO61 4BD
Tel: 01347 868204
Fax: 01347 868678
Email: abbeyinn@english-heritage.org.uk
Website: www.bylandabbeyinn.com
Map ref: 8, SE57
Directions: From A19 Thirsk–York road follow signs to
Byland Abbey and Coxwold
Open: 12–3 6.30–11 🍺 L 12–2 D 6.30–9 🍽 L 12–2
D 6.30–9 **Facilities:** Children welcome Garden
Parking: 30 **Notes:** ⊕ Free House ♇ 20

In one of North Yorkshhire's most spectacular locations, the Abbey Inn stands in the shadows of the
hauntingly beautiful ruins of Byland Abbey which was destroyed by order of Henry VIII in the 16th
century. The inn's interiors are as distinctive as its creeper-clad exterior – the rambling rooms have
big fireplaces, oak and stripped tables, carved oak seats and Jacobean-style dining chairs on old
wood or flagstone floors. Fine tapestries, fresh flowers and unusual objets d'art complete the picture.

Recommended in the area

Hambleton Hills; Rievaulx Abbey, Terrace and Temples; Helmsley Castle; Byland Abbey; Shandy Hall; York

The Fox & Hounds

Address: CARTHORPE, Bedale, DL8 2LG
Tel: 01845 567433
Fax: 01845 567155
Website: www.foxandhoundscarthorpe.co.uk
Map ref: 7, SE38
Directions: Off A1, between Leeming Bar and A1(M)
junct 49, signed from north and southbound direction
Open: 12–3 7–11 🍺 L 12–2 D 7–9.30 🍽 L 12–2
D 7–9.30 **Facilities:** Children welcome **Parking:** 22
Notes: ⊕ Free House ♇

Near the Great North Road, but in rural surrounds, The Fox and Hounds has been serving travellers for
the past 200 years, and for the last 20, the Fitzgerald family have been making a thoroughly good job
of continuing the tradition. The restaurant, once the village smithy, serves up imaginative dishes, and
the midweek set-price menu is particularly good value, with dishes such as pan-fried lamb's liver with
bacon and onion gravy; or, from the specials board, grilled whole Dover sole with parsley butter. Home-
made desserts might include chocolate fondue; or raspberry and almond tart with vanilla ice cream.

Recommended in the area

Ariel Extreme; Snape Arboretum; Black Sheep Brewery Visitor Centre

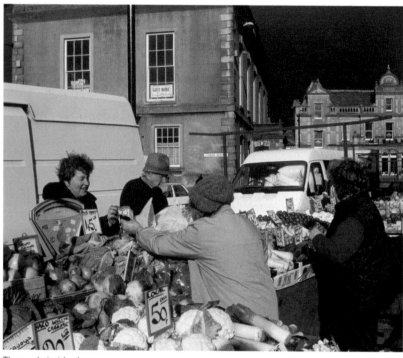

The market at Leyburn.

The Blue Lion

Address:	EAST WITTON, Nr Leyburn, DL8 4SN
Tel:	01969 624273
Fax:	01969 624189
Email:	bluelion@breathe.com
Website:	www.thebluelion.co.uk
Map ref:	7, SE18

Directions: From Ripon take A6108 towards Leyburn.
Open: 11–11 ⊕ L 12–2.15 D 7–9.30 ⊗ L 12–2.15
D 7–9.30 Facilities: Children welcome Garden
Parking: 30 Notes: ⌘ ⊕ Free House ♟ 12

In the late 18th century, coach travellers and drovers journeying through Wensleydale stopped at The Blue Lion. Its stone façades have hardly changed since, though the interior is now much more suited to 21st-century eating and drinking. The bar, with its open fire and flagstone floor, and the candlelit restaurant are just perfect. Diners will find, say, sautéed monkfish fillet in parma ham with tapenade sauce; and pan-fried breast of chicken stuffed with blue Wensleydale, with smoked bacon risotto. A vegetarian example would be sage and onion potato cake with creamed garlic mushrooms.

Recommended in the area

Jervaulx Abbey; Middleham Castle; Theakston Brewery Visitor Centre

The Tempest Arms

Address: ELSLACK, Skipton, BD23 3AY
Tel: 01282 842450
Fax: 01282 843331
Email: info@tempestarms.co.uk
Website: www.tempestarms.co.uk
Map ref: 7, SD94
Directions: From Skipton take A59 towards Gisburn, then left on A56; Elslack signed on left
Open: 7–11 ⓑ/⊚ L 12–2.30 D 6–9 **Facilities:** Garden
Parking: 120 **Notes:** ⊘ on premises ⊞ Free House ♟ 10

The Tempest Arms is set in magnificent countryside, close to the market town of Skipton – gateway to the Dales – in the tiny hamlet of Elslack. On the edge of the Pennine Way, the village has its own Roman Fort site, and the pub itself dates back to 1690. The Pickhill Barn, built in 1786, is a romantic setting often used for civil weddings, family gatherings, meetings and conferences, while the Tempest Room is a club style room, also suitable for small parties or private dining. Inside, the main pub instantly induces relaxation, particularly when sitting in a cosy corner by a crackling log fire and enjoying a fine wine or one of the hand-pulled Yorkshire ales on offer. There are two dining styles, the informal bar and the more formal restaurant. The seasonal specials and vegetarian menu is known as the 'hymn sheet' here. You will find dishes like warm salad of crispy bacon, sauté potatoes, pint nuts, crispy croutons, herbed mayonnaise and tomato basil dressing to start followed by award-winning Mr Chamley's Raised Pork Pie with piccalilli, minted gravy and mushy peas. Other options range from pan-fried tuna steak to butter bean, leek and sweet potato hotpot. The bar menu is served throughout the bar and dining room and features starters like roast black pudding, locally made in Skipton, with Bramley apple chutney, English mustard and brown bread and butter. Main courses include cottage pie or lamb 'thingymebob' (a famous local dish). Sandwiches and side orders are also on offer.

Recommended in the area

Skipton Castle; Yorkshire Dales National Park; Embsay & Bolton Abbey Steam Railway

The Plough Inn

Address: Main Street, FADMOOR, York, YO62 7HY
Tel: 01751 431515
Fax: 01751 432492
Map ref: 8, SE68
Directions: 1m N of Kirkbymoorside off the A170
Pickering–Helmsley road
Open: 12–2.30 6.30–11 &L 12–1.45 D 6.30–8.45
&L 12–1.45 D 6.30–8.45 Facilities: Children welcome
Garden Parking: 20 Notes: ⊕ Free House ♀ 6

A well-established country inn located on the edge of the North York Moors National Park and offering genuine northern hospitality. Overlooking the tranquil village green, The Plough also has views towards the Vale of Pickering and the Wolds. Stylishly refurbished, with snug little rooms, real ales and open fires, it attracts local people and visitors alike, and the imaginative food is another draw. Most of the kitchen produce is locally sourced and the extensive selection of dishes includes a separate seafood menu: expect seafood paella; butterfly filleted kippers; pan-seared king scallops; peeled jumbo scampi deep-fried in light batter; and basil and parmesan crusted cod to feature here.

Recommended in the area

Rievaulx Abbey, Terrace and Temples; Duncombe Park; North Yorkshire Moors Railway

Stone Trough Inn

Address: Kirkham Abbey, KIRKHAM, YO60 7JS
Tel: 01653 618713
Fax: 01653 618819
Email: info@stonetroughinn.co.uk
Website: www.stonetroughinn.co.uk
Map ref: 8, SE76
Directions: 1.5m E of A64, between York and Malton
Open: 12–2.30 6–11 (Sat 12–11, Sun 11.45–10.30)
&L 12–2 D 6.30–8.30 &L 12–2.15 D 6.45–9.30
Facilities: Children welcome Garden Parking: 100
Notes: ⊕ Free House ♀ 11

Adam and Sarah Richardson, here since 1999, have taken the inn to new gastronomic heights. After studying all aspects of cooking, Adam specialised in pâtisserie, a passion that inspires his desserts today. The pub name comes from the trough-like stone base of a long-lost cross erected by a 12th-century French knight in memory of his son, killed in a riding accident. The restaurant offers dishes like roast rump of Flaxton lamb; fillet of Escrick beef; and skewer of monkfish, halibut and tiger prawns.

Recommended in the area

Castle Howard; Eden Camp; City of York

Sandpiper Inn

Address: Market Place, LEYBURN, DL8 5AT
Tel: 01969 622206
Fax: 01969 625367
Email: hsandpiper@aol.com
Website: www.sandpiperinn.co.uk
Map ref: 7, SE19
Directions: From A1 take A684 to Leyburn
Open: 11.30–3 6.30–11 (Sun 12–3, 6.30–10.30)
L 12–2.30 D 6.30–9 L 12–2.30 D 6.30–9
Facilities: Children welcome Garden
Notes: on premises Free House 8

Although the Sandpiper Inn has been a pub for only 30 years, the building is the oldest in Leyburn, dating back to around 1640. It has a beautiful terrace, a bar, snug and dining room, and the menu offers a varied mix of traditional (fish in real ale batter and chips; steaks) and more unusual dishes, which might include apple-smoked black pudding on a garlic mash with a port wine jus; warm goat's cheese on rocket and beetroot salad; and crispy duck leg with fried potatoes and oriental dressing.
Recommended in the area
Wensleydale Railway; Forbidden Corner; Leyburn Model Village

The Sportsmans Arms Hotel

Address: Wath-in-Nidderdale, PATELEY BRIDGE,
Harrogate, HG3 5PP
Tel: 01423 711306
Fax: 01423 712524
Map ref: 7, SE16
Directions: From Harrogate take A61 N, then B6165 W
to Pateley Bridge. Pub is 2m N nr Gouthwaite Reservoir
Open: 12–2 7–11 (closes 10.30 Sun) L 12–2 D 7–9
L 12–2 D 7–9.30 **Facilities:** Garden **Parking:** 30
Notes: Free House 12

This very special pub is in one of the loveliest areas of the Yorkshire Dales. A custom-built kitchen, run by chef/patron Ray Carter for nearly 25 years (now assisted by his son), is the heart of the operation. True to the best pub traditions, real ales and wines accompany dishes served in an informal bar, while daily restaurant menus tempt all comers. Delights include loin of pork with mustard and mushroom sauce; and roast Scottish salmon with spring onions and stem ginger. Round off the meal in style with double chocolate roulade or the ever-popular Sportsman's summer pudding.
Recommended in the area
Fountains Abbey and Studley Royal; Stump Cross Caverns; Brimham Rocks

Fox & Hounds Country Inn

★ ★   75% ® HOTEL

Address: Sinnington, PICKERING, YO62 6SQ
Tel: 01751 431577
Fax: 01751 432791
Email: foxhoundsinn@easynet.co.uk
Website: www.thefoxandhoundsinn.co.uk
Map ref: 8, SE78
Directions: 3m W of Pickering, off A170
Open: 12–2 6–11 (Sun 6–10.30) ͏ L 12–2 D 6.30–9
͏ L 12–2 D 6.30–9 **Rooms:** 10 en suite, S £59 D £80
Facilities: Children welcome Garden **Parking:** 35 **Notes:** ͏ ⊕ Free House ͏ 7

Set in a pretty village with a river running by, and a large green with a small pack-horse bridge, this 18th-century inn offers good drinking, imaginative modern cooking, and well-designed rooms. In the bar, oak beams, wood panelling and an open fire make ideal surroundings for a pint of Black Sheep Special or a glass of house wine. The menus range from sandwiches and light lunches to dishes like pan-seared local lamb cutlets with red cabbage. The rooms are equipped with TV and drinks trays.

Recommended in the area

North Yorkshire Moors Railway; Rievaulx Abbey; Nunnington Hall

Nags Head Country Inn

★ ★   72% HOTEL

Address: PICKHILL, nr Thirsk, YO7 4JG
Tel: 01845 567391
Fax: 01845 567212
Email: enquiries@nagsheadpickhill.freeserve.co.uk
Website: www.nagsheadpickhill.co.uk
Map ref: 8, SE38
Directions: From A1(M) junct 49, continue N on A1 for
4m, then go rt at rdbt for 1m
Open: 11–11 ͏ L 12–2 D 6–9.30 ͏ L 12–2 D 7–9.30
Rooms: 16 en suite, S £50 D £75 **Facilities:** Children welcome Garden **Parking:** 40
Notes: ͏ ⊕ Free House ͏ 8

This 200-year-old establishment, with beamed ceilings, stone-flagged floors and cosy winter fires stands in the village of Pickhill, a perfect spot for exploring Yorkshire's famed 'Herriot Country'. All this exercise will whet your appetite nicely for the likes of Nag's Head hors d'oeuvres platter; roast chump of lamb; and dark chocolate torte with wild cherry ice cream.

Recommended in the area

Yorkshire Dales; Lightwater Valley Theme Park; Falconry Centre

The Carpenters Arms

Address: THIRSK, YO7 2DP
Tel: 01845 537369
Fax: 01845 537889
Website: www.carpentersarmfelixkirk.co.uk
Map ref: 8, SE48
Directions: 2m outside Thirsk on the A170
Open: 11.30–3 6.3–11(Sun 12-8) ᇤ L 12–2 D 7–9 ⵏⵓⵍ
L 12–2 D 7–9 Facilities: Children welcome Parking: 50
Notes: ⊗ on premises ⬚ Free House ⵏ 12

Karen Bumby and her mother, Linda, won't forget 2000: their dog, Lloyd, featured in the Disney film *102 Dalmatians*, and they became the landladies here. Introducing oil lamps, big cushions and soft seating, they renamed the bar the Bistro, adding old carpenters' tools and toy hot-air balloons for good measure. White linen, crystal glasses and stylish furniture formalise the restaurant. Dishes, essentially traditional English/European, are all very attractively arranged. Smoked salmon and Norwegian prawns with lime, dill and pink peppercorn dressing could start a meal, followed by breast of duck, vegetable stir-fry and five spice sauce; or scallop, king prawn, langoustine and bacon tagliatelle.

Recommended in the area

North York Moors National Park; Rievaulx Abbey; Lightwater Valley Theme Park

The Buck Inn

◆◆◆
Address: THORNTON WATLASS, Ripon, HG4 4AH
Tel: 01677 422461
Fax: 01677 422447
Email: inwatlass1@btconnect.com
Website: www.buckwatlass.co.uk
Map ref: 7, SE28
Directions: From A1 at Leeming Bar take A684 to
Bedale, then B6268 towards Masham. Village 2m on rt
Open: 11–11 ᇤ L 12–2 D 6–9.30 ⵏⵓⵍ L 12–2 D

6.30–9.30 Rooms: 7 (5 en suite) S £55 D £75 Facilities: Children welcome Garden Parking: 40
Notes: ⵏ ⬚ Free House ⵏ 7

Margaret and Michael Fox have to refit the occasional tile on the inn, but this is a small price to pay for its idyllic situation on the boundary of the village cricket pitch. Five real ales are served, most from local independent breweries, and the menu offers such specialities as Masham rarebit (Wensleydale cheese with local ale on toast, topped with bacon); deep-fried fresh Whitby cod; and chicken hotpot.

Recommended in the area

Lightwater Valley Theme Park; Theakson Brewery Visitor Centre; Yorkshire Dales National Park

The Wensleydale Heifer Inn

★★ 79% ● HOTEL

Address: WEST WITTON, Wensleydale, DL8 4LS
Tel: 01969 622322
Fax: 01969 624183
Email: info@wensleydaleheifer.co.uk
Website: www.wensleydaleheifer.co.uk
Map ref: 7, SE08
Directions: From the A1 at Leeming Bar, take the A684
W through Leyburn to West Witton; the inn is at the west
end of the village
Open: 11–11 ⓑ L 12–2 D 6–9 ⓘ L 12–2 D 6.30–9 Rooms: 9 en suite, S £90 D £110
Facilities: Garden Parking: 30 Notes: ⬡ Free House ⓦ 7

The 17th-century former coaching inn, with a whitewashed stone exterior, has a sculptured garden
and an attractive area of decking for sitting outside in fine weather. Despite its inland location in the
heart of Wensleydale, fish features strongly on the menus, and the Wensleydale Heifer was the AA's
Seafish Pub of the Year for England 2007. The inn is owned and run by award-winning chef David
Moss and has its own chic restaurant and fish bar. The restaurant offers the ideal setting for a special
occasion meal, with its chocolate brown leather chairs, linen covered tables and original Doug Hyde
pictures. Alternatively, the fish bar and snug are less formal in style, with sea grass flooring, rattan
chairs and wooden tables, perfect for a light meal in relaxing surroundings. If you want to relax in more
comfort with a coffee, a pint or a glass of the finest malt, you can retire to the Whisky Club Lounge,
where an open fire burns in cooler weather. Overnight accommodation is provided in lovely bedrooms
that each have their own individual character. Some rooms have four-poster beds and all are equipped
with fluffy towels, Egyptian cotton sheets and luxurious Molton Brown toiletries. Hot drinks-making
facilities are also provided.

Recommended in the area

Yorkshire Dales National Park; Aysgarth Falls; Wensleydale Railway

Roche Abbey near Maltby.

Huddersfield's Victorian station.

Cubley Hall

Address:	Mortimer Road, Cubley, PENISTONE, S36 9DF
Tel:	01226 766086
Fax:	01226 767335
Email:	cubley.hall@ukonline.co.uk
Website:	www.cubleyhall.co.uk
Map ref:	7, SE20

Directions: From M1 junct 36, take A616 W; just beyond Stocksbridge, turn rt into Mortimer Road
Open: 11–11 ⬟ L 12–9.30 D 12–9.30 ⓧ L 12–9.30
Facilities: Children welcome Garden **Parking:** 100 **Notes:** ⊕ Free House ⓟ 7

Steeped in history, Cubley Hall started out in the 1700s as a farm on a Pennine packhorse route, was later transformed into a gentleman's residence, and then became a children's home. Many original features survive, including the oak-beamed restaurant that was tastefully converted from a barn. The menu offers a choice of pizzas, pastas, chargrills and blackboard specials. Favourites include 'posh fish and chips' and English brisket beef with fondant mash, tarragon carrots and caramelised shallots.

Recommended in the area

Yorkshire Sculpture Park; Millennium Galleries; Peak District National Park

Yorkshire Sculpture Park, West Bretton.

Shibden Mill Inn

♦♦♦♦ ◉

Address: Shibden Mill Fold, HALIFAX, HX3 7UL
Tel: 01422 365840
Fax: 01422 362971
Email: shibdenmillinn@zoom.co.uk
Website: www.shibdenmillinn.com
Map ref: 7, SE02
Directions: From M62 junct 26, take A58 towards Halifax; after 4th sets of traffic lights (junct with A6036), turn immediately right beside Stump Cross Inn into Kell Lane; follow sign left for Shibden Mill Inn

Open: 12–2.30 5.30–11 ▐ L 12–2 D 6–9.30 ▐◯▌ L 12–2 D 6–9.30 **Rooms:** 11 en suite, S £68 D £85 **Facilities:** Children welcome Garden **Parking:** 120 **Notes:** ⊞ Free House ♟ 14

When Simon Heaton purchased the whitewashed, 17th-century Shibden Mill, he made his friend Glen Pearson a business proposition he couldn't refuse: to run a traditional country inn offering excellent beers, wines, food and accommodation, in a warm and welcoming atmosphere, and to a consistently high standard. Glen didn't refuse and he's now general manager. The pub is set in the Shibden valley overlooking Red Beck, which once powered the mill-wheel. It has been sympathetically renovated, and retains all its original charm and character, especially in the cosy, friendly oak-beamed, open-fired bar and intimate candlelit restaurant. A whole team of chefs collude to produce a broad and varied menu, to which the word conventional simply doesn't apply. Starters, for example, might include Nidderdale ham hock with lentils, white stilton and celeriac pudding; or an aubergine, ricotta and saffron tart. Among the main courses are gilt-edge sea bream with baby spinach rösti and laska sauce; pumpkin risotto cakes with a red pepper sauce and pak choi; and wild venison served with red cabbage, apples and roast chestnut sauce.

Recommended in the area

Shibden Hall and Folk Museum; Keighley and Worth Valley Railway; Eureka! The Museum for Children

The Three Acres Inn

Address: SHELLEY,
Huddersfield, HD8 8LR
Tel: 01484 602606
Fax: 01484 608411
Email: 3acres@globalnet.co.uk
Website: www.3acres.com
Map ref: 7, SE21
Directions: From M1 junct 38 follow Huddersfield signs past the Yorkshire Sculpture Park, turn left at rdbt for Denby Dale, then right after approx 0.5m to Emley and continue 0.75m. From junct 39, follow signs Denby Dale; after 2m straight on at rdbt, then right after 0.5m to Emley; continue for 0.75m
Open: 12–3 7–11 (Sat 7–11 only) ⓑ L 12–2 D 7–9.45 ⑩ L 12–2 D 7–9.45 **Facilities:** Children welcome Garden **Parking:** 100 **Notes:** ⊕ Free House ⓨ 9

The Three Acres Inn has been co-owned for well over 30 years by Brian Orme and Neil Truelove, and it has been in Neil's family since his father, Derrick, acquired the business in 1969. The Krug Room offers a private dining facility for up to 20 guests incorporating a Champagne bar listing an extensive range of premier marque Champagnes. In the bar, you can enjoy the 3 Acres Bitter, Tetley's and Black Sheep ales and there's a good selection of wines by the glass. Running your eyes down the menu reveals starters such as 'Bobby Baxter's' famous potted shrimps on home-made toasted granary bread with watercress and lemon; and main courses might include steak, kidney and mushroom pie under a grain mustard shortcrust; steamed game suet pudding; Lunesdale duck; and fennel roast loin of local pork, with a stew of home-made black pudding, haricot blanc, roast tomato and smoked paprika, with apple and green cabbage colcannon. The seafood bar offers a fruits de mer platter and whole fresh lobster among its selections.

Recommended in the area

National Mining Museum for England; Cannon Hall Country Park; Yorkshire Sculpture Park

Ring O'Bells

Address: 212 Hilltop Road, THORNTON,
Bradford, BD13 3QL
Tel: 01274 832296
Fax: 01274 831707
Email: enquiries@theringobells.com
Website: www.theringobells.com
Map ref: 7, SE03
Directions: From M62 take A58 for 5m, turn right
onto A644; 4.5m follow Denholme signs, onto Well
Head Rd into Hilltop Rd
Open: 11.30–3.30 5.30–11 (Sun 12–4.30, 6.15–10.30) 🍴 L 12–2 D 5.30–9.30 🍽 L 12–2
D 7–9.30 **Facilities:** Children welcome **Parking:** 25 **Notes:** 🛢 Free House 🍷 10

Set high on the hills of the Yorkshire Pennines, where dramatic moorland views stretch up to 30 miles
on a clear day, the Ring O'Bells is just minutes from the village of Thornton where the Brontë sisters
were born and where their father was the curate of the local church. The pub is actually a conversion
of a Wesleyan chapel, and the restaurant part was formerly two mill workers' cottages. The old-world
bar serves traditional hand-pulled ales and a decent selection of malt whiskies, speciality liqueurs
and wines by the glass. The Brontë Restaurant has a modern new contemporary look and is fully air-
conditioned, and a conservatory with beautiful valley views runs the whole length of the restaurant. The
Preston family have successfully run the pub for over 15 years and have built up a good reputation for
food service. Locally sourced produce goes into dishes prepared by a team of six professional chefs.
The menu is essentially British with some European influences, and features such starters as smooth
chicken liver and brandy pâté and deep-fried goat's cheese with spinach and sun-blushed tomato
risotto cake. Main courses include traditional roasts, pies and fried fish alongside more exotic choices
like pan-fried tiger prawns topped with sweet Thai caramel on a coconut and lime risotto cake.

Recommended in the area

National Museum of Photography, Film &Television; Keighley & Worth Valley Railway; Brontë Parsonage

The Ridings Shopping Centre, Wakefield.

Kaye Arms Inn & Brasserie

Address: 29 Wakefield Road, Grange Moor,
WAKEFIELD, WF4 4BG
Tel: 01924 848385
Fax: 01924 848977
Map ref: 8, SE32
Directions: On A642 Huddersfield–Wakefield road, east
of its junct with A637 Barnsley road
Open: 11.30–3 7–11 ⓑ/ L/⊚ 12–2 D 7.15–9.30
Parking: 50 **Notes:** ⊞ Free House ⓨ 15

A dining pub run by the same family for more than 35 years, the Kaye Arms Inn and Brasserie stands alone on the Huddersfield to Wakefield road. The bar menu offers open and closed sandwiches, snacks and bistro dishes such as smoked morteau sausages on braised Puy lentils or chicken Basquaise. Offerings from the main menu, which might include roast rump of lamb or grilled sea bass fillet, are supplemented by daily specials. The establishment is a free house serving Scottish Courage, John Smiths, Theakstons Best and Guinness, and the extensive wine list comprehensively roams the world, with 15 wines available by the glass.

Recommended in the area

National Coal Mining Museum for England; Yorkshire Sculpture Park; Oakwell Hall

SCOTLAND

Kilchurn Castle, Loch Awe.

Stonehaven.

The Lairhillock Inn

Address:	NETHERLEY, By Stonehaven,
	ABERDEENSHIRE AB39 3QS
Tel:	01569 730001
Fax:	01569 731175
Email:	lairhillock@breathemail.net
Website:	www.lairhillock.co.uk
Map ref:	10, NO89

Directions: From Aberdeen take A90; go rt on B9077 towards Durris, then left on B979 towards Stonehaven
Open: 11–2 5–11(Fri 11-2 & 5-12, Sat 11-12, Sun 11-11) ᵭ L 12–2 D 6–9.30 ⏹ L 12–1.30 D 7–9.30 Facilities: Garden Parking: 100
Notes: ⚑ ⊘ on premises ⊞ Free House ♇ 7

Only 15 minutes from Aberdeen, this 200-year-old inn offers real ales like Isle of Skye Hebridean Gold in the bar and real fires in the lounge. The bar and restaurant offer robust dishes using fresh, quality local produce. Try the locally smoked salmon with quails' eggs and horseradish crème fraîche to start, followed by venison layered with peppered potatoes, wild mushrooms and a port and thyme jus.
Recommended in the area
Dunnottar Castle; Crathes Castle and Garden; Storybook Glen

Crinan Hotel

Address: CRINAN, ARGYLL & BUTE PA31 8SR
Tel: 01546 830261
Fax: 01546 830292
Email: nryan@crinanhotel.com
Website: www.crinanhotel.com
Map ref: 9, NR79
Directions: From M8, cross Erskine Bridge (M898) to join A82, at Tarbert bear left onto A83 to Lochgilphead, then A816 Oban road. In 2m turn left to Crinan on B841
Open: 11–11 (11–12 May–Oct) ₤ L 12–2.30 D 6–8.30
🍴 D 7–8.30 **Facilities:** Children welcome Garden
Parking: 30 **Notes:** 🐾 ⊘ on premises ⊕ Free House

From its location on the northern end of the Crinan Canal, this establishment enjoys fabulous views across the Sound of Jura to the islands of Mull and Scarba. Though the hotel dates back some 200 years, it was rebuilt by owners Nick Ryan and his wife Frances Macdonald following a major fire in the mid 1970s. They retained many of the original features and all of its charm, restoring it to its rightful place at the heart of this tiny fishing village. The freshest imaginable seafood, landed daily just 50 metres away, is the speciality of the house, whether you eat in the exquisite Westward Restaurant, rent Lock 16 (the roof-level private dining room) or feast in the ground floor Panther's Arms and Mainbrace Bar. If you prefer to sit outside the Mainbrace has an attractive patio overlooking the sea lock, and there is also a secret garden to the rear of the hotel. Frances is a reknowned artist, regularly exhibiting in London and Edinburgh, so of course there are plenty of paintings hung in the hotel. Accommodation is provided in 20 bedrooms over three floors, all with beautiful views and some with private balconies. The hotel has a children's license and children's facilities are available. Dogs are also permitted.

Recommended in the area

Wonderful walks; Sea-fari Adventures; Kilmartin Museum; Dunadd Fort

Cairnbaan Hotel & Restaurant

★★★ 80% ❀ HOTEL

Address: Cairnbaan, LOCHGILPHEAD,
ARGYLL & BUTE PA31 8SJ

Tel: 01546 603668

Fax: 01546 606045

Email: info@cairnbaan.com

Website: www.cairnbaan.com

Map ref: 9, NR88

Directions: From M8, cross Erskine Bridge (M898) to
join A82, at Tarbert bear left onto A83 to Lochgilphead,
take A816 N for 2m; hotel is off B841

Open: 11–11 ᴸᴮ L 12–2.30 D 6–9.30 ᴵᴼᴵ D 6–9.30 **Rooms:** 12 en suite, S £72.5 D £92.5
Facilities: Children welcome Garden **Parking:** 50 **Notes:** ⊗ on premises ⊞ Free House ♈ 8

The Cairnbaan Hotel is owned by ex-*Queen Elizabeth II* catering officer Darren Dobson and his wife
Christine, who plans the menus and does all the baking. It has a long history of providing hospitality for
fishermen trading on the Crinan Canal, and has adapted perfectly to the waterway's current role, which
is almost entirely geared to the leisure industry. It has even played host to the likes of Bill and Hilary
Clinton and The Princess Royal. You too can enjoy a meal in the serene restaurant, where the carte
specialises in the use of fresh local produce, notably seafood and game. On the menu, look out for the
smoked salmon and smoked trout pâté starters, and for mains including pan-fried breast of pheasant
on sautéed cabbage and bacon with plum and sage glaze; lobster, either served thermidor or cold with
mayonnaise; fillet of halibut with pink peppercorns and lemon hollandaise; and Cairnbaan fish and
seafood stew with a home-made garlic baguette. Daily specials might include loin of tuna with pesto
sauce; wild mushroom Stroganoff; or tenderloin of pork in sweet ginger. Lighter meals in the lounge
bar and conservatory include the very tasty chicken stuffed with haggis.

Recommended in the area

Dunadd Fort; Carnasserie Castle; Kilmory Woodland Park

The Pierhouse Hotel & Seafood Restaurant

Address: PORT APPIN, ARGYLL & BUTE PA38 4DE
Tel: 01631 730302
Fax: 01631 730400
Email: reservations@pierhousehotel.co.uk
Website: www.pierhousehotel.co.uk
Map ref: 9, NM94
Directions: From the A85 Lochawe–Oban road, go N on
A828 towards Ballachulish; turn left just beyond Appin
Open: 11.30–11.30 (Sun 12–11.30) ⓑ L 12.30–2.30

D 6.30–9.30 ⓘ L 12.30–2.30 D 6.30–9.30 **Facilities:** Children welcome Garden **Parking:** 20
Notes: ⌗ ⊕ Free House

A spectacular setting on Loch Linnhe with stunning views over the island of Lismore and the Morvern
Hills makes The Pierhouse an unforgettable dining destination. It also happens to be one of the finest
seafood restaurants in the country, the AA Scottish Seafish Pub of the Year 2007. A narrow road from
Appin leads to the hotel, originally home to the pier master, and the tiny Lismore ferry, but you can
also arrive by sea, securing one of 10 private moorings in the harbour. Fish, including scallops, lobster,
hand-picked Lismore oysters, Loch Etive mussels and langoustines, and Inverawe salmon, is caught
fresh from local waters, and one of the many irresistible dishes is the enormous Pierhouse Platter.
Other house specialities are Pierhouse salmon cakes and delicious seafood pasta. Alternatives include
chicken fajita, beef stroganoff and vegetable bake. The restaurant also has an excellent cellar of
interesting wines, while the real ales on offer include Calders Cream, Calder 70/- and Belhaven Best.
There are also 12 en suite bedrooms, including two four-poster rooms and three rooms suitable for
families. All have TVs, direct dial telephones, Wi-fi internet hotspots and tea- and coffee-making facilities.
Recommended in the area
Scottish Sea Life Sanctuary; Dunstaffnage Castle; Bonawe Iron Furnace; Glencoe

Creggans Inn

★★★   72% ◎ HOTEL

Address: STRACHUR, ARGYLL & BUTE PA27 8BX
Tel: 01369 860279
Fax: 01369 860637
Email: info@creggans-inn.co.uk
Website: www.creggans-inn.co.uk
Map ref: 9, NN00
Directions: A82 from Glasgow, at Tarbet take A83 to
Cairndow, then A815 down coast to Strachur
Open: 11–11 ᴌ L 12–2.45 D 6–8.45 ⊚ D 7–9
Rooms: 14 en suite **Facilities:** Children welcome Garden **Parking:** 36 **Notes:** ⊘ on premises
⊕ Free House ♥ 7

Wonderful views are afforded from this small country hotel situated on the very edge of Loch Fyne, and from the hills that stand above it you can gaze across the Mull of Kintyre to the Western Isles beyond. Lunches and suppers are on offer in the bar, ranging from a simple sandwich to the chef's interesting daily specials, and include favourites like cullen skink. To make the most of the splendid vistas, the restaurant has five big picture windows overlooking the garden and the loch beyond, and there's also a baby grand piano here, for anyone with a mind (and the ability) to play. Flowers from the garden decorate the tables in summer, and in winter there are cosy log fires and candles. Loch Fyne mussels and oysters are a feature of the menus, along with other local seafood, fish and game. There is also a good choice of Scottish real ales, an enthusiast's wine list, and various Argyll malt whiskies with a range of characteristics. The Creggans was originally a coaching inn, dating from Mary, Queen of Scot's day, and now offers individually furnished bedrooms, including a suite with a separate sitting room. Standard and larger superior rooms are available. In addition to the car parking, there are two moorings for guests' boats.

Recommended in the area

Auchindrain Museum; Inveraray Castle; Crarae Gardens

The Bridge Inn

Address: 27 Baird Road, RATHO, Edinburgh,
EDINBURGH, CITY OF EH28 8RA
Tel: 0131 3331320
Fax: 0131 333 3480
Email: info@bridgeinn.com
Map ref: 10, NT17
Directions: From M8 junct 2 (Newbridge), take B7030
S and follow signs for Ratho
Open: 12–11 (Sat 11–12, Sun 12.30–11) 🍺 L 12–9
D 12–9 🍽 L 12–2.30 D 6.30–9 **Facilities:** Children

welcome Garden **Parking:** 40 **Notes:** ⊘ on premises 🍺 Free House 🍷 6

The Bridge Inn at Ratho offers all-day bar food in the lounge overlooking the canal, or more formal
dining in the waterways-themed restaurant. Typical dishes include pan-fried chicken breast stuffed
with haggis, served with a creamy Drambuie sauce; poached smoked haddock and salmon with prawn
sauce; casserole of Highland venison, cooked in whisky and port sauce; and pappardelle pasta with
spring onion sauce.
Recommended in the area
Suntrap Garden; Almondell & Calderwood Country Park; Malleny (NTS)

Ubiquitous Chip

🏵🏵

Address: 12 Ashton Lane, GLASGOW,
GLASGOW, CITY OF G12 8SJ
Tel: 0141 334 5007
Fax: 0141 337 1302
Email: mail@ubiquitouschip.co.uk
Website: www.ubiquitouschip.co.uk
Map ref: 9, NS56
Directions: In the west end of Glasgow, off Byres Road
Open: 11–12 (12.30–12 Sun) 🍺 L 12–4 D 4–11

🍽 L 12–2.30 D 5.30–11 **Facilities:** Children welcome **Notes:** 🍺 Free House 🍷 21

The Chip has been a Glasgow institution for more than 35 years. The main restaurant is a glass
covered mews with cobbled floors,water fountains and a plethora of plants. Traditional draught beers
(Deuchars IPA and their own specially brewed Chip 71), over 150 malt whiskies and first class wines
by the glass are served from 3 separate bars each with its own particular ambience.The food has two
AA Rosettes and offers a contemporary slant on traditional Scottish cooking.
Recommended in the area
Hunterian Museum and Art Gallery; McLellan Galleries; Glasgow School of Art

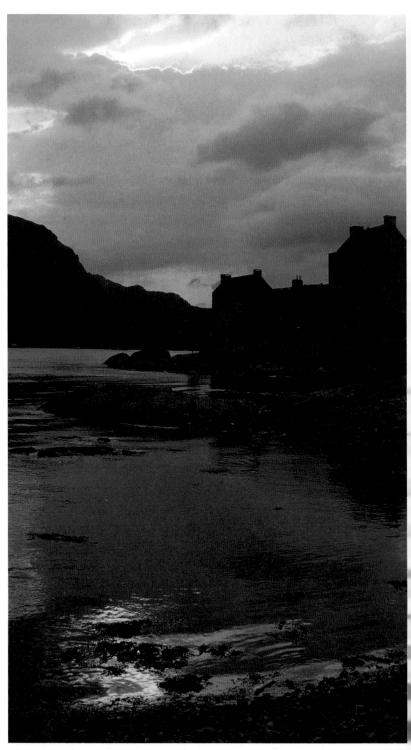

An autumn evening casts a golden glow over Eilean Donan Castle on Loch Duich.

The Unicorn

Address: 15 Excise Street, KINCARDINE, Alloa,
          FIFE FK10 4LN
Tel: 01259 739129
Email: info@theunicorn.co.uk
Website: www.theunicorn.co.uk
Map ref: 10, NS98

Directions: Exit M9 at Kincardine bridge, turn off across the bridge then bear left. Take 1st left then second left
Open: 12–2 5.30–12 🍺 L 12–2 D 5.30–9 🍽 D 7–9
Facilities: Children welcome **Parking:** 4 **Notes:** 🍷 8

A family-run business, the Unicorn aims to offer an unforgettable dining experience in an imaginatively refurbished 17th-century inn. There is a comfortable lounge bar, a grill room, and a more formal dining room upstairs, reserved for weekends and private functions. The modern décor and leather sofas are attractive, and there is a coal fire. Where possible, the food is locally sourced; seafood is a speciality and beef comes from the Buccleuch estate. There is also a good choice of coffees, malts and ales. Children's facilities are provided.

Recommended in the area

Falkirk Wheel; Culross Palace, Town House & The Study; Stirling Castle

Applecross Inn

Address: Shore Street, APPLECROSS, Wester Ross,
          HIGHLAND IV54 8LR
Tel: 01520 744262
Fax: 01520 744400
Email: applecrossinn@globalnet.co.uk
Website: www.applecross.uk.com
Map ref: 11, NG74

Directions: From A87 Skye rd, take A890, then A896 to Kishorn; turn left on unclassifed rd over 'Bealach Na Ba'
Open: 11–11 (Sun 12.30–11) 🍺 L 12–9 🍽 D 6–9
Facilities: Children welcome Garden **Parking:** 30 **Notes:** 🐾 ⊗ on premises 🍺 Free House 🍷 6

To reach this white-painted inn on its sandy cove, you must drive over Britain's highest mountain pass at Bealach Na Ba. The setting is lovely, facing Skye and the Cuillins, and there's a garden with tables right on the beach. The refurbished interior is full of Highland character and bedrooms have superb sea views. Enjoy Isle of Skye Cask Ales and your pick of 50 malt whiskies in the bar, plus bar food prepared from top quality local produce, notably fish.

Recommended in the area

Applecross Heritage Centre, Torridon Countryside Centre (NTS); Beinn Eighe Nature Reserve

Cawdor Castle.

Cawdor Tavern

Address: The Lane, CAWDOR, HIGHLAND IV12 5XP
Tel/fax: 01667 404777
Email: cawdortavern@btopenworld.com
Map ref: 12, NH85
Directions: From Inverness, take A96 Aberdeen rd; past airport, turn rt on B9006, then follow Cawdor Castle signs.
Open: 11–3 5–11 (May–Oct 11–11) ⅃ L 12–2
D 5.30–9 ⎰⎱ L 12–2 D 6.30–9 **Facilities:** Garden
Parking: 60 **Notes:** ⛺ 🍺 Free House 🍷 8

The Tavern is at the heart of a beautiful conservation village, close to the famous castle built by the Thane of Cawdor in 1375, and was formerly a joinery workshop for the Cawdor Estate. The handsome oak panelling in the lounge bar came from the castle and was a gift from the late laird. Roaring log fires keep the place cosy on long winter nights, while in the summer guests can sit out on the patio area at the front. The same menu is offered throughout, and options include prime meats, fresh local seafood, game and vegetarian specialities, complemented by a hand-picked wine list. Aficionados will also appreciate the cask and bottled real ales from the Tavern's own brewery and the range of malts.

Recommended in the area

Cawdor Castle; Fort George; Culloden Battlefield

The Plockton Hotel

★★ 76% HOTEL

Address: Harbour Street, PLOCKTON, HIGHLAND IV52 8TN
Tel: 01599 544274
Fax: 01599 544475
Email: info@plocktonhotel.co.uk
Website: www.plocktonhotel.co.uk
Map ref: 11, NG83
Directions: From A87 Kyle of Lochalsh/Skye road, turn northward at Balmacara and continue for 7m to Plockton
Open: 11–11.45 (Sun 12.30–11) ♨ L 12–2.15 D 6–9.15 ▮⊘▮ L 12–2.15 D 6–9.15
Rooms: 15 en suite, S £55 D £90 **Facilities:** Children welcome Garden **Notes:** ⊕ Free House

How's this for an unexpected sight: palm trees in the Northwest Highlands of Scotland. Incredible though it may be to anyone unaware of the warming effect the Gulf Stream up here, there they are, growing happily between the Plockton Hotel and the shores of Loch Carron. Rather distinctively, the hotel is painted in black pitch and pointed in white, which is the traditional way of weatherproofing coastal buildings, and it has stunning views across the bay to the old castle. Not surprisingly, seafood is something of a speciality here, and guests can eat prawns from the loch moments after they have been landed. The menu might also offer the freshest pan-fried herring in oatmeal; fillets of sole with a herb crust; grilled halibut with a ginger glaze; loch-caught wild salmon, poached with lime leaves and whole peppercorns, and served with a fresh lime and crème frâiche dressing; and monkfish and smoked bacon brochettes – a heavenly combination. Meat is served too, of course, including the most succulent locally-reared beef and lamb, and casseroled Highland venison. Mouthwatering home-made desserts and an excellent wine list ensure a meal that is as memorable as the setting and the unusual vegetation along the shore.

Recommended in the area

Eilean Donan Castle; Broadford Reptile Centre; Seal watching by boat

Plockton Inn & Seafood Restaurant

Address: Innes Street, PLOCKTON,
HIGHLAND IV52 8TW
Tel: 01599 544222
Fax: 01599 544487
Email: info@plocktoninn.co.uk
Website: www.plocktoninn.co.uk
Map ref: 11, NG83
Directions: From A87 Kyle of Lochalsh/Skye road, turn
northward at Balmacara and continue for 7m to Plockton
Open: 11–1am (Sun 12.30–11pm) 🍺 L 12–2.30 D 5.30–9.30 🍽 L 12–2.30 D 5.30–9.30
Facilities: Children welcome Garden **Parking:** 10 **Notes:** 🐾 ⊗ on premises ⊕ Free House

The location of this inn is ideal, in one of Scotland's most beautiful fishing villages, just 100 metres
from the harbour – a great base from which to explore the Isle of Skye and the Torridon mountains.
Popular with locals and tourists alike, the inn has regular music nights in the bar, and in winter a pub
quiz on Fridays, making for a lively atmosphere. When the season demands, fires are lit in both bars
making it the perfect place to come in from the cold. A good choice of real ales is offered, plus more
than 50 malt whiskies. There are two eating areas inside, the Dining Room and Lounge Bar, plus
an area laid with decking outside. Fresh West Coast fish and shellfish are the speciality of the house,
delivered directly to the restaurant door by the fishermen, though the meat alternatives are also worthy
of consideration: best West Highland beef, game, lamb and locally grown produce. Some of the 14
bedrooms have lovely sea views, 13 are en suite, and all have the usual home comforts. There are two
gardens with sloping lawns and trees. Children's facilities are available and the inn has a children's
license. Dogs are also allowed.

Recommended in the area

Eilean Donan Castle; Lochalsh Woodlands (NTS); Strome Castle (NTS)

Shieldaig Bar

Address: SHIELDAIG, HIGHLAND IV54 8XN
Tel: 01520 755251
Fax: 01520 755321
Email: tighaneileanhotel@shieldaig.fsnet.co.uk
Map ref: 11, NG85
Directions: From A87 Skye rd, take A890, then turn off A896 to Kishorn; continue N towards Torridon, then turn left on to village road signed Shieldaig; bar on the Loch front
Open: 11–11 ⬛ L 12–8.30 **Facilities:** Children welcome
Parking: 12 **Notes:** ⊘ on premises ⬛ Free House ♟ 12

The welcome here is friendly and the views across Loch Torridon to the sea beyond are just stunning. Inland the mountains and lakes of Wester Ross stretch east and north, providing a glorious backdrop for this coastal community. The bar is a lively meeting point for that community, too, and on a summer Friday night the bar is likely to be alive with the sound of local musicians. Owner Chris Field will be in the thick of things, playing guitar, banjo and pipes. Throughout the day a full range of both alcoholic and non-alcoholic beverages is served to suit the hour, and there's a ready supply of newspapers and magazines to settle down and read. The pub has a fine reputation for its bar snacks, such as home-made soups, sandwiches and salads, and for its daily-changing specials, which might include a fresh crab bisque; local seafood stew; and Hebridean scallop mornay. In addition to the fish specialities, there might be venison, hare and other game in season; steak and ale pie; Tuscan-style leek tart with home-made bread; and haggis, neeps and tatties. Vegetarians can look forward to such dishes as feta, olive and vine tomato frittata, with a side salad and home-baked walnut bread. A good range of real ales – Isle of Skye Brewery, Black Isle and Tenants Superior – will please lovers of the hop. It's the sort of place you'll want to linger, so take note that the Fields also own the Tigh an Eilean hotel next door.

Recommended in the area

Torridon Visitor Centre (NTS); Beinn Eighe Nature Reserve; Applecross Countryside Centre

Killiecrankie House Hotel

Address:	KILLIECRANKIE, Nr Pitlochry,
	PERTH & KINROSS PH16 5LG
Tel:	01796 473220
Fax:	01796 472451
Email:	enquiries@killiecrankiehotel.co.uk
Website:	www.killiecrankiehotel.co.uk
Map ref:	10, NN96

Directions: Take B8079 N out of Pitlochry for 3m; hotel is just after National Trust for Scotland Visitor Centre

Open: 12–2.30 6–11 ⓑ L 12.30–2 D 6.30–9 ⓘ D 7–8.30 **Facilities:** Children welcome Garden **Parking:** 20 **Notes:** ⌗ ⊘ on premises ⊞ Free House ⌘ 8

This long-established hotel is set in four acres of neat grounds overlooking Killiecrankie Pass, a deep river gorge formed by the River Garry cutting its way through the surrounding granite hills, and there are fabulous views. Delightful gardens include lawns, a rose garden, herbaceous border and woodland. Built as a private residence in 1840, the house was converted in 1939 and stands near the site of the Battle of Killiecrankie and the intriguingly named Soldier's Leap. A National Trust for Scotland Visitor Centre nearby is dedicated to the area's interesting history and rich wildlife. Locals and visitors alike frequent the panelled bar and the snug to enjoy real ales, a great range of Scottish malts and fine wines available by the glass. The menu draws on the finest of local produce, including vegetables, fruits and herbs from the garden, and the restaurant has two AA Rosettes. Food is served in the bar, the elegant dining room and the conservatory, and might include game casserole with mashed potato and fresh vegetables, or roast fillet of monkfish wrapped in Parma ham. There is also a notable wine list. Ten individually decorated en suite bedrooms are offered and equipped with televisions, radios, direct dial telephones, hairdryers, tea- and coffee-making facilities and shoe cleaning materials.

Recommended in the area

Queen's View Visitor Centre; Blair Castle; Scottish Hydro Electric Visitor Centre

Moulin Hotel

Address: 11–13 Kirkmichael Road, Moulin,
PITLOCHRY, PERTH & KINROSS PH16 5EH
Tel: 01796 472196
Fax: 01796 474098
Email: enquiries@moulinhotel.co.uk
Website: www.moulinhotel.co.uk
Map ref: 10, NN95
Directions: From A9, turn off onto A924 into Pitlochry
(Atholl Road), then take West Moulin Road (also A924) to
reach Moulin in 0.75m
Open: 12–11 (Fri–Sat 12–11.45) 🍴 L 12–9.30 D 12–9.30 🍴 D 6–9 **Facilities:** Children welcome
Garden **Parking:** 40 **Notes:** ⊘ on premises 🛢 Free House ♟ 20

Owners Chris and Heather Tomlinson race ocean-going yachts in whatever spare time running the
hotel permits, and in 2004 they took part in the Atlantic Rally for Cruisers as entrants of the only craft
sponsored by two breweries – Stella Artois and their own Moulin brewery. Their hotel lies at the heart
of a small conservation village on the edge of the Tay Forest Park, below 841m Ben Vrackie, and has
a long history. In fact, by the time of the Jacobite rebellion of 1745, it had been up and running for
half a century. You'd have to search a wide area to find a better example of a traditional Scottish pub,
especially one that brews its own beers. It has a pretty courtyard garden for summer use, and blazing
log fires for the winter. The Moulin micro-brewery produces Braveheart, named during the filming of
Mel Gibson's film, and three other real ales. It's the Braveheart that gives the local venison dishes their
extra flavour. A typical menu might include a starter such as Tombuie smoked lamb; fillet of haddock
for the main course; and a deliciously wicked chocolate fudge cake. Vegetarians are sure to warm
to such offerings as sautéed mushroom pancakes; stuffed peppers; and vegetable goulash. Meals,
prepared by a French chef, can be enjoyed in the pub or the more formal Garden Restaurant.
Recommended in the area
Scottish Hydro Electric Visitor Centre; Edradour Distillery; Pass of Killiecrankie

The Black Bull Hotel

◆◆◆◆

Address:	Market Place, LAUDER,
	SCOTTISH BORDERS TD2 6SR
Tel:	01578 722208
Fax:	01578 722419
Email:	enquiries@blackbull-lauder.com
Website:	www.blackbull-lauder.com
Map ref:	10, NT54

Directions: Lauder is on the A68, 28m SE of Edinburgh; hotel is on main road, in the Market Place in town centre

Open: 12–2.30 5–9 (winter 12–2, 5.30–9) ♿ L 12–2.30 D 5–9 **Rooms:** 8 en suite, S £50 D £80 **Facilities:** Children welcome **Parking:** 10 **Notes:** ✝ ⊘ on premises ⊞ Free House ♟ 16

A handsome white-painted former coaching inn, the Black Bull stands three storeys high and dates from 1750. It is run by proprietors Tony and Maureen Rennie, with Maureen as head chef, and they have restored the building to create a cosy haven in the heart of the Borders, just 20 minutes' drive from Edinburgh. The interior is full of character with lots of interesting pictures and artefacts. The large dining room used to be a chapel and the church spire remains in the roof. Food is also served in the Harness Room Bar or the cosy lounge. The same seasonal menu is served throughout, specialising in quality country fare prepared from locally grown produce where possible. Aberdeen Angus beef and Texel lamb from Wedderlie Farm features regularly. Additional dishes are also offered from the specials board, and there's an interesting choice of wines and Broughton Ales. The hotel is a recent recipient of the coveted AA Pub of the Year for Scotland award. The accommodation is beautiful, and includes three bedrooms that are suitable for family occupation. All have hairdryers, TV, telephone, Internet access, luxurious Gilchrist and Soames toiletries, and tea- and coffee-making facilities. Decorated in period style, the rooms have modern baths and/or showers.

Recommended in the area

Thirlstone Castle; Mellerstain House; Melrose Abbey

Linlithgow Palace.

Champany Inn

Address: Champany, LINLITHGOW,
WEST LOTHIAN EH49 7LU
Tel: 01506 834532
Fax: 01506 834302
Email: reception@champany.com
Website: www.champany.com
Map ref: 10, NS97
Directions: N off M9 junct 3; at Champany turn rt A904
Open: 12–2 6.30–10 (all day Fri–Sun) L 12–2 D
6.30–10 L 12.30–2 D 7–10 Facilities: Children welcome Garden Parking: 50
Notes: on premises Free House

Under the ownership of well-known restaurateurs Anne and Clive Davidson for more than 20 years, the inn is renowned for the sourcing, handling and cooking of prime Scottish beef – it has been described as the 'Rolls Royce of steak restaurants'. Menus offer several choices of Aberdeen Angus steaks and a range of Angus steak burgers, plus Scottish lamb, home-made sausages and chargrilled chicken.

Recommended in the area
Linlithgow Palace; Blackness Castle; House of the Binns (NTS)

WALES

Caernarfon Castle and the River Seiont.

Mermaid Quay, Cardiff Bay.

Caesars Arms

Address: Cardiff Road, CREIGIAU, CARDIFF CF15 9NN
Tel: 029 2089 0486
Fax: 029 2089 2176
Email: caesarsarms@btconnect.com
Map ref: 2, ST08
Directions: 1m from M4 junct 34; take A4119 N, right at Castell Mynach pub, thru Groesfaen & left signed Creigiau
Open: 12–2.30 6–10.30 (Sun 12–4) 🍴/🍽️ L 12–2.30 D 6–10.30 **Facilities:** Children welcome Garden
Parking: 100 **Notes:** ⊕ Free House

Some ten miles out of Cardiff, and tucked away down winding lanes, the Caesars Arms attracts a well-heeled clientele to its heated patio and terrace overlooking countryside. The inn prides itself on its selection of fresh fish and seafood, displayed in shaven-ice display cabinets before being turned into starters like Bajan fish cakes; crispy laver balls; or crayfish cocktail, and main courses such as hake, salmon or monkfish; Dover sole, crawfish tails and lobster are priced by weight. Meat includes Welsh beef steaks, honeyed crispy duck and roast Welsh lamb, and there's a help-yourself salad counter.

Recommended in the area

St Fagans: National History Museum; Castell Coch; Llandaff Cathedral

The Groes Inn

★ ★ ★ 78% ◉ HOTEL

Address:	CONWY, CONWY LL32 8TN
Tel:	01492 650545
Fax:	01492 650855
Email:	thegroesinn@btinternet.com
Website:	www.groesinn.com
Map ref:	5, SH77

Directions: Take A55 to Conwy; at mini rdbt by Conwy Castle go S on B5106, inn is 2.5m on right.

Open: 12–3 6.30–11 ⓛ L 12–2.15 D 6.30–9

🍽 L 12–2.15 D 6.30–9 Rooms: 14 en suite S £79 D £95 Facilities: Garden Parking: 90

Notes: ⊕ Free House 🍷 10

Built in the 15th century as a small two-storey dwelling, this was the first licensed house in Wales, established as an inn in 1573. The location is stunning, with a panorama over the River Conwy and the surrounding hills from the front, and slopes rising towards Snowdonia at the rear. For centuries the inn has maintained a tradition of welcoming travellers, and today it makes a great base for exploring the mountains, coastline, castles and gardens of North Wales. Rambling rooms with beamed ceilings and antique settles are jauntily decorated with stone cats, military hats, saucy Victorian postcards and old advertisements. The elegant Gallery Suite, comprising the Library and the Wellington Room, provides a perfect setting for a special occasion. Traditional British and Welsh dishes are prepared from quality ingredients – Welsh salt marsh lamb, Conwy crab and local game – and you can enjoy it in the bar, restaurant, conservatory, or outside in the garden, with its lovely views of the river and Snowdonia. Accommodation is available at The Groes all year round. The bedrooms are spacious, with sitting areas, televisions, radios, direct dial telephones, hairdryers and hospitality trays. Each of the rooms has its own distinctive style, and some have the added attraction of a private terrace or balcony.

Recommended in the area

Snowdonia; Bodnant Gardens; Conwy Castle

The Kinmel Arms

Address: ST GEORGE, Nr Abergele, CONWY LL22 9BP
Tel: 01745 832207
Fax: 01745 822044
Email: info@thekinmelarms.co.uk
Website: www.thekinmelarms.co.uk
Map ref: 5, SH97
Directions: Off A55 St Asaph–Abergele road junct 24A;
take slip road, then 1st left; pub is on left at top of hill
Open: 12–3 6.30–11 (Sun 12–5; BH wknds all day Sun
and Mon) ⅃ L 12–2 D 7–9.30 ⅃○⅃ L 12–2 D 7–9.30
Rooms: 4 en suite D £135 Facilities: Garden
Parking: 60 Notes: ⊘ on premises ⊞ Free House ⅃ 19

Despite its neo-Elizabethan appearance, the Kinmel Arms
dates from the last decade of the Victorian era. Nestling in
the foothills of the stunning Elwy Valley, the rural free house is handy for the coast, mountains and
valleys of North Wales. The building, stylishly renovated by owners Lynn and Tim Watson, features their
own mountain photography. Cask ales are a passion, with weekly changing guests and two regulars,
and there is an extensive wine list. The tempting seasonal menus range from sandwiches and light
lunches to a selection of more adventurous dishes and daily specials, with an emphasis on local fish,
meat and game. There's regular live music here, too. Accommodation is provided in individually styled
luxurious suites on two floors, with natural materials used to great effect. Particularly worthy of note
are the hand-made king-size beds in oak and maple, Welsh green oak balconies, and bathrooms with
Spanish limestone and Indian quartzite floors and walls. The rooms are handsomely furnished and are
equipped with tea-, coffee- and breakfast-making facilities, broadband, LCD TV and DVD, hairdryers,
fridges and ironing facilities. There is a small walled garden with trees and an area of decking.

Recommended in the area

Bodelwyddon Castle; Conwy Castle; Bodnant Gardens

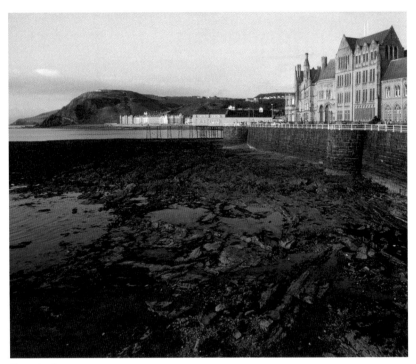

Aberystwyth.

Penhelig Arms

★★ 82% ⦿ SMALL HOTEL

Address:	Terrace Road, ABERDYFI,
	GWYNEDD LL35 0LT
Tel:	01654 767215
Fax:	01654 767690
Email:	info@penheligarms.com
Website:	www.penheligarms.com
Map ref:	2, SN69
Directions:	On A493 W of Machynlleth

Open: 11.30–3.30 5.30–11 (Sun 12–3.30, 6–10.30) ▣
L 12–2.30 D 6.30–9.30 ▣ L 12–2.30
D 7–9.30 **Rooms:** 16 en suite S £49 D £78 **Facilities:** Children welcome Garden **Parking:** 12
Notes: ⌁ ⊕ Free House ⚱ 30

The inn, built in 1870, offers spectacular views over the tidal Dyfi estuary, real ales, 24 malt whiskies and a fabulous choice of some 300 wines, including 30 by the glass. The menu is strong on fresh fish, crab and lobster arriving straight from the quay, and might include plaice grilled with a parmesan crust.

Recommended in the area

Centre for Alternative Technology; Tal-y-Llyn Railway; Celtica

The Brigands Inn

◆◆◆◆

Address: MALLWYD, GWYNEDD SY20 9HJ
Tel: 01650 511999
Fax: 01650 531208
Website: www.brigandsinn.com
Map ref: 2, SH81
Directions: From Dolgellau, take A470 east for 11m; Mallwyd is at junct with A458. From Machynlleth, take A489 E for 5m, at rdbt take A470 N for 6m
Open: 10am–11pm 🍴 L 12–2.30 D 6–9 🍽 L 12–2.30 D 6–9 **Rooms:** 11 en suite S £50 D £80 **Facilities:** Children welcome Garden **Parking:** 80 **Notes:** ⊕

In the heart of the Cambrian Mountains, on the upper banks of the River Dovey, lies the Brigand's Inn, the AA Pub of Year for Wales 2006–7. A renowned 15th-century coaching inn, it was once the haunt of the Gwylliaid Cochion Mawddwy (Red Bandits). The impressive setting makes it a popular base for exploring this spectacularly scenic corner of Wales. Fly-fishing is popular here, as is walking, and one well-worn route leads up the Camlan Mountain to inspect the reputed site of King Arthur's last battle. Alternatively, or afterwards, opt for a glass of wine in the pub's large landscaped garden. Inside, there is a bar, a cosy snug and a residents' dining room, as well as facilities for private functions. The chef sources the finest local produce to create a fusion of contemporary and classic Welsh cuisine. Menus reflect the changing seasons, with a good selection of fish, meat and game, and might include grilled fillet of sea bass with sun-dried tomato and pesto; grilled sirloin steak with onions, mushrooms and tomato; and loin of venison on caramelised red onions with a port and juniper sauce. The bedrooms include doubles, twins and a family room. All are spacious and full of character, with oak furniture, televisions, telephones and internet access, plus fresh cafetière coffee and mineral water. Four-poster and half-tester beds – and even a slipper bath – are available in the deluxe rooms.

Recommended in the area

King Arthur's Labyrinth; Centre for Alternative Technology; Cymer Abbey

Beaumaris Castle.

Ye Olde Bulls Head Inn

★ ★   83% ◉ ◉   HOTEL

Address:	Castle Street, BEAUMARIS,
	ISLE OF ANGLESEY LL58 8AP
Tel:	01248 810329
Fax:	01248 811294
Email:	info@bullsheadinn.co.uk
Website:	www.bullsheadinn.co.uk
Map ref:	5, SH67

Directions: Town centre, on A545 from Britannia Bridge

Open: 11–11 (Sun 12–10.30) ♿ L 12–2 D 7–9 ⓘ D

7–9 **Rooms:** 13, S £75 D £98.5 **Facilities:** Children welcome **Parking:** 10 **Notes:** ⊞ Free House ♟ 16

A short walk from the castle, this historic watering hole dates back to 1472. There's a traditional bar leading to the popular brasserie where light lunches can be enjoyed. In the evening, mount the ancient staircase to the smartly decorated restaurant, where you might start with carpaccio of Welsh beef with pickled walnuts and hazelnut oil, or the sea trout terrine with caper mayonnaise. Main courses might include grilled line-caught local sea bass with a Conwy mussel ravioli, or Hereford duck breast.

Recommended in the area

Beaumaris Castle; Plas Newydd; Din Llugwy Ancient Village

Fishing boats moored at Porthcawl.

The Greyhound Inn

Address:	LLANTRISANT, Usk, MONMOUTHSHIRE NP15 1LE
Tel:	01291 672505
Fax:	01291 673255
Email:	enquiry@greyhound-inn.com
Website:	www.greyhound-inn.com
Map ref:	2, ST39

Directions: From M4 junct 24 take A449 Monmouth rd; at 1st junct take A472 to Usk, left onto Usk Sq, then 2nd left signed Llantrisant; 2.5m to inn

Open: 11–11 (Sun 12–4, 7–11) 🍽 L 12–2.15 D 6–10 🍽 L 12–2.15 D 6–10.30 **Rooms:** 10 en suite S £54 D £74 **Facilities:** Children welcome Garden **Parking:** 60 **Notes:** ⊕ Free House ♀ 10

Built in the 17th century as a Welsh longhouse and becoming an inn in 1845, The Greyhound has been run by the same family for over 20 years and its beautiful gardens have won awards. Visitors will find a good range of home-made dishes such as steak and kidney pie; medium-fruity chicken curry; chilli con carne; lasagne verde; and various fresh fish dishes. Vegetarians also have a good choice.

Recommended in the area

Chepstow Castle; Caerleon and Caerwent Roman sites; Tintern Abbey

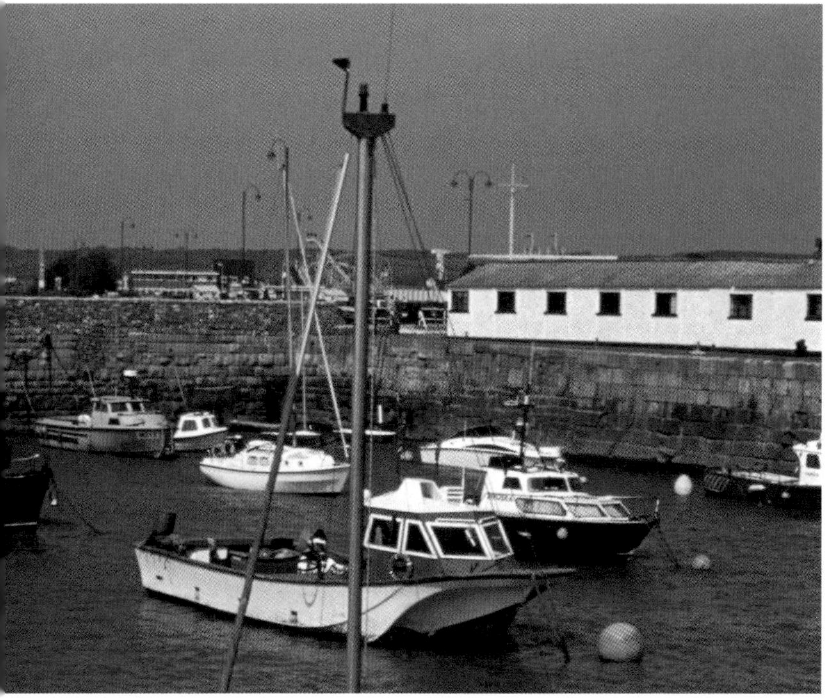

The Beaufort Arms

★★ 75% HOTEL

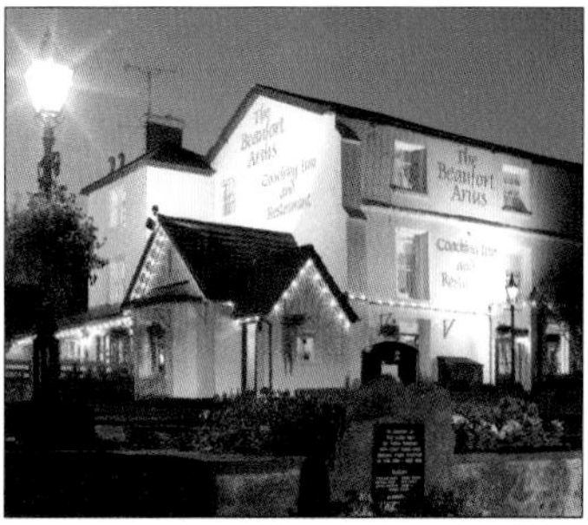

Address: High St, RAGLAN, Monmouthshire NP15 2DY
Tel: 01291 690412
Fax: 01291 690935
Email: enquiries@beaufortraglan.co.uk
Website: www.beaufortraglan.co.uk
Map ref: 2, SO40
Directions: 0.5m from junct A449/A40 Abergaveny, Monmouth. 1/4 hr from M4 junct 24
Open: 7–11 (Sat 8–11, Sun 8–10.30) and L 12–3 D 6–9 **Rooms:** 15 en suite S £55 D £65 **Facilities:** Garden Private dining room Function suite **Parking:** 30 **Notes:** Free House 12

This atmospheric inn has been at the heart of village life since the 15th century, and Parliamentarian soldiers used it during the Siege of Raglan Castle in 1646. Beautifully refurbished, it still resonates with history and legend, with log fires in winter and a garden with a south-facing terrace for summer. In the bars and stylish brasserie, traditional dishes sit comfortably alongside innovative modern food.

Recommended in the area

Raglan Castle; Big Pit National Mining Museum of Wales; Tintern Abbey

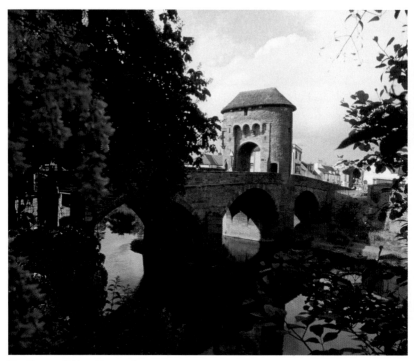

The Monnow Bridge, Monmouth.

The Bell at Skenfrith

♦♦♦♦♦ ◉◉

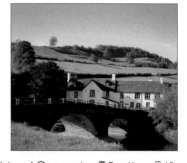

Address:	SKENFRITH, MONMOUTHSHIRE,NP7 8UH
Tel:	01600 750235
Fax:	01600 750525
Email:	enquiries@skenfrith.co.uk
Website:	www.skenfrith.co.uk
Map ref:	2, SO42

Directions: From Monmouth take A466 Hereford Rd. At B4521, go left towards Abergavenny. Bell is 3m on left

Open: 11–11 ⬛ L 12–2.30 D 7–9.30 ⓘ L 12–2.30 D 7–9.30 Rooms: 8 en suite S £75 D £100 Parking: 36 Notes: 🐾 ⊘ on premises ⊞ Free House ♈ 13

Refurbished to the highest standard, this 17th-century coaching inn nestles in the Monmouthshire hills, just inside the Welsh border, overlooking the Monnow River and Skenfrith Castle. Flagstone floors, beams and antiques characterise the interior. The restaurant utilises local, seasonal produce including produce from its own organic kitchen garden. The wine list is large and wide ranging with a particularly interesting half bottle selection.

Recommended in the area

Skenfrith, Grosmont and White castles; Offa's Dyke; Forest of Dean

The Lion Inn

Address: TRELLECK, Monmouth,
MONMOUTHSHIRE NP25 4PA
Tel: 01600 860322
Fax: 01600 860060
Email: debs@globalnet.co.uk
Website: www.lioninn.co.uk
Map ref: 2, SO50
Directions: From A40 just S of Monmouth take B4293
and follow signs for Trellech. From M48 junct 2, straight
across rdbt, 2nd left at 2nd rdbt onto B4293 for Trellech

Open: 12–3 6–11 (Thu–Sat 6–12, Mon 7–11; all day summer Sat) ♿ L 12–2 D 6–9.30 ⸾◎⸾ L 12–2
D 6–9.30 **Facilities:** Children welcome Garden **Parking:** 40 **Notes:** ⊨ ⊕ Free House

This popular and well established free house stands in a scenic village location opposite St Nicholas's
Church. Guests are greeted by welcoming real fires in the winter months, while in the summer drinks
and meals can be served in the garden, which overlooks fields and features a stream and large aviary.
The former brew house has won many accolades for its food and hospitality over the years, and its
reputation is growing among locals and those travelling from further afield. Visitors aiming to explore
the nearby walking trails and notable historic buildings, or visit Trelleck's own archaeological dig, will
find it a useful staging post. The extensive pub menu caters for all tastes, from bar snacks and basket
meals to blackboard specials, including fresh fish dishes. There is also an adventurous menu featuring
wild and hedgerow ingredients, such as nettles and wild mushrooms. Real ales include Bath Ales, Wye
Valley Butty Bach, Rhymney Best, Cottage Brewery and many more regularly changing brews. Anyone
who wants to extend their visit to the Lion can stay overnight in the pub's one-bedroom cottage, which
is suitable for up to three guests. It features an en suite bathroom and kitchenette. Dogs are allowed
at the pub, and water and biscuits are provided for them.

Recommended in the area

Tintern Abbey; Chepstow Castle; Wye Valley Forest Park

The Georges Restaurant/ Cafe Bar

Address: 24 Market Street, HAVERFORDWEST,
PEMBROKESHIRE SA61 1NH
Tel: 01437 766683
Fax: 01437 760345
Email: llewis6140@aol.com
Map ref: 1, SM91
Directions: From A40 on edge of Haverfordwest, take
A4076; at next rdbt turn right onto A487 then left into
Picton Pl. Continue along Victoria Pl onto High St, taking
3rd left into Market Street
Open: 10.30–5.30 (Sat 10.30–11) ⬛ L 12–5.30 D 6–9.45 ⧉ L 12–2.30 D 6–9.30
Facilities: Garden **Notes:** ⬛ Free House ♟ 10

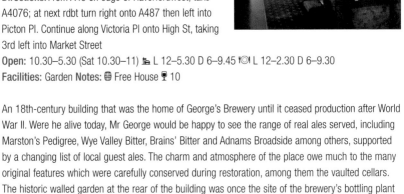

An 18th-century building that was the home of George's Brewery until it ceased production after World War II. Were he alive today, Mr George would be happy to see the range of real ales served, including Marston's Pedigree, Wye Valley Bitter, Brains' Bitter and Adnams Broadside among others, supported by a changing list of local guest ales. The charm and atmosphere of the place owe much to the many original features which were carefully conserved during restoration, among them the vaulted cellars. The historic walled garden at the rear of the building was once the site of the brewery's bottling plant and old stables, and still offers a splendid view over the ruins of Haverfordwest's 12th-century castle. The global menu offers something for every palate, from tasty local sausages and Welsh lamb with Mediterranean flavours, to spicy dishes that draw their influences from India, China, Thailand and Mexico. In addition to old favourites, the dessert menu features a range of Pembrokeshire ice-cream sundaes, luxury Italian hot chocolates, and herbal teas.

Recommended in the area

Oakwood Park Theme Park; Scolton Visitor Centre; Pembroke Castle

The Usk Inn

◆◆◆◆ ◉

Address: Talybont-on-Usk, BRECON, POWYS LD3 7JE
Tel: 01874 676251
Fax: 01874 676392
Email: stay@uskinn.co.uk
Website: www.uskinn.co.uk
Map ref: 2, SO02
Directions: Off A40 Brecon–Abergavenny rd, approx 6m SE of Brecon; turn S onto minor road at Llansantffraed
Open: 8am–11pm ⬧ L 12–3 D 6.30–9 ⬧ L 12–3 D 6.30–9 **Rooms:** 11 en suite **Facilities:** Garden **Parking:** 35 **Notes:** ⬧ ⬧ Free House ⬧ 8

Mike Taylor is a fourth-generation innkeeper, his wife Barbara's parents ran a successful Thameside club at Chiswick, and together they have years of experience in the hospitality industry. A background such as this meant they had little difficulty transforming an ordinary village boozer into what became the AA's Welsh Pub of the Year 2004–5. Originally it was a bank, but by the 1840s was licensed and when, in 1878, a wayward locomotive was derailed in the station opposite and crashed into the street outside, drinkers had something to talk about for weeks. The railway has long gone, leaving today's visitors to arrive by other means, the possibilities including by narrowboat on the Monmouth & Brecon Canal. While the bar areas retain a traditional feel, with open fires, flagstone floors and wooden tables, the restaurant has a Mediterranean feel. Here, imaginative menus make use of fresh local produce, as testified by dishes like Welsh rib-eye steak with red wine and caramelised shallot sauce; Caerphilly cheese-stuffed breast of chicken with cream and tarragon sauce; and whole boned trout with diced shallot, white wine, cream and fresh dill. Blackboard specials might include starters like fresh figs wrapped in cured ham, stuffed with goats' cheese, or slow-roasted lamb on mashed potato, with diced vegetables and a hint of mint. The long wine list includes many countries, from Argentina to the USA.

Recommended in the area

Brecon Beacons National Park; Tretower Court and Castle; Brecon Mountain Railway

The Bear

Address:	Brecon Road, CRICKHOWELL, POWYS NP8 1BW
Tel:	01873 810408
Fax:	01873 811696
Email:	bearhotel@aol.com
Website:	www.bearhotel.co.uk
Map ref:	2, SO21
Directions:	Approx 6m N of Abergavenny on A40 Brecon rd

Open: 11–3 6–11 (Sun 12–3, 7–10.30) 🏨 L 12–2 D 6–10 🍴 L 12–2 D 7–9.30 **Facilities:** Garden **Parking:** 45 **Notes:** 🐾 🛢 Free House ♟ 12

The social hub of the pretty little town of Crickhowell, The Bear is also popular with travellers – hardly surprising, since it is not only right on the main route to the Brecon Beacons, but is appealingly historic (dating from 1432), very convivial, and has won many accolades for its food and drink. Stephen and Judith Hindmarsh have been here for nearly 30 years, and though they have made changes along the way, this has never threatened the character of this splendid old building. From the cobbled forecourt, an archway leads to an inner courtyard where stage coaches between Fishguard and London changed horses. Inside, you'll find a low-beamed, antique-filled interior. Two bars have open fires and there are two dining rooms, one small and intimate, one longer and busier. Eat in the bar and enjoy a sandwich, a meal from the bistro-style menu, or a dish from the daily changing specials board. For a more formal option there's a candlelit restaurant. An extensive wine list is offered, plus a good choice of local beers and seasonal guest ales. There are 35 en suite bedrooms for anyone who wants to stay overnight, with some in the main building and the rest in converted stables in the courtyard area. All the rooms have TV, direct-dial telephones with Internet access, hairdryers, and tea- and coffee-making facilities. Some rooms are suitable for family occupation and some have Jacuzzis.

Recommended in the area

Tretower Court and Castle; Big Pit National Mining Museum of Wales; Llanthony Priory

The Old Black Lion

★★ 75% ◉ HOTEL

Address: Lion Street, HAY-ON-WYE, POWYS HR3 5AD
Tel: 01497 820841
Fax: 01497 822960
Email: info@oldblacklion.co.uk
Website: www.oldblacklion.co.uk
Map ref: 2, SO24
Directions: From A438 Hereford–Brecon road, take the B4350 from either Whitney-on-Wye or Glasbury, depending on your approach direction, or the B4351 from Clyro. Pub is in town centre
Open: 11–11 ♿ L 12–2.30 D 6.30–9.30 ⏹ D 6.30–9 **Rooms:** 10 en suite S £42.5 D £80
Facilities: Garden **Parking:** 20 **Notes:** ⊞ Free House

Hay-on-Wye has a great deal to commend it to the visitor. It is well known that this picturesque town, set in the stunning Wye Valley, in the shadow of the Black Mountains, is the largest second-hand book centre in the world, and that it hosts a renowned annual literary festival. Another excellent reason for a detour off the main road is The Old Black Lion, which dates from the 1300s but is a predominantly 17th-century – and reputedly the place where Oliver Cromwell stayed during the siege of Hay Castle. Today its cosy environment, with oak-timbered bar, scrubbed pine tables and comfy chairs, tempts people inside, and while savouring a pint of Old Black Lion ale or Wye Valley bitter you can muse over the justly acclaimed menu. The regularly changing offerings are written around seasonal local produce, including locally reared meat, fresh seafood and herbs from the garden. Restaurant main courses include supreme of guinea fowl filled with spinach and garlic; herb crusted rack of local spring lamb; and banana and pineapple curry with jasmine rice. Simpler bar food includes snacks; baguettes; liver, bacon and onions with Madeira gravy; and baked cod on braised leeks and fennel with cheese sauce.

Recommended in the area

Black Mountains and Brecon Beacons National Park; Llanthony Priory; Hergest Croft Gardens

View across the hills of New Radnor.

Red Lion Inn

Address: Llanfihangel-nant-Melan, NEW RADNOR,
Presteigne, POWYS LD8 2TN
Tel: 01544 350220
Fax: 01544 350220
Email: theredlioninn@yahoo.co.uk
Map ref: 2, SO26

Directions: From Llandrindod Wells, go N on the A483
to Crossgates, then E on the A44 towards Kington
Open: 12–2.30 6–11 (all day summer) ᴸ L 12–2
D 6–9 ⏐◎⏐ L 12–2 D 6–9 **Facilities:** Children welcome
Garden **Parking:** 30 **Notes:** ⚐ ⊕ Free House

Built in 1592 as a pit stop for drovers, the Red Lion Inn stands next to St Michael's Church. It is easily
reached from the A4, and is ideally placed for exploring the beautiful surrounding countryside. Inside
this pub, the old world bars serve a pint of Woods real ale or a glass of wine by a big log fire, and a
blackboard lists the daily food. Welsh black steaks are a favourite, along with the fish of the day.
Recommended in the area
Brecknock Museum & Art Gallery; South Wales Borderers (24th Regiment) Museum; Tretower
Court & Castle

The Castle Coaching Inn

Address: TRECASTLE, nr Brecon, POWYS LD3 8UH
Tel: 01874 636354
Fax: 01874 636457
Email: guest@castle-coaching-inn.co.uk
Website: www.castle-coaching-inn.co.uk
Map ref: 2, SN82
Directions: On A40 between Brecon and Llandovery
Open: 12–3 6–11 ⓑ L 12–2 D 6.30–9.00 ⓘ L 12–2 D
6.30–9 **Facilities:** Children welcome Garden
Parking: 25 ⊞ Free House

Once a Georgian coaching inn on the old London to Carmarthen coaching route, The Castle sits right on the northern edge of the Brecon Beacons/Black Mountain area, with myriad streams flowing down to join the River Usk nearby. The inn has been carefully restored in recent years, and retains lovely old fireplaces and a remarkable bow-fronted bar window, and has a peaceful terrace and garden. A good selection of real ales is on offer, including Fuller's London Pride, Breconshire Brewery Red Dragon and Timothy Taylor Landlords, and there are nine malt whiskies to choose from. Food can be eaten in the bar or more formally in the restaurant, and bar lunches feature tasty, freshly-cut sandwiches (maybe roast beef, turkey or stilton), a ploughman's with cheese or perhaps duck and port pâté, and hot crusty baguettes with fillings such as steak with melted stilton or bacon with mushrooms and melted mature cheddar. Of the more substantial offerings, specialities include mature Welsh 12oz sirloin steak served with mushrooms and onion rings; home-made lasagne with parmesan cheese; and supreme of chicken with a Marsala and mascarpone sauce. The tasty desserts, worth saving room for, and might include strawberry crush cake, hot jaffa puddle pudding; and Dutch chunky apple flan. Or sample the selection of Welsh farmhouse cheeses. There is a separate children's list that runs through the usual favourites – turkey dinosaurs, fish stars, or jumbo sausage, all served with chips and baked beans.

Recommended in the area

Dan-yr-Ogof The National Showcaves Centre; Brecon Beacons National Park; Usk Reservoir

Blue Anchor Inn

Address: EAST ABERTHAW, Nr Barry,
VALE OF GLAMORGAN CF62 3DD
Tel: 01446 750329
Fax: 01446 750077
Website: www.blueanchoraberthaw.com
Map ref: 2, ST06
Directions: From Cardiff take the A4226 W, passing the airport turn-off. At rdbt, keep forward to B4265, then turn right for Eat Aberthaw

Open: 11–11 🍺 L 12–2 D 6–8 🍽 L 12–2.30 D 7–9.30
Facilities: Children welcome Garden **Parking:** 70 **Notes:** ⊕ Free House 0

With Cardiff International Airport practically on the doorstep, the Blue Anchor Inn provides the perfect antidote to jet-setting modern living. Dating back to the 1380s, its mellow, ivy-covered stone walls are broken up with tiny windows and low doors, the whole picturesque ensemble topped by a thatched roof. Brightly coloured hanging baskets and flower-tubs grace the frontage in summer, and there are tables and benches on the courtyard and terrace. Inside is a warren of small rooms separated by thick walls, and with low, beamed ceilings. Real ales are on hand for travellers lucky enough to drop in, with a couple of guest ales always available from the hand pumps. In the bar, sandwiches, soup and baked potatoes can be ordered at lunchtime, with more substantial, exotic choices available on the evening restaurant menu. Here, the emphasis continues on a theme of firm favourites, and you might find such starters as fragrant king prawns on a lemongrass skewer with egg fried rice; or seared chicken livers on toasted French bread. These could be followed by glazed shank of Welsh lamb, pan-fried pork loin chop with Dijon mustard; seared fillet of salmon; or Mexican-style chilli corn carne. Save some room for a dessert such as apricot and ginger pudding; strawberry Bakewell tart; or classic crème brûlée, then, over a digestif or coffee contemplate the 600 years of hospitality of which you are now a part.

Recommended in the area

Welsh Hawking Centre; Dyffryn Gardens; St Fagans: National History Museum

Sgwd-Isaf-Clun-Gwyn Falls in the Vale of Neath.

The Bush Inn

Address: ST HILARY, nr Cowbridge,
VALE OF GLAMORGAN CF71 7DP

Tel: 01446 772745

Map ref: 2, ST07

Directions: From M4 junct 34 take A4119 N. At rdbt,
turn left on A473, then go S on A4222 to Cowbridge.
Here, turn left on A48 and right on minor road to St Hilary

Open: 11.30–11 (Sun 12–10.30) 🍴 L 12–2.30
D 6.45–9.30 🍽 L 12–2.30 D 6.45–9.30

Facilities: Children welcome Garden **Parking:** 60

Notes: 🐾 🍺 Punch Taverns 🍷 10

This thatched pub is in a picturesque Vale of Glamorgan village, with seating at the front overlooking
the 14th-century church. It has been a meeting place for people for over 200 years and its inglenook
fireplace, flagstone floors and spiral staircase are features of the cosy interior. Between them, the bar
and restaurant offer choices that range from light bites, sandwiches and salads to chargrilled steaks,
a fresh fish special of the day, and vegetarian options.

Recommended in the area

Old Beaupre Castle; Welsh Hawking Centre; St Fagans: National History Museum

The West Arms Hotel

★★★ 75% ◉◉ HOTEL

Address: LLANARMON DYFFRYN CEIRIOG,
nr Llangollen, WREXHAM LL20 7LD
Tel: 01691 600665
Fax: 01691 600622
Email: gowestarms@aol.com
Website: www.thewestarms.co.uk
Map ref: 5, SJ13
Directions: Leave A5 Oswestry–Llangollen road at Chirk
and follow signs for Ceiriog Valley onto the B4500. The
hotel is 11m from Chirk
Open: 8am–11pm ⓑ L 12–2 D 7–9 ⊙ L 12–2 D 7–9 **Rooms:** 15 en suite **Facilities:** Children
welcome Garden **Parking:** 30 **Notes:** ⚑ ⊕ Free House ♈ 10

In the eastern lea of the Berwyn mountains, The West Arms has been offering hospitality since the
16th century, first to weary drovers and now to locals, tourists and hunting parties drawn by food
that has earned it two AA Rosettes and the AA Seafood Pub of the Year for Wales award 2005. The
new owners, Grant Williams and Lee and Siân Finch welcome visitors from all over the world,
charmed by the warmth of the welcome and character of the building's undulating slate floors,
ancient timberwork and vast inglenook fireplaces. Award-winning chef Grant Williams has global
kitchen experience and serves his food in substantial portions, whether from the menu or the
blackboard. You might find such starters as gravad lax, mussel and leek tart; or perhaps chargrilled
vegetable terrine as a precursor to the main courses, which might include pan-fried breast of guinea
fowl with thyme, bacon, chestnuts and wild mushrooms; medallions of Welsh beef on crushed
potatoes and wild mushrooms; panaché of grilled sea bass, red mullet and seared scallops; or fillet
of sole with saffron butter sauce.

Recommended in the area

Chirk Castle; Llangollen Railway; Horse Drawn Boats Centre

MAPS

KEY TO ATLAS PAGES

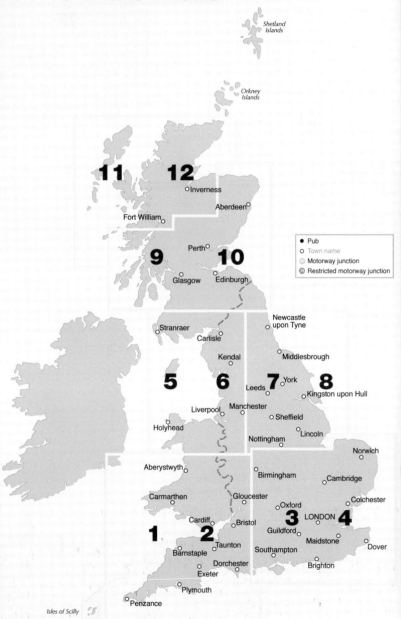

Shetland Islands

Orkney Islands

11   12

Inverness

Aberdeen

Fort William

• Pub
○ Town name
⊕ Motorway junction
⊕ Restricted motorway junction

Perth

9   10

Glasgow   Edinburgh

Stranraer

Newcastle upon Tyne

Carlisle

Kendal   Middlesbrough

5   6   7   York   8

Leeds

Kingston upon Hull

Liverpool   Manchester

Holyhead   Sheffield

Nottingham   Lincoln

Norwich

Aberystwyth

Birmingham   Cambridge

Carmarthen   Gloucester   Colchester

Cardiff   Oxford

1   2   Bristol   3   LONDON   4

Guildford   Maidstone

Barnstaple   Taunton   Southampton   Dover

Dorchester   Brighton

Exeter

Isles of Scilly   Plymouth

Penzance

315

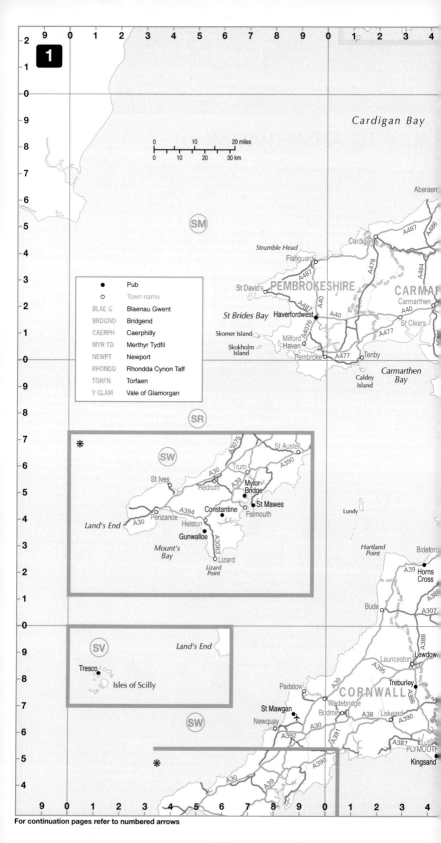

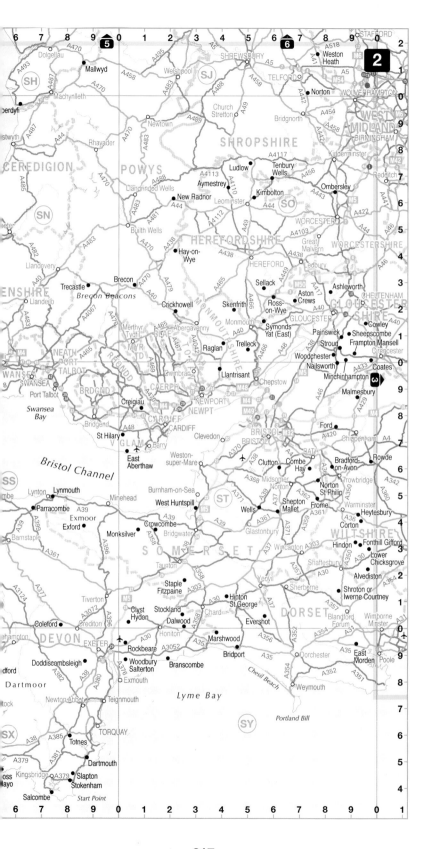

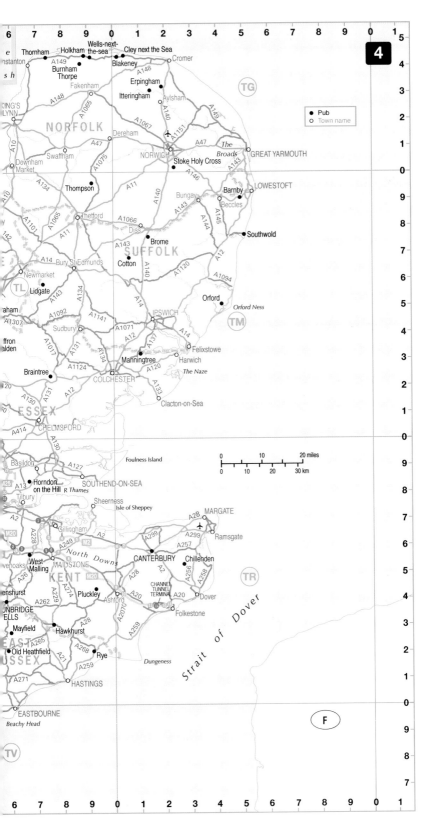

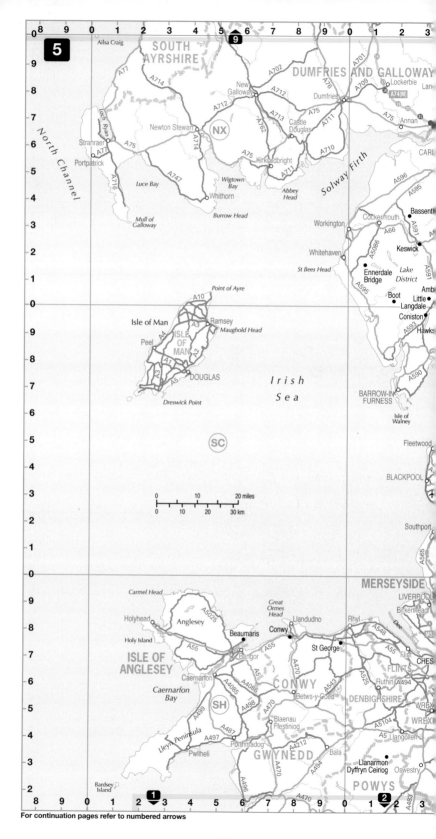

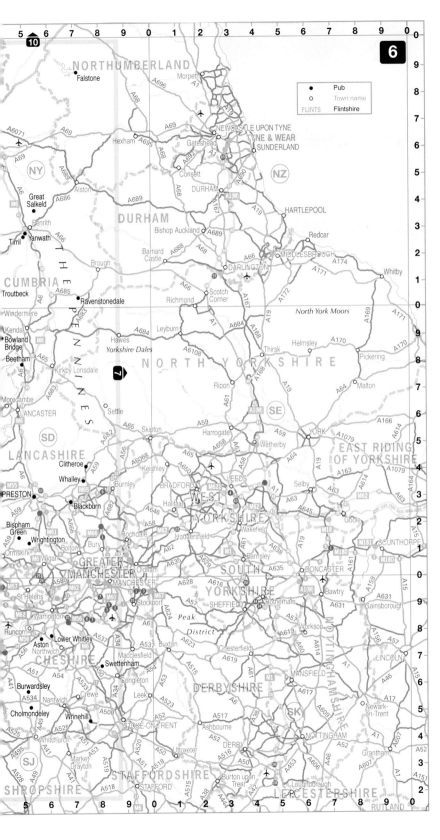

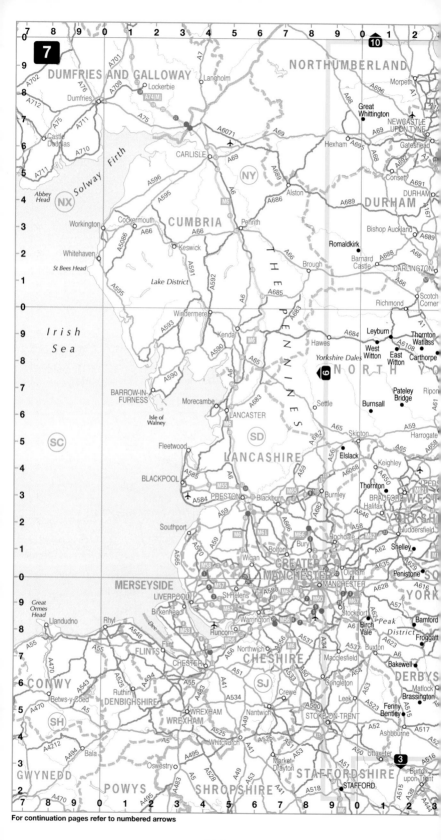

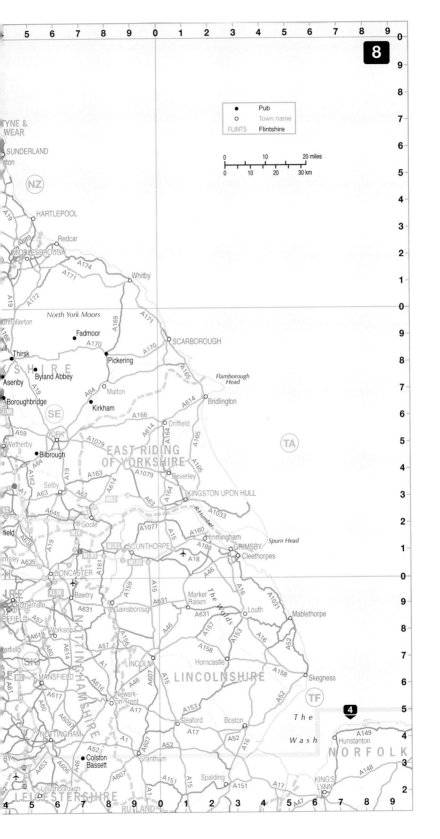

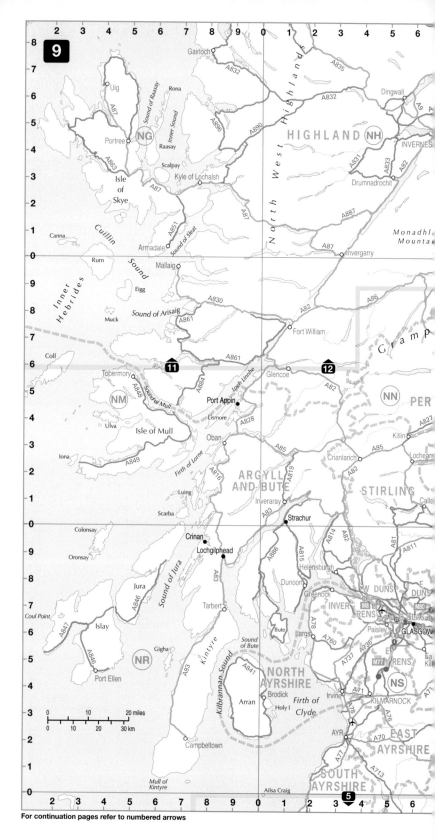

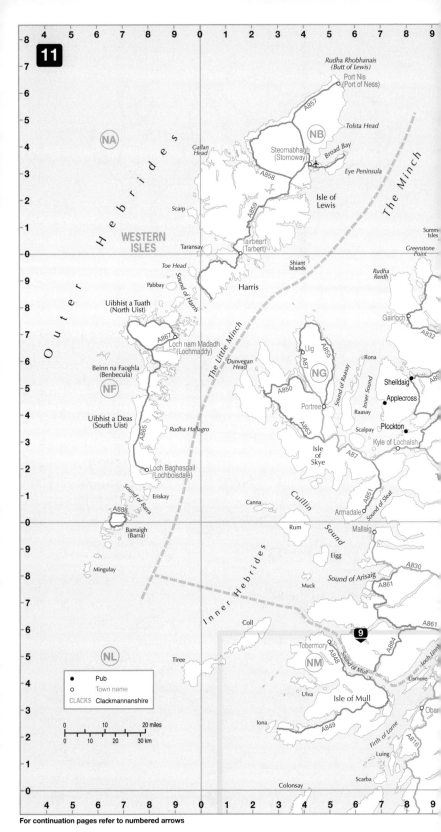

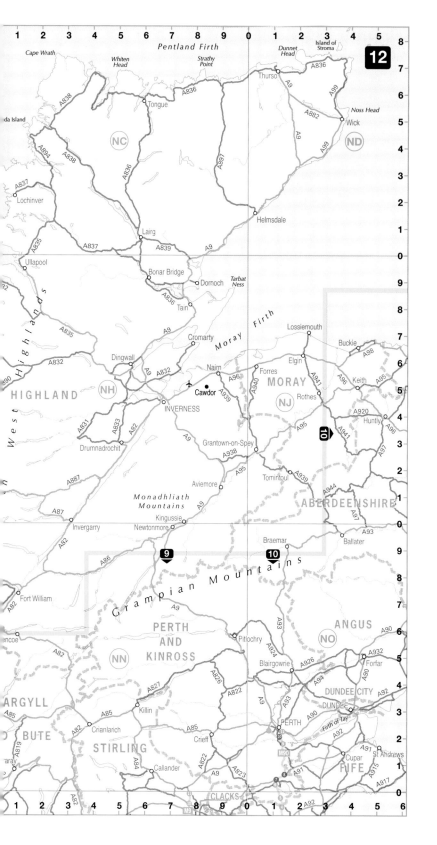

County Map

England
1 Bedfordshire
2 Berkshire
3 Bristol
4 Buckinghamshire
5 Cambridgeshire
6 Greater Manchester
7 Herefordshire
8 Hertfordshire
9 Leicestershire
10 Northamptonshire
11 Nottinghamshire
12 Rutland
13 Staffordshire

14 Warwickshire
15 West Midlands
16 Worcestershire

Scotland
17 City of Glasgow
18 Clackmannanshire
19 East Ayrshire
20 East Dunbartonshire
21 East Renfrewshire
22 Perth & Kinross
23 Renfrewshire
24 South Lanarkshire
25 West Dunbartonshire

Wales
26 Blaenau Gwent
27 Bridgend
28 Caerphilly
29 Denbighshire
30 Flintshire
31 Merthyr Tydfil
32 Monmouthshire
33 Neath Port Talbot
34 Newport
35 Rhondda Cynon Taff
36 Torfaen
37 Vale of Glamorgan
38 Wrexham

Location Index

Location Index

Location Index

Location Index

Location Index

Pub Index

Pub Index

Pub Index

Picture credits

The following photographs are held in the Automobile Association's own photo library (AA World Travel Library) and were taken by these photographers:

4 AA\C Sawyer; 5 AA\C Sawyer; 9 Photodisc; 10 AA\C Sawyer; 12/13 AA\T Mackie; 14 AA\M Birkitt; 16 AA\J Tims; 20 AA\C Jones; 22 AA\J Tims; 30 AA\C Jones; 31 AA\C Coe; 37 AA\A Tryner; 41 AA\J Beazley; 42 AA/J Wood; 49 AA\T Mackie; 51 AA\E A Bowness; 53 AA\A Mockford & N Bonetti; 57 AA\A J Hopkins; 59 AA\P Bennet; 62 AA\P Sharpe; 63 AA\P Baker; 67 AA\T Mackie; 68 AA\C Jones; 70 AA\N Hicks; 76 AA\A Lawson; 82 AA\P Baker; 84 AA\C Jones; 86 AA\A Burton; 89 AA\R Czaja; 90 AA\G Rowatt; 91 AA\R Coulam; 92 AA\J Miller; 98 AA\D Hall; 99 AA\S & O Mathews; 101 AA\P Baker; 104 AA\S Day; 108 AA\D Hall; 112 AA\F Stephenson; 114 AA\K Doran; 115 AA\A Burton; 119 AA\A Burton; 121 AA\A Burton; 124 AA\D Forss; 126 AA\H Palmer; 127 AA\C Jones; 132 AA\M Birkitt; 135 AA\S & O Mathews; 136 AA\D Forss; 138 AA\J Miller; 144 AA\M Busselle; 146 AA\T Griffiths; 148 AA\J Beazley; 152 AA\S Day; 153 AA\R Newton; 154 AA\M Adelman; 155 AA\W Voysey; 159 AA\T Mackie; 160/161 AA\S & O Mathews; 169 AA\A Baker; 170 AA\M Birkitt; 173 AA\M Birkitt; 175 AA\C Lees; 179 AA\R Newton; 181 AA; 182 S Day; 189 AA\S Day; 192 AA\M Birkitt; 194 AA\M Birkitt; 195 AA\M Haywood; 196 AA\C Jones; 199 AA\S Day; 207 AA\R Moss; 208 AA\P Baker; 211 AA\T Mackie; 214 AA\M Birkitt; 216 AA\W Voysey; 217 AA\D Forss; 218 AA\J Tims; 221 AA\J Miller; 222 AA\T Souter; 226 AA; 228 AA; 231 AA; 236 AA\P Baker; 239 AA\H Palmer; 241 AA\W Voysey; 246 AA\W Voysey; 251 AA\S & O Mathews; 252 AA\M Moody; 253 AA\C Jones; 256 AA; 257 AA\T Mackie; 259 AA\J Beazley; 262 AA\L Whitwam; 269 AA; 270 AA\P Wilson; 271 AA\P Wilson; 275 AA\P Wilson; 276/277 AA\J Carnie; 278 AA\E Ellington; 284 AA\D Hardley; 286 AA\J Carnie; 293 AA\K Paterson; 294/295 AA\P Aithie; 296 AA\N Jenkins; 299 AA\C Molyneux; 301 AA\I Burgum; 302/303 AA\I Burgum; 304 AA\H Williams; 310 AA\C & A Molyneux; 313 AA\I Burgum;

Every effort has been made to trace the copyright holders, and we apologise in advance for any accidental errors. We would be happy to apply the corrections in the following edition of this publication.